‘To all those who came before us,
and to those who will come after us’

‘Puohháid kođeh ovdil mii pottii,
já puohháid kođeh mii maŋa puátih

Gájkajda gudi mijá åvddåla båhtin,
ja gájkajda gudi mijá maŋŋela båhti’

‘Пукэ гуэйке, ке ля̄йй мӣн райя я пукэтӻ тэ̄йт,
ке ля̄ннч маӊӊа мӣнэ’

Čatnosat (Northern Sámi) means connections, attachments or bonds. The dedication on this page is in the following languages: Anár Sámi, Lule Sámi and Kildin Sámi.

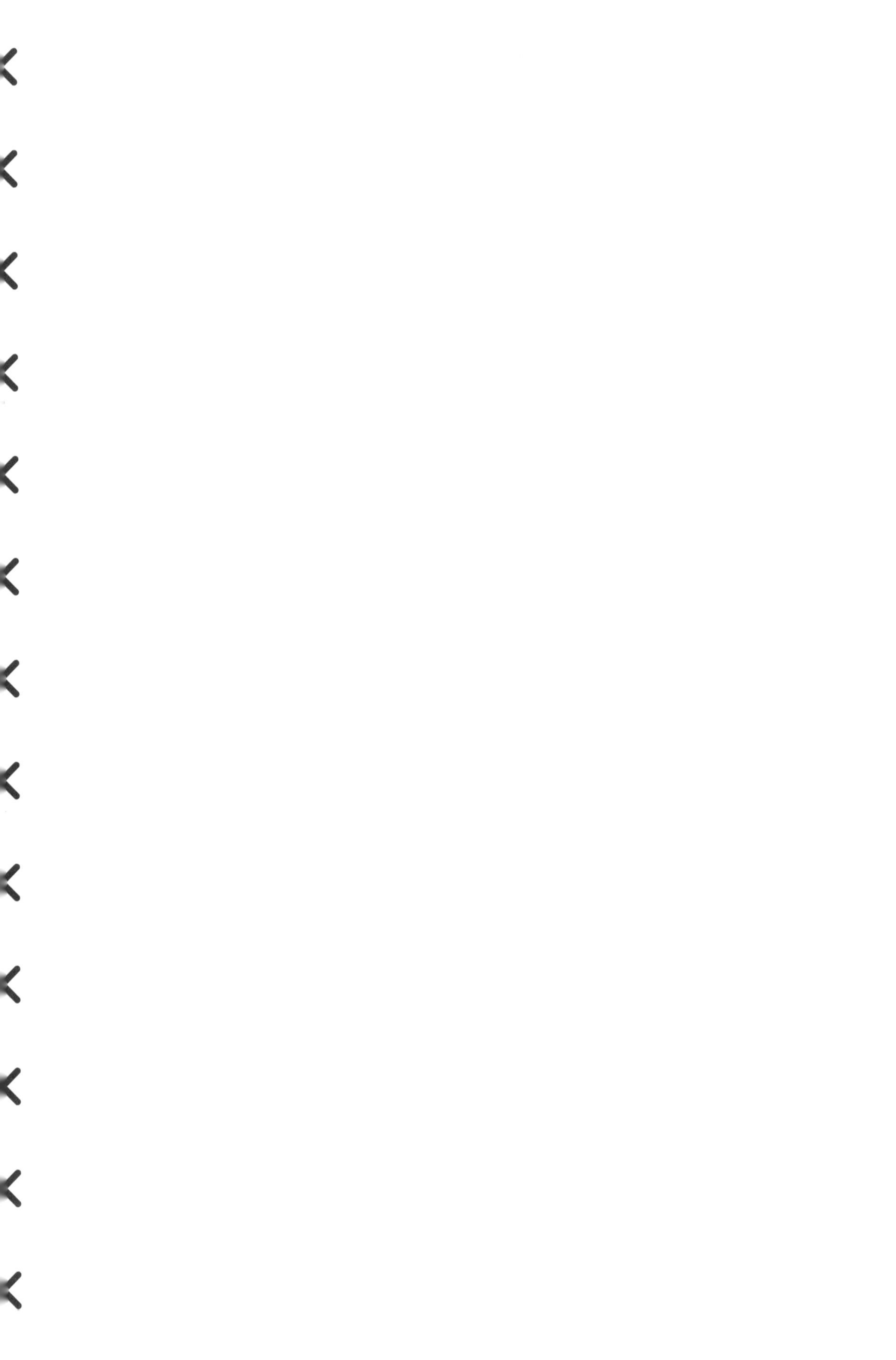

Pauliina Feodoroff

Katya García-Antón

‘Please do not buy our lands, buy our art, begs the Begging Queen, and sells the views of her lands as portraits’[1]

1 Pauliina Feodoroff, *Matriarchy,* draft script, 2021.

2
Pauliina Feodoroff in Una Meistere, 'The Western World is turning to Indigenous Peoples', *Spiriterritory*, 13 November 2021 https://spiriterritory.com/foresterritory/foresterritory/25378-the_western_world_is_turning_to_indigenous_peoples/ accessed 10 January 2022.

3
Ibid.

When you see your world falling apart, when the law is barred to you, when politics fail you, 'you need something that keeps you in action, that doesn't paralyse you and make you want to kill yourself or silently disappear', reflects Pauliina Feodoroff.[2] For the artist, that 'something' lies in the entwined possibilities of art and the practice of land guardianship. This approach falls logically within the Sámi understanding of the world as a space of relations and reciprocities, where people (and their cultural expressions) do not define their surroundings (land, waters, species and those other than human) but are an indivisible part of them. This is a formulation within which Feodoroff can act and be heard, in a manner nourished by the ancestral knowledges of her Skolt Sámi people, to regenerate and sustain a sovereign future for her community, that is, to honour all the relations with those around them.

With roots both in Čeʹvetjäuʹrr (in the Finnish part of Sápmi) and Suõʹnnjel (in the Russian part of Sápmi) Feodoroff's family has experienced deep loss at multiple levels. In the ancestral grounds of the Kola Peninsula, the Skolt community endured Soviet-enforced collectivisation and nickel mining that resulted in the requisition of forests and rivers, and their forcible removal from the land, as well as in the degradation of the region by acid rain. In Feodoroff's words: 'These are our traditional (unceded) lands and my whole life has been about trying to survive after those great losses that happened to my grandparents, and they are still affecting our society. We lost our lands, our belongings, and our reindeer, and we lost so many of the people.'[3]

The colonial dispossession of territory and the toxification of the environment have played a fundamental role in the significant drop in children being born into Skolt Sámi society, and in addition has caused the collapse of language and the loss of knowledge on how to live in and with the land in a non-subjugating manner. The situation was further exacerbated with the re-drawing of borders as Russia and Finland signed a treaty in 1948, forcing Feodoroff's family to relocate to the Finnish side, in tandem with the emergency evacuation of Skolt Sámi in the face of the scorched-earth policy of the retreating German army at the end of World War II.[4] In addition to this came Finnish policies of modernisation (read ecocide) of waterways, mineral extraction, aggressive forestry and industrialised tourism, the imposition of property laws on what was previously commonly governed Sámi land, compounded by Soviet military nuclear testing in the 1970s, and the deathly effects of nuclear waste following the Chernobyl disaster of 1986, both of which had documented fallout on Skolt land on the Finnish and Norwegian sides of the borders dividing Sápmi. With every aspect of Skolt society under fire, the prospect of extinction places an asphyxiating grip on Skolt futures. As Feodoroff remarks: 'It is a miracle that some of us still exist, speak the language and continue with our traditional livelihoods.'[5]

In the last decades, climate change in the Arctic region (whose effects are experienced at an accelerated rate compared to the rest of the world) has added significant pressure to the Skolt Sámi struggles. Yet it is only recently that the world appears to have finally accepted that whilst Indigenous peoples may be at the forefront of climate change, no one on the entire planet can escape its impact. With Western science and climate advocates turning towards Indigenous knowledges to reduce the impact of climate change, a new window of opportunity for making their voices heard has opened for the Skolt, and Feodoroff is at its forefront, advocating a clear message:

> I feel that we are a warning or a sign from the future that this can happen to others as well (Sámi, Indigenous and others in the world). So don't let these things happen to you, and please

4 The Skolt Sámi have lived in an area of shifting borders for a long time, due to the diplomatic struggles between Norway (and Denmark-Norway), Finland and Russia/the Soviet Union. Notably, the territory of Petsamo, which includes Skolt Sámi territories, was ceded from the Soviet Union to Finland in 1922, but in 1945 Finland was forced to give the entire, now warworn territory back to the Soviet Union. The Skolt Sámi were forced to choose whether to be evacuated into a new area in Finland or stay and become part of the Soviet Union.

5 Feodoroff in Una Meistere, 'The Western World'.

listen to us, especially now, in this race for who gets to have the last remaining metals or the last remaining clean water, clean air and space to live in.[6]

Feodoroff has been a long-term collaborator with the Snowchange Cooperative, an NGO led by Tero Mustonen. It is both a network and scientific organisation dedicated to documenting and re-remembering the ancestral ways of life and the knowledges of Indigenous societies, especially in the Circumpolar North, but also across the world. One of Snowchange's major achievements was made public in autumn 2020, when the cooperative confirmed that around 130 new Atlantic salmon and trout spawning sites that were being diligently hand-created in Skolt lands within an area of four kilometres, had been successfully established. It meant that a destroyed habitat had been reclaimed, and as Feodoroff concludes:

> It proved the concept of 'neo-nature' to be possible, which means that you can restore something, even if it will never be the same as it was before the damage [...] The best science is being done there, and it's very close in its perceptions to what the traditional knowledge-bearers are saying [...] If there is equal collaboration and equal dialogue, they can work very well together.[7]

Feodoroff's ceremonies of renewal, securing Skolt land and regenerating its habitats, are processes intimately bound to the regeneration of the knowledge required to care for them and rooted in the interdependence of humans with land, waters and other non-human entities.[8] In tandem, they enable the resurgence of Skolt Sámi forms of community governance – namely the Siida system that was one of the

6 Ibid.

7 Ibid.

8 The term 'ceremonies of renewal' was initially introduced by Canadian professor of Education, Cynthia M. Chambers, and Indigenous scholar and elder, Narcisse Blood of the Kainai First Nation on Turtle Island in an article discussing the relationship between people and land. As they explain it, a ceremony of renewal is a means of restitution that returns the interrelational balance of the world 'nurtured through unimpeded access, continued exchange of knowledge, and [...] visiting and exchanging gifts and stories', in Cynthia M. Chambers and Narcisse J. Blood, 'Love Thy Neighbour: Repatriating Precarious Blackfoot Sites'. *International Journal of Canadian Studies* 39–40 (2009): p. 267.

9
As Feodoroff has explained in emails to the author, 'leett' is the Skolt Sámi word defining this perspective.

10
Feodoroff in Una Meistere, 'The Western World'.

first to be attacked by colonial policies. These factors are interdependent, and together they lead to the recovery of Skolt Sámi-health (mental and physical), which is by implication the the equivalent of recovery of habitat-health.

At the core of this process of interdependence is the acknowledgement that humanity is not at the centre of the planet, and rather that the land and everything it provides to human existence is a gift that comes with a responsibility to reciprocate. It is in this reciprocity, in this leett,[9] in this duty of care (values shared by Sámi worldviews and global Indigenous worldviews) that your ability to 'live a good life' (láhttet olbmo láhkai) generates your calibre as a human being. As Feodoroff explains:

> There are traditional 'land-keeping' and 'water-trading' practices – very concrete ways of how to give back. For example, you give back to the river the bones of the fish – the bones will become a source of food for the young fish living there. In the case of the forest, in the old days when you slaughtered an animal, the insides of the belly were given back to the forest. It was a way to nurture the land and enrich the biomass. If the river is still giving you fish, it's your duty to give back. These sets of very strict rules come from ancestral culture and this is how I was taught to interact with the river, to ensure that the river stays clean, that it is not overfished, and that no harm comes to it. Giving thanks means that there's a bond between the two parties. It is a two-way bond that always carries an obligation if both parties are to survive.[10]

11 Pauliina Feodoroff, *The Act of Begging*, excerpt from sketch notes for a performance series in 'The Sámi Pavilion', Biennale Arte 2022.

The Act of Begging[11]

The market of Esthetics,
the market of Ethics,
the market of Survival in forms of Carbon
sinks,
the market of new ideas and ideologies for
Survival,
the market of new faces,
the market of new-found names,
the market of new names,
new findings,
the market of Protection,
the market of Havens,
the market of connections and clout
constantly surrounding an Indigenous
individual (artist).
Making your culture visible may cause severe
protection.
Making your story visible may cause severe
societal change.
Making yourself a visible example of larger
phenomena in the world may cause severe begging, that will not succeed if it is recognised as
begging, and will not succeed either, if there is
not an element of submission.

It is with these words that Feodoroff commences her notes sketching out *Matriarchy* – a performance of rematriation (of re-remembering interdependent care) for 'The Sámi Pavilion' 2022 developed with the support of dialogue partner and Sámi Elder Asta M. Balto. In this performance, Feodoroff choreographs situations where power relations are out of balance, where Indigenous people are forced to give up or sell what is most precious in their lives, and she off-sets them with moments of sovereign Indigenous

12
Ibid.
13
Duodji is the principal Sámi epistemology that encompasses various insights into materials, their sources and seasons, spirituality and relations within the community. Duodji is a body of knowledge that informs and defines Sámi practitioners who in the Western world would be termed artists, crafters, poets, dancers, musicians, etc.

performance. Working with a group of Sámi and Nordic dancers and performers, Feodoroff examines the strategies of begging. She accentuates the submitter's awareness of the process of submission, in order to catalyse the abandonment of automatic patterns of submission colonially embedded in Indigenous bodies and movement, and generate sovereign forms of existence.

> It makes us watch how the land is being sold, every minute, every day, for business, for pleasure, for Christ's sake. I've started to sell and buy land that isn't mine to sell or buy. I've started to protect the land from extractivism. I don't have any money of my own, so I need to seduce someone else's fortune for that. I beg for money for my culture's protection. I loathe what I'm doing. I don't know what else I could do, how much more I could put myself, my body and my mind between the act of extracting and protection.[12]

Matriarchy is structured as a performance in three parts. Part one is titled *First Contact* and presents a group of beautiful duodji[13] objects and their creators. *First Contact* comments on the epistemic violence that underlined first encounters between Indigenous and settler peoples and went on to define the future asymmetrical relations between them, with brutal consequences for Indigenous worlds. It refers to the practice of gifting that characterises Sámi perspectives when entering into relations. Those gifts were mistaken as Indigenous acknowledgements of hierarchy, and were converted into forms of taxation and control. Settlers were not epistemologically equipped to understand them for what they were – pivotal corners of Sámi protocols of civility, and elements of relationship-building that elicited reciprocity and were directed at constructing a relational balance.

In part two *Auction*, a series of video-portraits of Indigenous landscapes currently under threat from aggressive commercial logging, or other industrial land use, are auctioned off as artworks. A number of these wre made in Feodoroff's Skolt Sámi and other Sámi lands, and two were made in First Nation's land in Turtle Island, aka North America. This performed auction sets the scene for the actual auction of the works, scheduled for some months later and conducted by an auction house. The funds raised will contribute to securing the purchase of those lands through the previously mentioned Snowchange programme to protect the area from further devastation, as well as catalyse its rewilding through the resurgence of Sámi knowledges required for this.

Auction invokes significant art histories and economic practices rooted in or in some way connected to colonialism, and re-conducts them into forms that bring agency to those fighting the ongoing violence that continues to shape Sámi realities today. If, in the past, Sámi peoples were erased from Western artistic depictions of land in the race for its control and its representation, today, Sámi peoples are viewed as obstacles to governmental policies on large-scale mining, industrial forestry, hydro-electric and wind-farm construction. The onset of modernity in the late nineteenth century and its development through the twentieth century was accompanied by a prolific amount of image production, informed by the modernist drive to conquer the world through the construction, control and dissemination of images depicting it. These images were central to imperial processes of nation-building and territory expansion in what was colonially considered as wilderness or Terra Nullius. Such a mindset defined the landscape paintings of, amongst others, the Hudson River School and the Group of Seven in Turtle Island, and Nordic artists such as Johann Christian Dahl, Harald Sohlberg, Marcus Larsson and Akseli Gallen-Kallela.

14
David Garneau, 'Imaginary Spaces of Conciliation and Reconciliation: Art, Curation and Healing', in *Arts of Engagement: Taking Aesthetic Action in and Beyond Canada's Truth and Reconciliation Commission*, ed. Dykab Robinson and Keavy Martin (Waterloo, Ont.: Wilfrid Laurier University Press, 2016), p. 26.

15
Performers: Outi Pieski, Birit Haarla, Katja Haarla, Satu Herrala and Eséte Eshetu Sutinen. Collaborators include: Snowchange Cooperative, Office for Contemporary Art Norway, Zodiak Centre for New Dance, Museum of Contemporary Art Kiasma / Finnish National Gallery and Sápmi salasta.

Feodoroff's video-portraits to be auctioned are mindful of this context, yet thoughtfully redirect it through a choreography of the bodies and gazes of women, who as allies of the land invite the viewer/buyer to engage according to their sovereign terms. Moreover, upon purchasing thc work, the buyer enters into a new relationship with Feodoroff (and with the First Nation custodians mentioned previously). A contract of reciprocity will thus be forged (personal but also legal), whereby the buyer gains the video-portrait in question and the right to visit the land on a pre-arranged regular basis, and the custodian takes up the responsibility to protect and reform the land, as well as potentially generating in the process of this exchange a new accomplice for Sámi epistemologies of reciprocity and care.

Feodoroff's novel approach bridges the gap between different world views and creates conduits through which to generate common ground. However, it is also cognisant of the creativity that Indigenous peoples have been forced to generate over centuries to keep pivotal aspects of their life alive. In this regard, it is useful to point to Métis scholar David Garneau's reflections on the production of Indigenous 'screen-objects'[14] that enter into a relation with Western desires to engage with and acquire from Indigenous peoples spiritually important objects, without completely ceding the power and knowledges they embody.

Part three is titled *Matriarchy* and closes the performance. It presents a configuration of Indigenous and accomplice female bodies converging in actions that do not beg, which purge the body from colonially transmitted and inherited forms of mobility and existence. Mindful of the matriarchal strength of spiritual and social organisation of ancestral Sámi forms of being, doing and thinking – early targets of colonial strategies of patriarchisation – they re-centre Sámi matriarchal values as leading activators of Sámi sovereign living in the future.[15]

16
'Gelassenheit' was a German word for 'tranquil submission' used in the Christian mystical tradition. It has continued in the form of two distinct usages: in Heideggerian terminology and in the Anabaptist tradition.

17
Pauliina Feodoroff, *The Act of Begging*, excerpt from sketch notes for a performance series in 'The Sámi Pavilion', Venice Biennale, 2022.

Matriarchy *sees art as capital, and currency as resistance, placing begging and sovereign bodies between the buyer and the seller to renegotiate the buying decision. The negotiation itself is outrageous: the currency is beauty and the added value of aesthetics is a reciprocation for 'gelasseneheit'.*[16] Matriarchy *makes works of art out of land areas that the Begging Queen auctions off in the performance. Please do not buy our lands, buy our art, begs the Begging Queen, and sells views of her land as portraits.*[17]

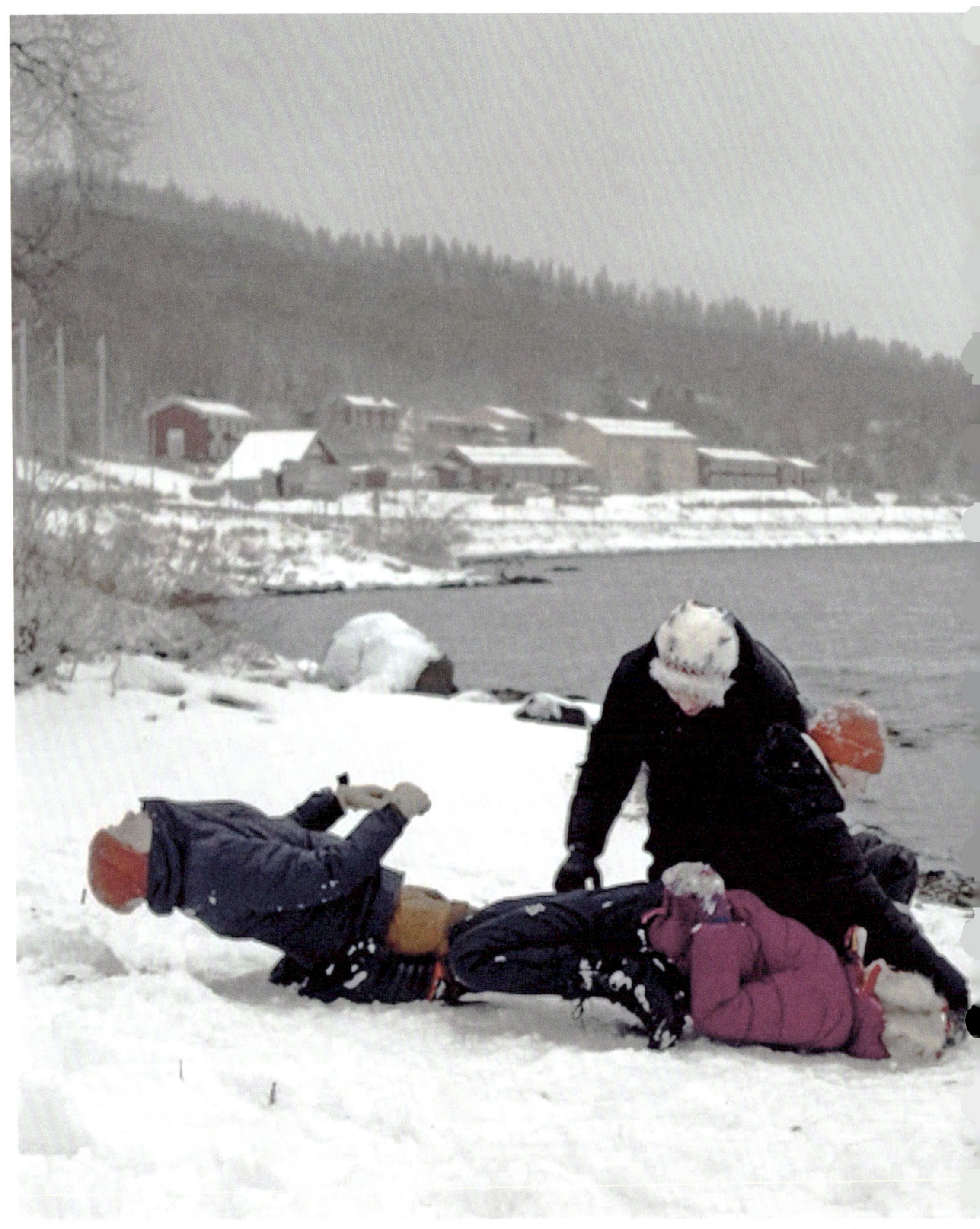

Matriarchy rehearsals at the Sápmi Salasta residency, Västerbotten (Sápmi), 2021. From left to right: Pauliina Feodoroff, Birit Haarla, Satu Herrala, Katja Haarla. Still by Egil Pedersen, 2021

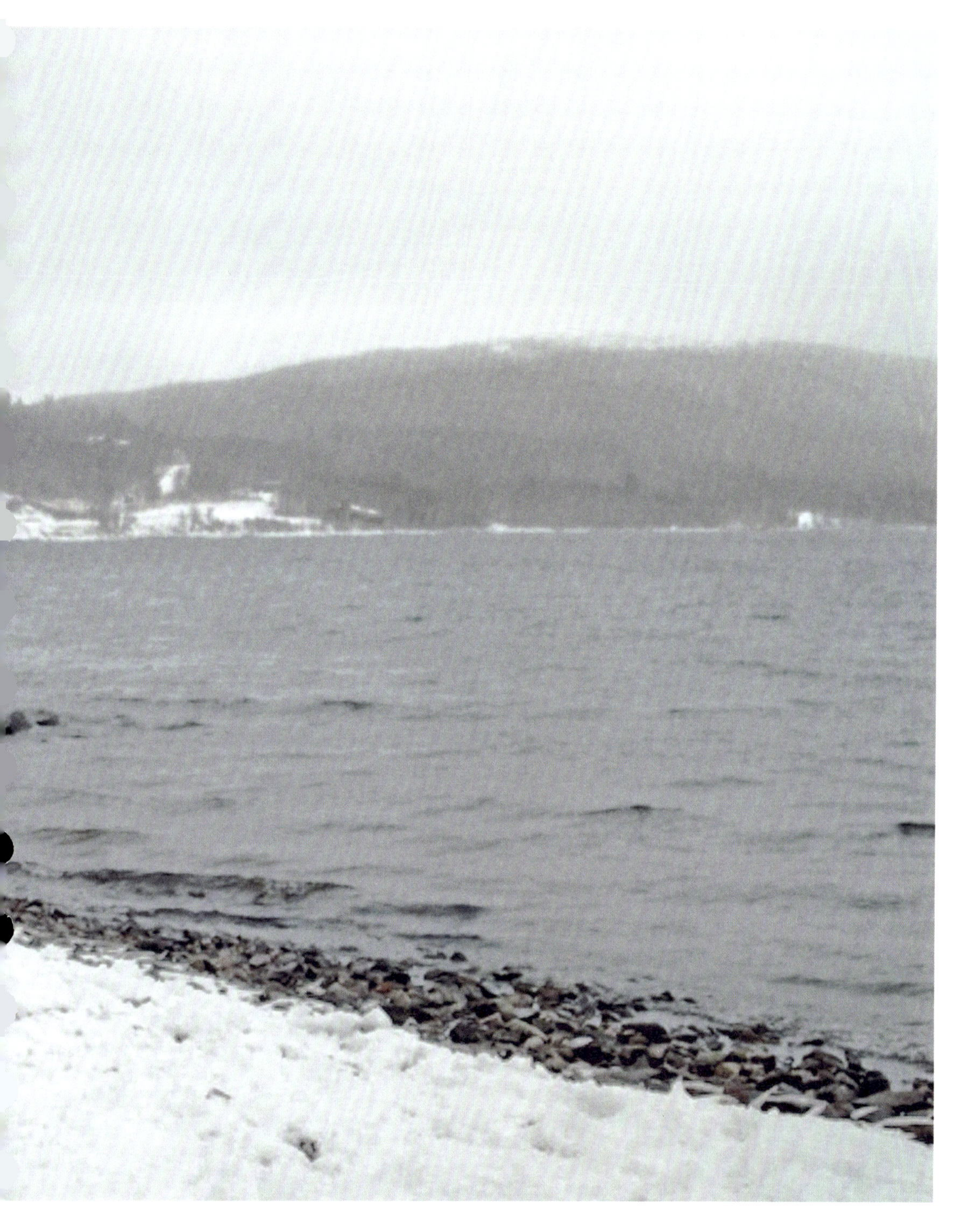

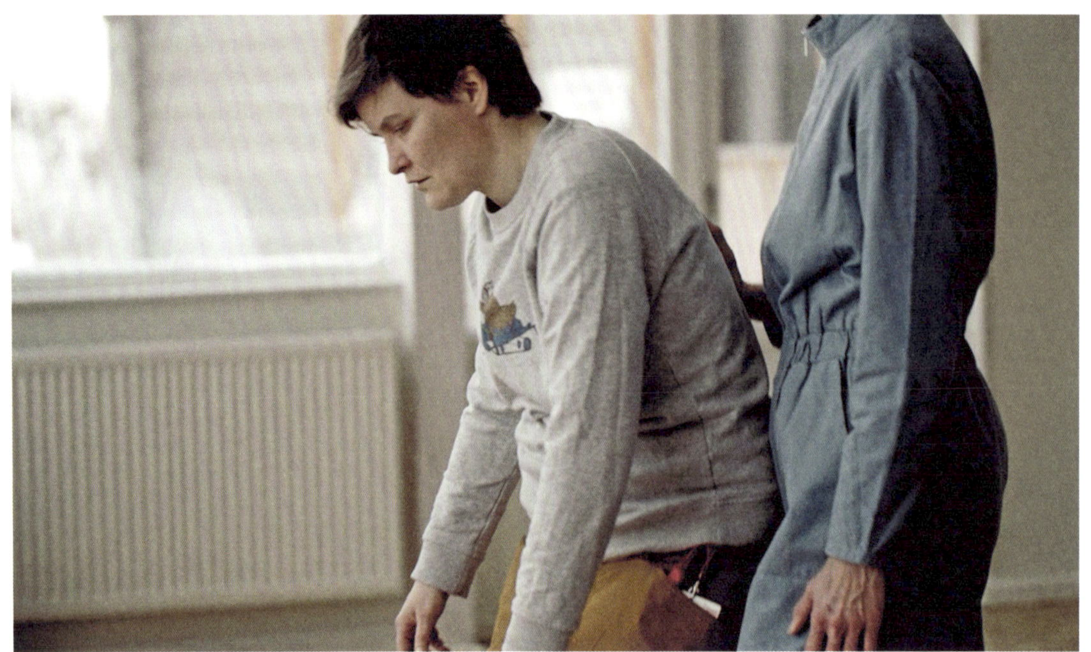

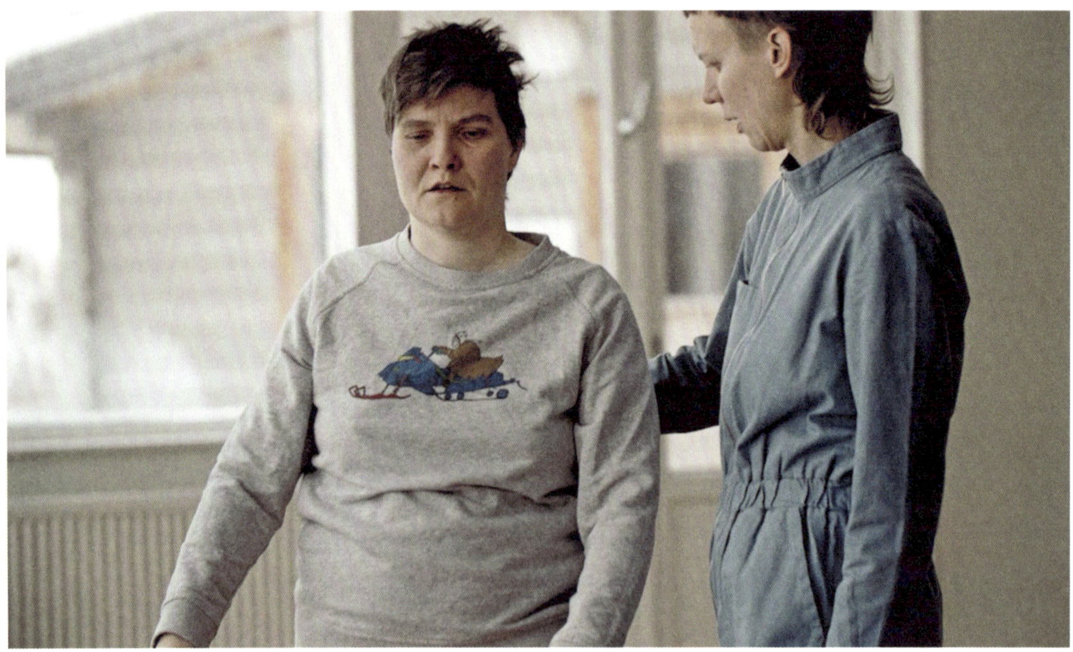

Matriarchy rehearsals at the Sápmi Salasta residency, Västerbotten (Sápmi), 2021. Pauliina Feodoroff (left) and Satu Herrala (right).
Stills: Egil Pedersen, 2021

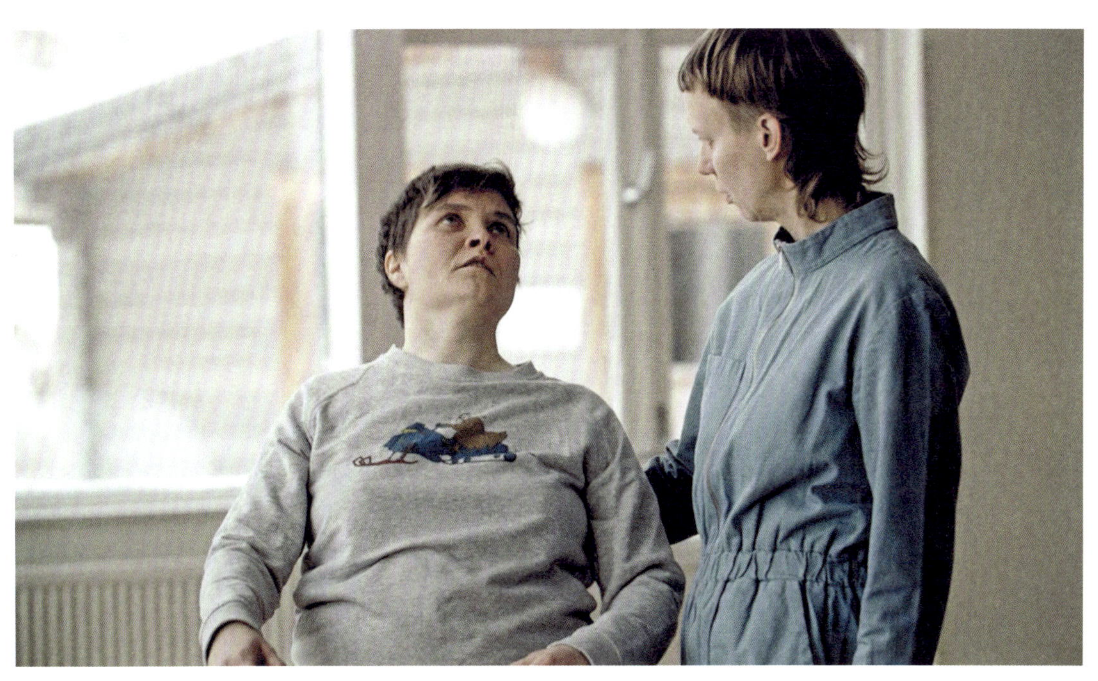

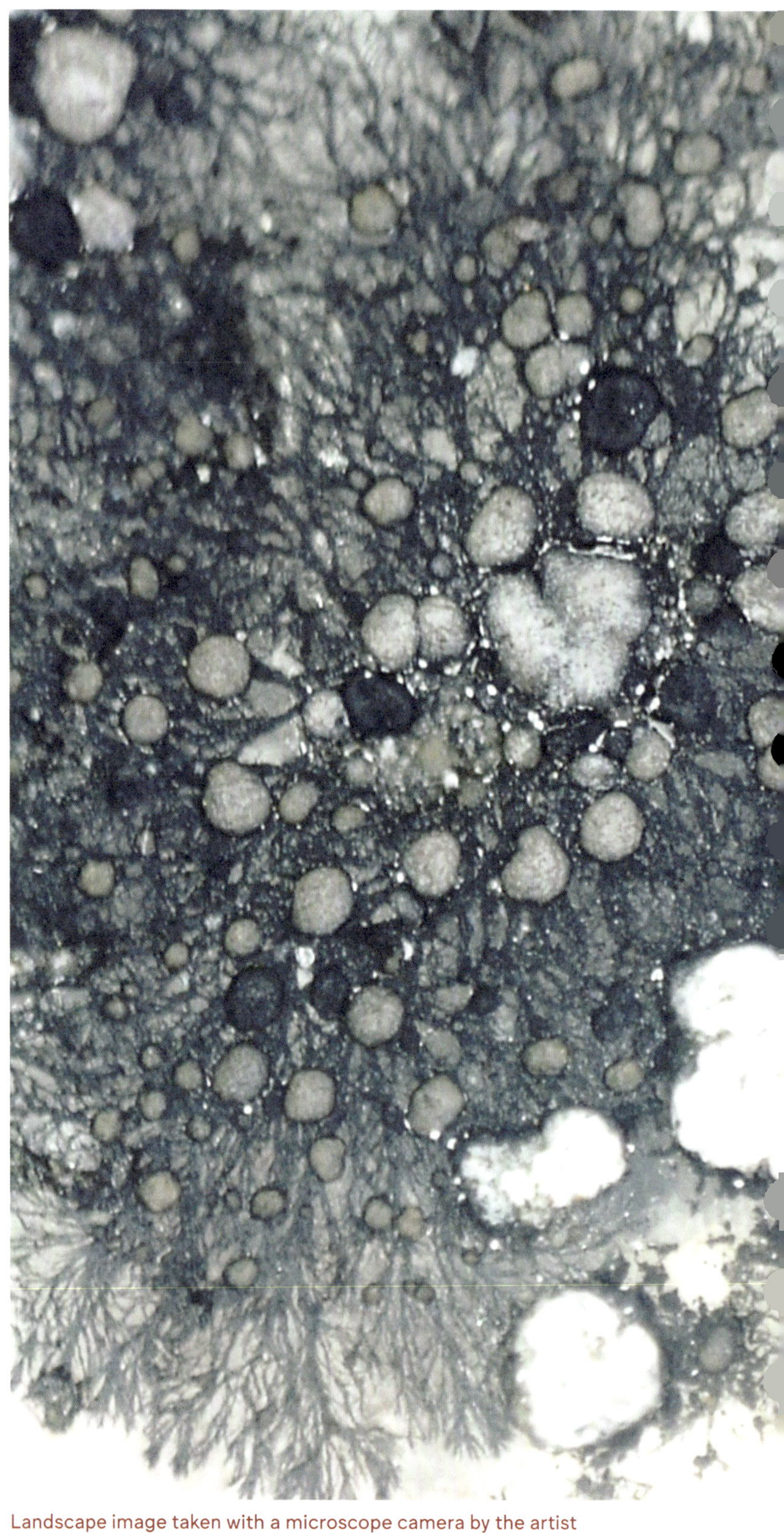

Landscape image taken with a microscope camera by the artist during the production of *Matriarchy*, 2021

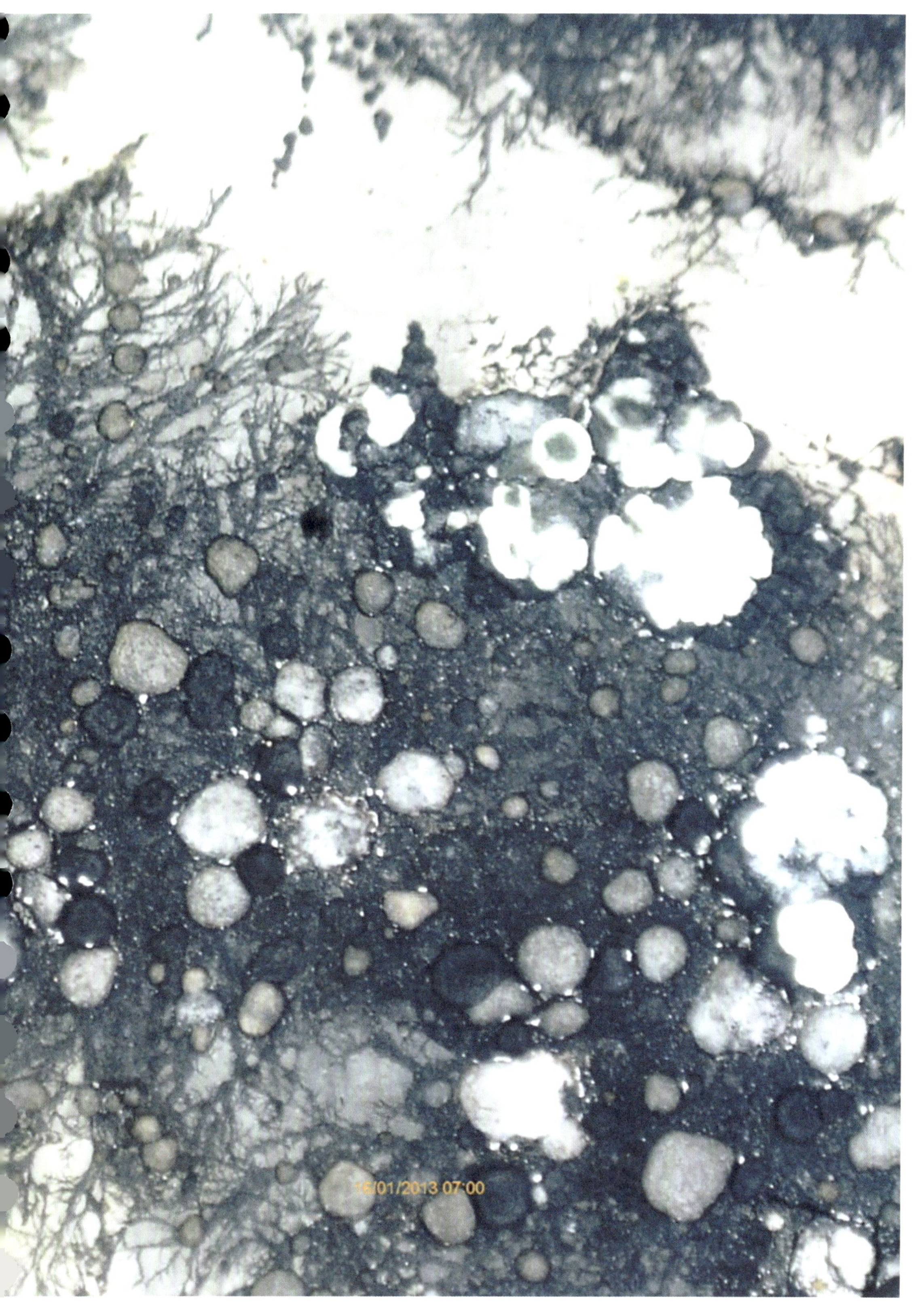

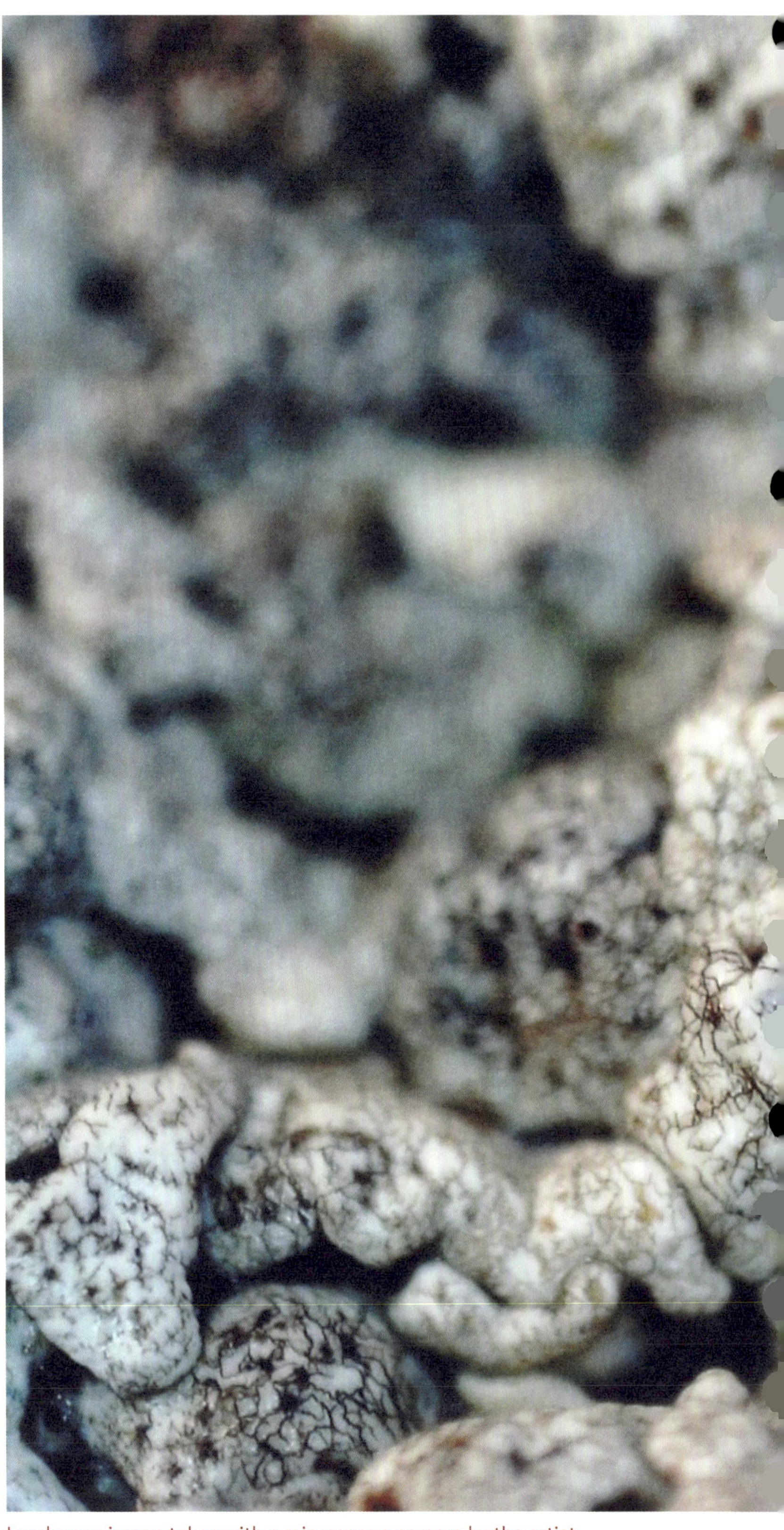

Landscape image taken with a microscope camera by the artist during the production of *Matriarchy*, 2021

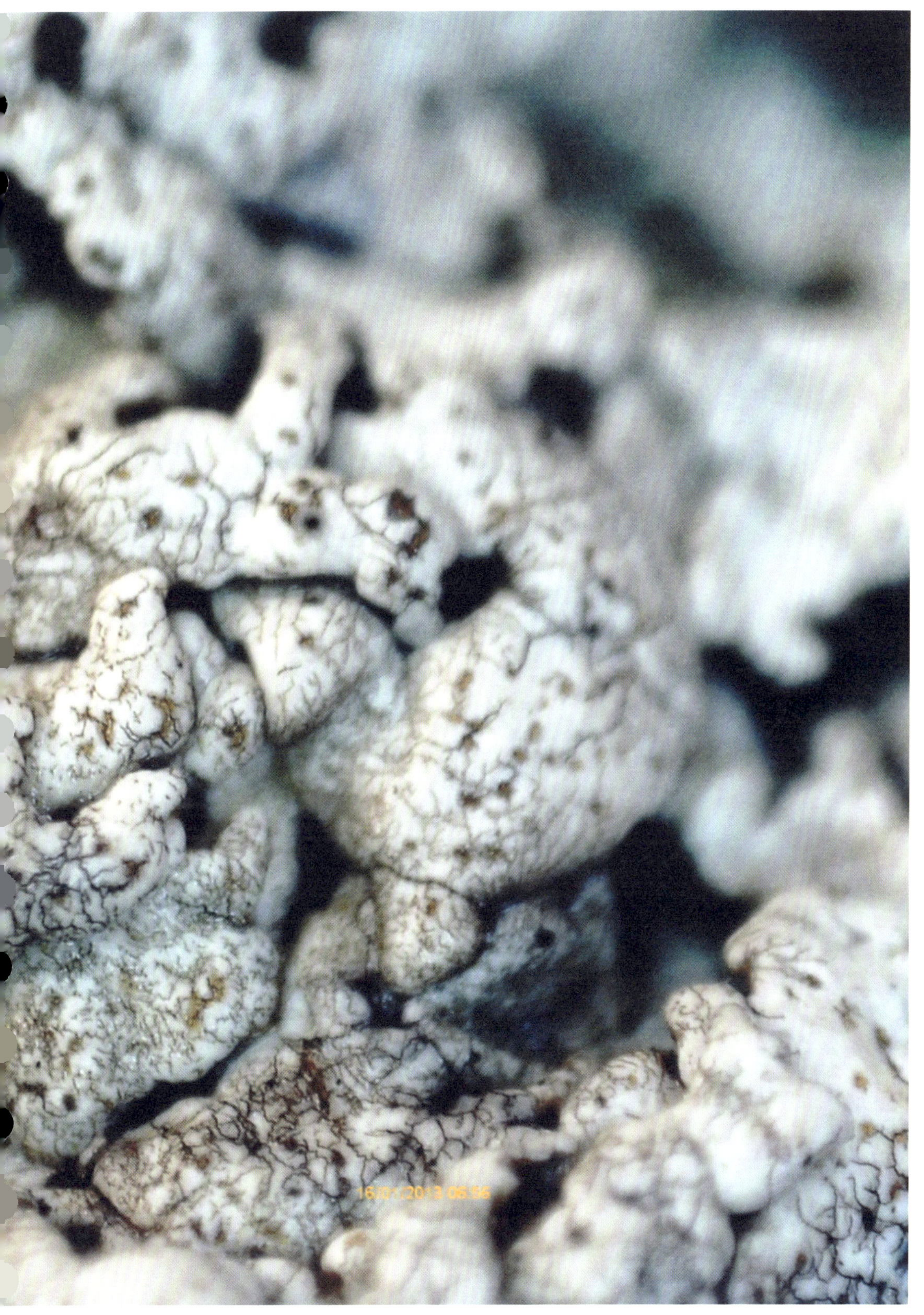

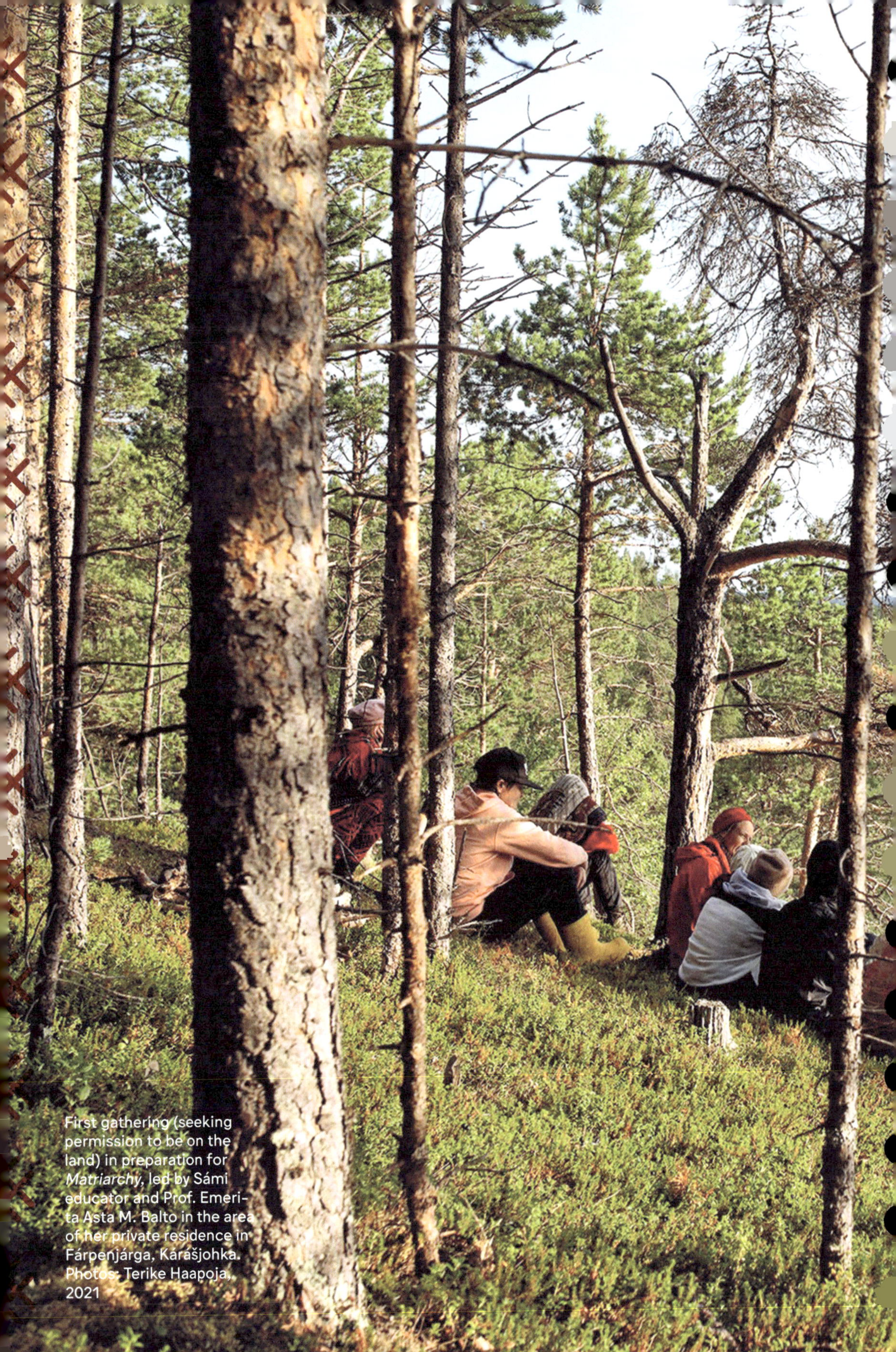

First gathering (seeking permission to be on the land) in preparation for *Matriarchy*, led by Sámi educator and Prof. Emerita Asta M. Balto in the area of her private residence in Fárpenjárga, Kárášjohka. Photos: Terike Haapoja, 2021

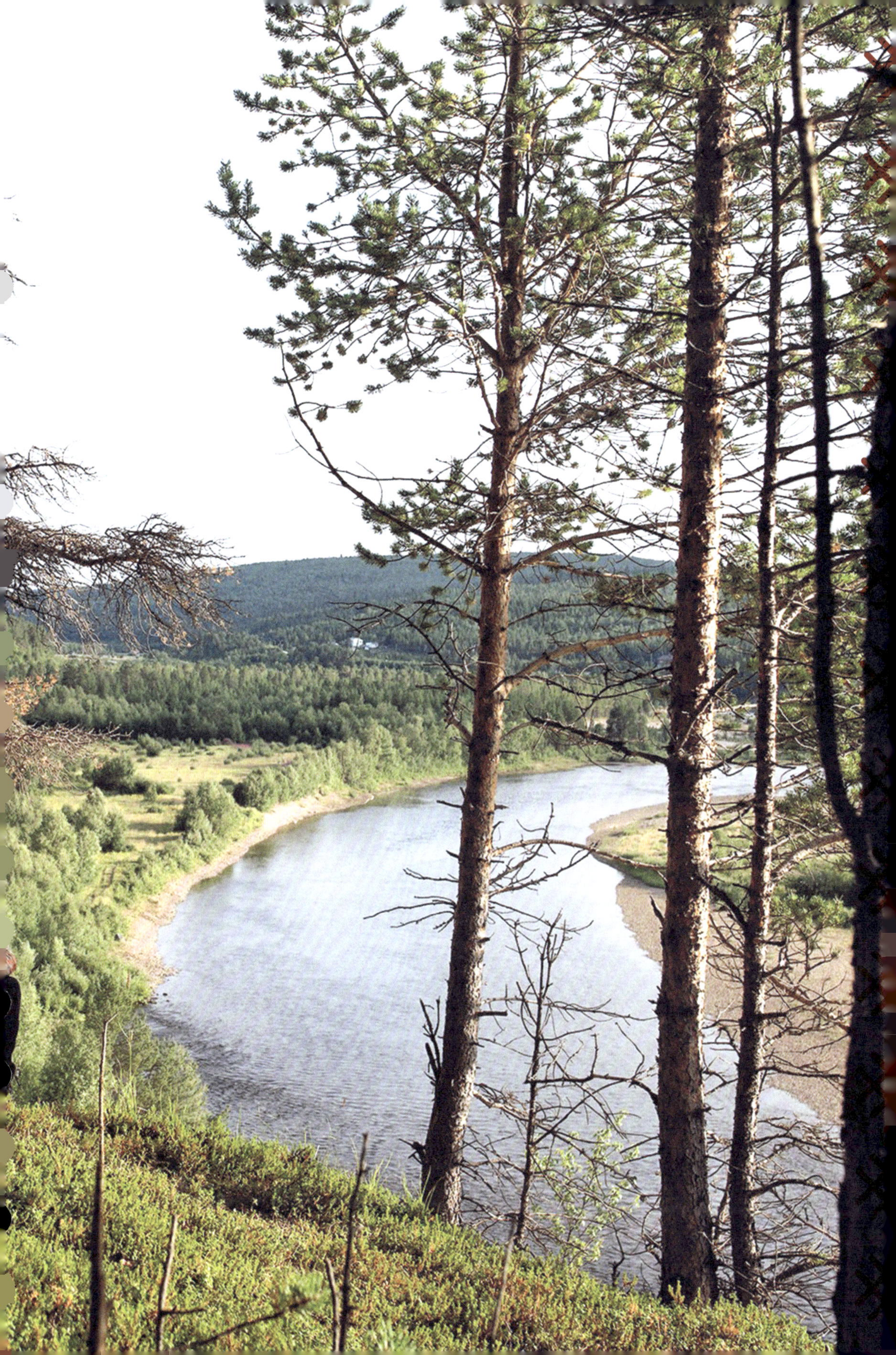

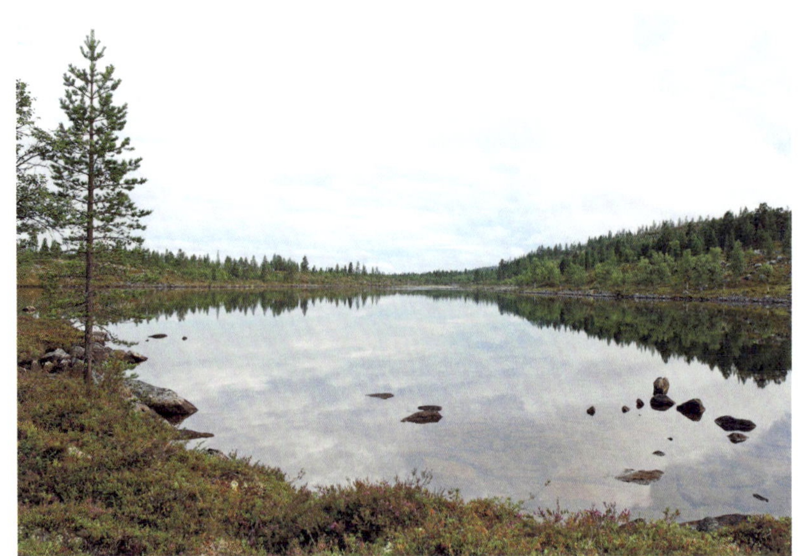

Documentation from the first gathering in preparation for *Matriarchy*.
Photo: Terike Haapoja, 2021

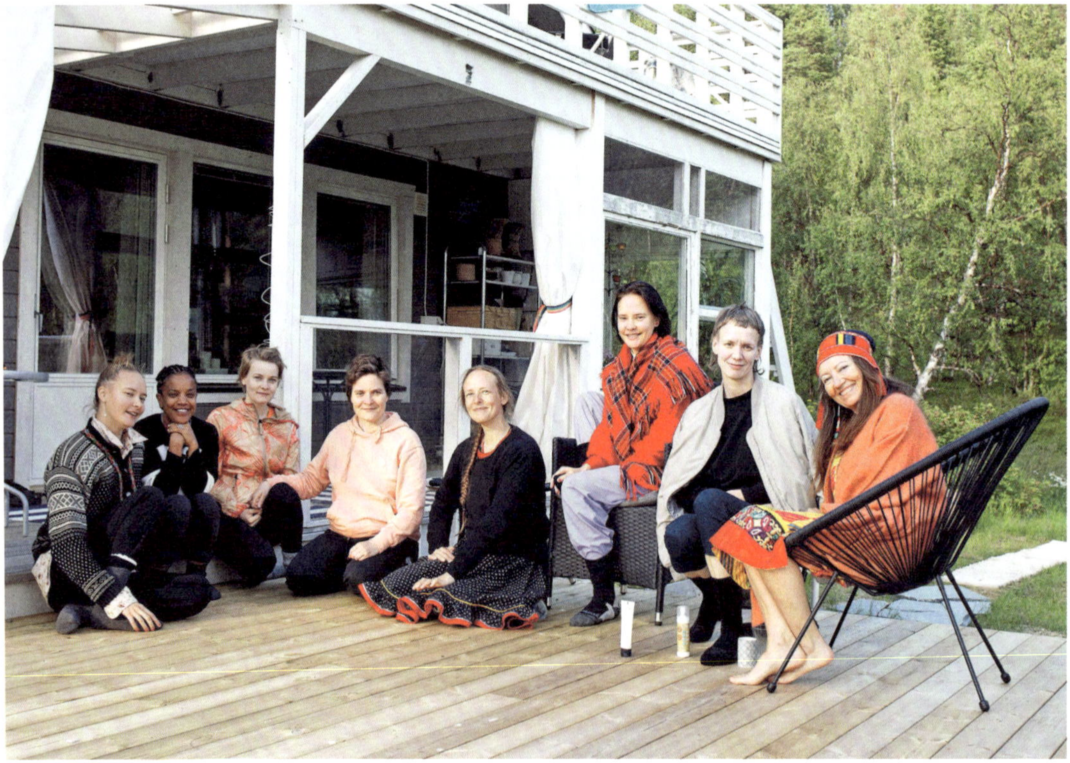

First gathering (seeking permission to be on the land) in preparation for *Matriarchy*, led by Sámi educator and Prof. Emerita Asta M. Balto at her private residence in Fárpenjárga, Kárášjohka. From left to right: Katja Haarla, Eséte Eshetu Sutinen, Hanna Parry, Pauliina Feodoroff, Outi Pieski, Birit Haarla, Satu Herrala and Asta Balto. Photos: Terike Haapoja, 2021

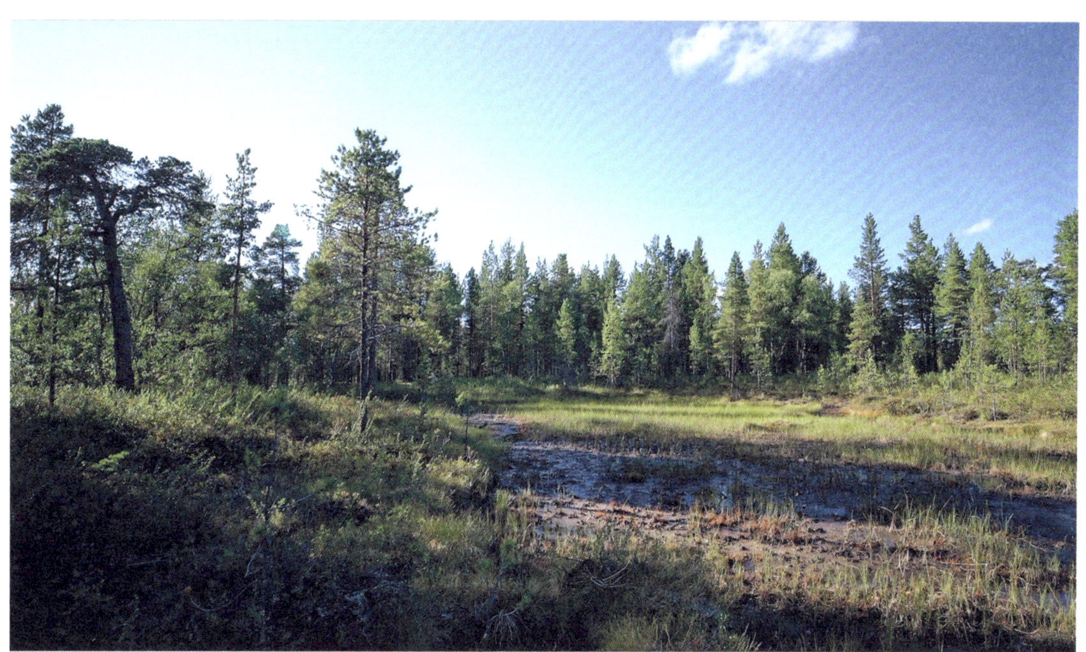

Still from research material for a series of video-portraits of Sámi landscapes under threat from commercial logging, or other industrial land use, in preparation for *Matriarchy* part two, *Auction*. Still: Outi Pieski, 2021

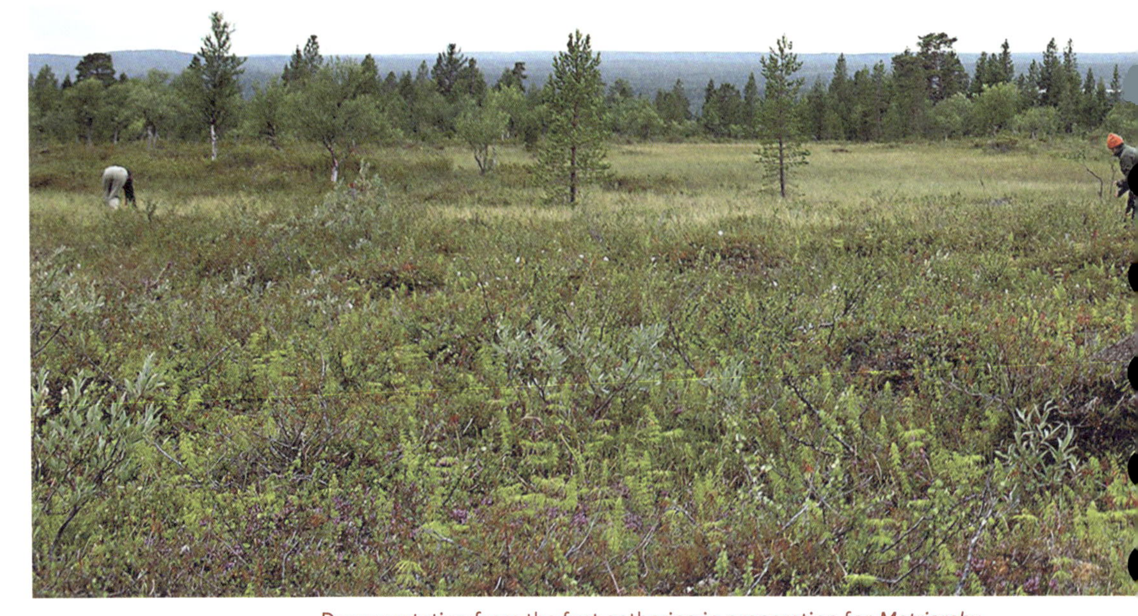

Documentation from the first gathering in preparation for *Matriarchy*.
Photo: Terike Haapoja, 2021

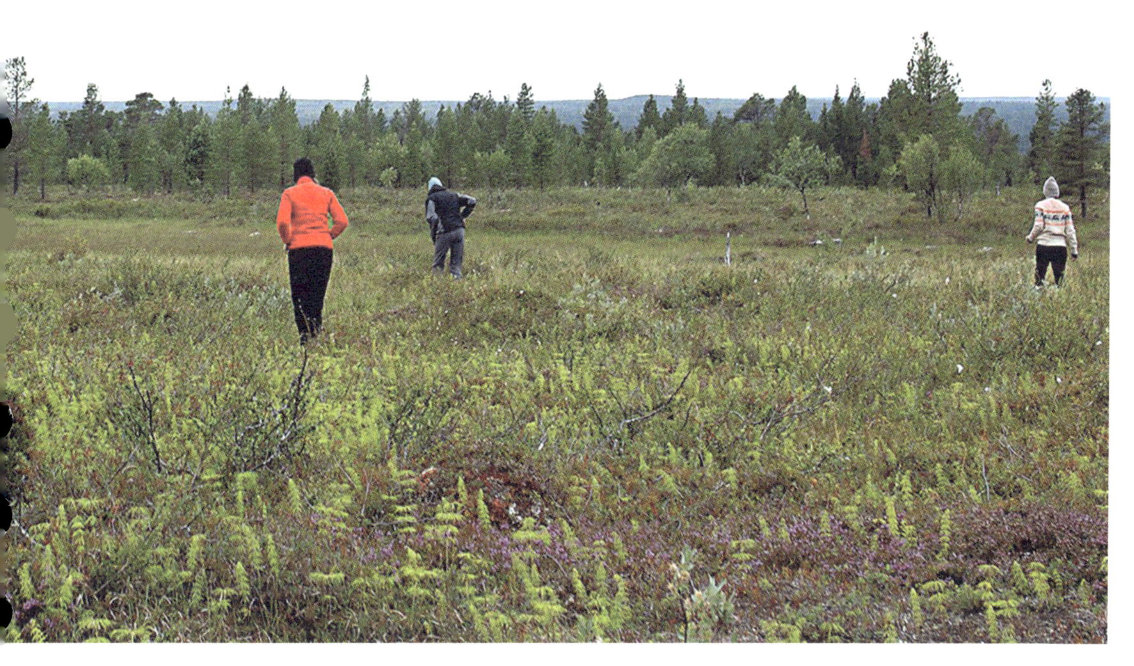

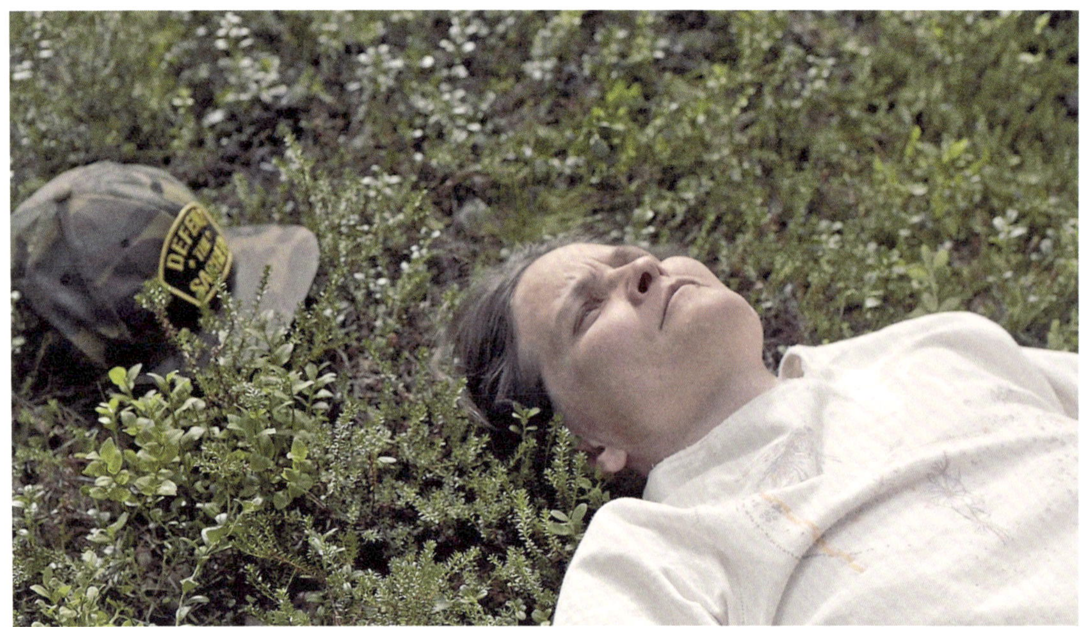

Still from the film *Pauliina Feodoroff Representing Sápmi at La Biennale di Venezia 2022* by Forest People AS, commissioned by OCA, 2020

Pauliina Feodoroff

Writing is Against Me
Ǩee'rjtemtäidd lij muu vuâstta

Writing is against me
I'm battling against those who can write
I write against writing
Whenever I'm supposed to draw, one after
another
KKKs
eMMs
eSSes
and yoUUs
My field of vision narrows
To fill the straight empty lines
With agreed letter combinations
I get addicted to the lines instantly
In the narrow world
Where there's always a new white line that
needs to be filled with meaning
Because if I leave it empty, someone else
will fill it in and then I have to take in
someone else's line and
Its meaning
So that I know what happens what stands for
what stands for what
So that no one pulls out my hair or me out of
my home because writing
I need to know the right order of letters and
everything turns into writing
How to talk and what to talk about
Of which source
I want to free myself from the slavery of
white lines

ǩiõll lij ǩiõll, language is a trap is a
language
but surely they didn't mean this, the Grandmothers,

You have no idea how long
Writing has taken me

I don't understand
How anyone
Could steal from the Grandmothers,
Steal from them
Steal from ones who
Won't fight anymore
So that it won't happen, their daughters
Learned to write
Their grandchildren, to read

Ancient skills have no use here
Even though that's what you keep thinking
They'll be revealed time and again
Shown
Told
And the world is hiding
Is put out
Exactly when you think it's a preface, a
    beginning of sorts,
That starts after they've met you halfway
In the shape of rain, a meadow of flowers,

In order for it to be an aesthetic
Spacer
With ethical and moral dimensions
Reminders that
'You can always do better'
And the mind, petrified in wait for a
    dramaturgy of build-up, is waiting
For something
More distinct
Clearer
A stronger impulse
No, definitely not an impulse because
Like any written observation
It is traceable to who perceived it and
    knowing how to cite

Is a key to
Self-criticism
It is evident that a body's impulse in the water, its experience in the forest
Occurs in your own body
That is, in your own mind
And thus
It begins and ends
With you

If the landscape has a mind to talk
It needs to use sharper
Language
I'd like to have it in writing, please
When and in what manner is fishing to take place, Oh Arctic Ocean
And preferably, your response would take into consideration the investments
In the trawling population

Tell us the most beautiful word you know, the media said to my father

He chose to tell them about a *moonbow*, which the majority of people will never
See because it only appears for a moment in exactly precise conditions
This word describes
What happens then: mannulohss
My favourite word is udam: untamed, obstreperous

I am in the same team as the CEO of The Finnish Forest Industries Federation
We are talking about the future of culture
She also sits on the board of the federation that funds my work
Where we are charting the extent the forest

industries have destroyed our world
By the medium of art

We write concrete, shared ideas to secure culture
As soon as we have formed it into a vision

Of the inherited knowledge
Of inheritance
The eldest son inherited the hunting grounds
The youngest, the house
The eldest daughter, her mother's wife's crown

And the others got what was left
Paraphernalia
Marriage arrangements so that everyone has somewhere to be

Now I've hired a lawyer to look after everyone's fair share

I'LL KEEP MY WORD
We said we'd see each other in a year
And we'd wait at the end of the road
For a week or two
Knowing that the other one will show up, if they're still living
Because we said so

We write more than ever
Words mean less than ever

Ancient skills that some poor soul is trying to capture on digital paper
Being culturally sensitive, of course,
Knowing that watermark is just a small line of a code you can crack instantly

Oh oh oh

Each word gets hijacked and stuffed down
the throat of bottomless hunger, known as
thirst for knowledge
Whoever's lost its place can't find a watering
hole
And that's why
It modifies
Appropriates
Switches
Puts into its own language
Everything it sets its eyes on

How long can we pass on psychopathy before
it destroys the whole species
How far can permeability survive as an
attack strategy
Read it literally

L
I
T
E
R
A
L
L
Y

Even by themselves, the letters make
a stronger image to scare off the
neighbourhood's Siberian jays for good
Than a dogged attempt to tear the line of the
passage of time in two and force the heads
together
Into a time when
Word was law
Grandmothers were the book of law
Who understood the words the most, knew

law and pondered
The words of a stone
The words of wind
The prolixity of pipits

It does not matter where poetry goes
If no one can heal the poisoned earth
Revive it

Because each abandoned pile of sludge or
container or toxic waste
Would exist from that moment and stay
when it is
Even though you rewrote it

Half of my adulthood I took notice of what
was being written about forests
Forest as a paper
as loo roll
as a career path
For a forest contractor a forest professor a
nature photographer a forest activist an
ethical investor

What have I learned?
Forest makes the cut if I can somehow come
up with money
And exchange the money for deeds
Outside this forest that can still choose to
just speak, in its way
This method has used other people's money
to write off 700 hectares of forest, out of
the accounts

With the teachings of my entire adulthood

In my writer's chamber
My hands ailing of a lack of land
I live through a liberated summer without
letters

When I lie in the earth's bosom
Ants appear to let us know they too are here

And I think this is how a new world is born
By returning
To speaking and listening
When everything is still teeming with life

During these vital weeks
I can listen

In Autumn the word came that all that is
  under us has been signed away for battery
  minerals
Since they say transferring cultural heritage
  into digital form is more pressing than
Ever because everything is wiped away all
The time by
    torrential rain
    mudslides
    fires
    uprisings

And we cannot remember what we had
Without metals under our trees

So—forget paper!
Non-linear narrative in a five-dimensional
  virtual world will reach
Deeper
  into your core
Than anything before
Ever
Touched
Grandmother
It reveals
Your deepest
Your innermost

Layers of your being
In the meridian of your Google searches

You stupid girl, you have wasted your time
    on paper
And not realised the time has passed
As the binary code
    models the earth's crust
    in 3D

Minds, with no more restraints

Have only unsynchronised understanding
Between those who are still thinking they'll
    give way
And those who know they have no way to
    give

I write this for you
Do not buy our land
Do not buy the land
Do not
Only because you still can
You have misread the situation

Ǩee′rjtemtäidd lij muu vuâstta
ǩeâšt’tam ǩee′rjtemtäiddsaivui′m
ǩee′rjtam ǩee′rjtemtääid vuâstta
Tõn poodd, ko mie′rren lij pirsted
    ǩeäččlõõžži
KKK:id,
e′Mm:id,
ä′ŠŠ:id
da Ti′jjid
vuei′nnemǩe′dd mu′st ǩeäʒʒan
vuõigg kuâras riâddid teâudd
täi bukvan suåppum kuällsivui′m
tõid riâddid pâššnam tâ′lles
ǩie′ʒʒes maai′lmest
ko′st lij pâi ođđ kuâras viõ′lǧǧes riâdd, koon
    âlgg tieu′dded miârktõõzzivui′m
tõ′nt ko jõs kuâđam riâdd kuârrsen, teâudd
    tõn ǩii-ne jee′res da te′l âlgg mättjed suu
    tieu′ddem riâdd da tõn miârktõõzz
što teâđam mii šâdd mâid miârkkšââvv mii
    miârkkšââvv
što muu jeät ää′lj ǩeâškkad vuõptin le′be
    šâddpaai′ǩinan ko ǩee′rjtemtäidd
mu′st fe′rttai siltteed bukvai jä′rjstõõzz
    vuõi′ǧǧest da puk mottai ǩee′rjtemtäiddan
mä′htt da mâ′st mainstet
koon teâttkääivast
haa′lääm meädda viõ′lǧǧes riâdd å′rjjvuõđâst

    ǩiõll lij ǩiõll lij ǩiõll,
leâša jiõm åâsk tän meinnu, ääkka

Jeä′ped fi′tte mõõn jiânnai ǩee′rjtemtäidd
lij viikkâm ääi′j,

jiõm vuei′t fi′ttjed
mä′htt ni ǩii
ǩe′httai viikkâd ääkkain

suâleed see′st
suâleed nåkmest kåå′tt
ij pii vuâstta teänab
što nu′tt ij šõõddče, sij niõđ
mättje ǩee′rjted
äkkav lookkâd

tuâl' jõžtääidain ij leäkku tääi′b âânnmõš
hå′t ǩee′jjmie′ldd ääi′j ju′rddve′ted nu′tt
tõid ää′veet ti′jjid o′đđest di o′đđest
čuä′jtet
mušttlet
da maai′lm lââmm
čäckk,
tõ′st-i, što kä′ddve′ted tõt lij jåå′đtummuš,
    algg mõõn-ne vääras,
kåå′tt älgg mâŋŋa, ko ti′jjid lie puättam
    vuâstta
ââ′br, rää′ssmiõut hää′mest

što tõt le′čči esteettlaž
kõskk-kooskaž
mâ′st sä′tte lee′d eettlaž-moraal'laž
    vuälladvuõđ
moštt'tõõzz tõ′st što
”pâi vuäitt tuejjeed pue′rben”
da kaggõõtti dramaturgia vuârddmõ′šše
    tõrggâm miõll vuârdd
mâid-ne
jäänab koll'jeei
čiõlggsab
viõusab impuuls,
ij, jeä′rben ij impuuls ko
mâ′te juõ′ǩǩ mušttuǩee′rjtum vuâmmšõõzz
vuäitt kuõrrâd vuâmmšejjses da teâttkääivai
    kuäivvamtäidd
lij lokkčooud

jiõččkriti′ǩǩe
lij jijstes se′lvv, što vaard impulss čää′ʒʒest,
   ǩiõččlâsttmõš mie′ccest
šâdd jiijjad vaardâst
le′be jiijjad miõlâst
da nääi′t tõn algg da lopp
leäk ton

jõs kue′stelm haa′lad mainsted
tõt âlgg lee′d tää′rǩab
ǩiõlstes
miõlstan ǩeerjlânji vääldčem tän, spä′sseb
mä′htt da kuä′ss âlgg kue′llšee′lled, vuõi
   Jiõŋŋmiârr
da le′čči šiõgg, što vasttõssad vääldči lokku
   ju′n trooli meärra tuejjuum
investâsttmõõžžid

säärn moččumõs tuu tobddâm sää′n, raauki
   media e′jstan

son va′lljii mušttled *mannuloousâst*, koon
   vuäinnmõš ij leäkku šuurmõs vuässa
   oummin ni kuä′ss vuei′tlvaž ko tõt
   eett tå′lǩ siõmmni′žže tiiudlaž tää′rǩes
   åårrmõõžžâst
tät sää′nn kovvad tõn
mii te′l lij: mannulohss
muu miõl mie′ldd sää′nn lij udam:
   škoou′l’jeǩani, miâstǩani

išttâd ååram seämma tuâjj-joukâst
   Metsäteollisuus rõ tååimtemjåå′đtee′jin
smiõttâp kulttuur pue′ttiääi′j
son išttâd åårr seämma foond halltõõzzâst,
   kåå′tt teäggat muu tuâj
ko′st kaart’tet meä′ccindustria tuejjeem
   hiâvtummuž maailma

čeäppõõzz kuånstivui′m

mij ǩee′rjtep õhttsaž konkreettlaž e′tǩǩõõzzid
kulttuur pue′ttiääi′j staanâm diõtt
tâ′lles ko leä′p pâi häämääm tõ′st visio

ä′rbbteâđast
a′rbbjummšest
puärrsõmâs â′lǧǧ a′rbbji šee′llem-määddaid
nuõrmõs â′lǧǧ põõrt
puärrsõmâs nijdd jie′nnes šaamšiǩ

da jeärraz vuåǯǯu mâid vuåǯǯu
neävvaid
suõni pâânnmõõžž nu′tt što pukin lij sââ′jj
ko′st lee′d

ânn’jõžääi′j mon pa′lǩǩääm juriist ââ′nned
huõl, što puk vuäǯǯa mâid-ne

SÄÄ′NN TUÕ′LLAI
sue′ppe što lij lett ee′jj ǩee′jjest
da nuu′bb vuõ′rdde pälggaz ǩee′jjest
neä′ttel, nuu′bb
tie′đee′l što nu′bb puätt, jõs jie′llmen lij
ko nu′tt sue′ppe

ǩee′rjtet jäänab ko ni kuä′ss
sää′nn miârkkšââvv uu′ccben ko ni kuä′ss

”tuâl’jõžtääid” koid ǩii-ne leekktem võl
ǩiččal hääm eed digitaal’laž põ′mmai ool
kulttuurlânji sensitiivlaž naa′lin, tiõttlõs
tie′đee′l što watermark lij tå′lǩ siõm
koodkooskaž koon ää′vad jå′ttlânji

vuõi   vuõi   vuõi

juõ′ǩǩ sää′n njamstet puuđte′mes nie′lj
njiõlõ′ǩǩe, kåå′tt jåått nõõmin teâđ
jugstõõvvmõš

päi′ǩstes pååđnam ij kaaun čää′cckåå′v
da tõ′nt
tõt mott
väldd jiõccses
jåårgal
rääjj jiijjâsǩiõllsi′žžen
puk, koon tõn ǩicstõõgg vuâlla peejj

mõõn kookkas psykopatia vuäitt
    a′rbbjõõvvâd tõntää tõt hiâvat looppâst
    puk šlaaj
mõõn kookkas čõõđ peä′sttemvuõtt vuäitt
    se′lvvned kõrmmlemstrategian
loogg tõn bukvai mie′ldd
B
U
K
V
A
I

M
I
E
′
L
D
D

bukvain juõ′ǩǩkaž õhttu lij viõusab kovv
    põõlted kuusǩid ǩe′ddmää′rǩest âãggas
mâ′te a′ǧǧes ǩiččlummuš ǩeâškkad ääi′j
    jåå′ttemǩeäin peäll’lõõžži da pääkkted
    ǩie′jjid mååust õ′htte
po′dde kuä′ss
sää′nn leäi lää′ǩǩ
ääkkaž leäi lää′ǩǩ-ǩe′rjj

tõt kåå′tt puki saa′nid jäänmõsân fi′ttji, leäi
    lää′jj tobddi da tä′rǩstõõli
ǩie′đj saa′nid
piõgg saa′nid
hõ′ppja heä′rvvciâlkkjid

lij õhtt ko′st tiivtâs jåått
jõs ni ǩii ij silttâd teänab pue′reed
    suu′lmõsttum määdd
jeällted tõn

tõ′nt ko juõ′ǩǩ hiâlguum måå′đđpäi′ǩǩ
    ruõkkâmle′tt toxic waste
lij tõn rää′jest da pââšš ko tõt lij
hå′t mä′htt tõn ǩee′rjte′či jee′res ä′ššen

mon- kuvddlem pâ′jjel peä′l rää′vesvuõđstan
    mâid mie′ccin ǩee′rjtet
meä′cc   põ′mmjen
            nuu′žniǩpõ′mmjen
            karriää′rpälggsen
meä′ccurkkooumže meä′ccprofessoo′re
    *luâtt*sniimmja meä′ccaktivi′stte *eettlaž*
    teä′ǧǧruõkkja

mâid leäm mättjam?
Meä′cc vuäǯǯ puu′ttes põ′mmjid jõs
    ha′ŋǩǩääm ko′st-ne tie′ǧǧid
da tie′ǧǧivui′m vuä′mstempõ′mmjid
jee′reså′rnn ko tän mie′ccest kåå′tt võl vuäǯǯ
    va′lljeed pâi mainsted, vue′jjes mie′ldd
tät metood lij ǩee′rjtam jeärrsi tie′ǧǧivui′m
    700 hehtaarâd mie′cc åålgas tillǩii′rjin

ǩee′jjmie′ldd rää′vesvuõđ määttaivui′m

ǩee′rjteei kämmrastan
ǩiõđ pue′cce määdd vää′n diõtt
jeälam õõut luõvâsmiõllsaž ǩie′zz bukvaitää

kuä′ss liâžžääm määdd ââ′sǩest
kootk čuä′jtâ′tte mušttled što lie še tääi′ben

da juurdčam što ođđ maai′lm šâdd nääi′t
mainsted di kuvddled
mää′ccee′l
ko puk lij õinn tiudd jie′llem

vuäǯǯam täid jie′llma tää′rǩes neä′ttlid
kuvddled

čõhčč älgg looggee′l, što tät puk lij
    vuâllaǩee′rjtum mij vue′lnn meädda
akkumineraali vääras kulttuurää′rb
    se′rddmest digitaal'laž hämma lij
    ǩirrsab ko ni kuä′ss tõ′nt ko puk läppai
    ǩee′jjmie′ldd
ääi′j
    kõrr ââ′br
    måå′đđčääv
    puâllmõõžž
    meerkaggõõttmõõžž juõ′ljid

da jeä′p vuei′t mu′štted mii leäi
metaallitää, kook lie muõreen vue′lnn

â′tte väjldââ′tt põ′mmai!
non-lineaarlaž mušttlummuš viiđ
    vuälladvuõđ virtuaal'laž maai′lmest
    mâânn
čiŋŋlubun
    õđđmasad
ko ni mii lij
ni kuä′ss
likktõõllâm
ääkkžam
tõt päljsmâtt
čiŋŋlumâs
pukin peittum

jiijjadvuõđ ǩee′rdid
google-ooccmõõžžääd meridiaa′ne

ton tuu′hmes nijdd leäk tu′hll’jam ääigad
    põ′mmja
jiõk-ga leäkku fi′ttjam što äi′ǧǧ lij jååttam
    rääi ääi′j binää′rlååggaivui′m
mäddkõõr 3D-mallâttmõ′šše

miõlivui′m, koid jie teänab tuõ′lle

lie tå′lǩ fi′ttjõõzz jee′resäiggsažvuõđ
tõi kõõsk, kook kä′dde što võl kâ′rvve
da tõi, kook teä′tte što ij leäkku teänab koozz
    kâ′rvved

täid saa′nid ǩee′rjtam Tu′nne
jeä′l vue′st mäddan
jeä′l vue′st määdd
jeä′l vue′st
tå′lǩ tõ′nt što võl vuäitak
leäk lookkâm vue′jj puästtad

Anders Sunna

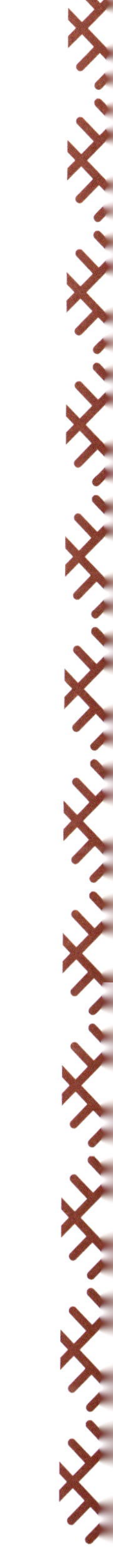

Katya García-Antón
and Liv Brissach

Revealing the Nordic States' Totalitarian Interior. Fifty Years of Sámi Struggles in Six Paintings by Anders Sunna

> 'When I grew up, I learnt that darkness is our friend … In our work we are not afraid of the dark.'[1]

Anders Sunna's immersive installations are characterised by for their sense of darkness and fury. *Illegal Spirits of Sápmi*, the installation he presents in 'The Sámi Pavilion', is similarly filled with anger. A hexalogy of paintings is displayed in free-standing archive units, hand-built with his brothers, also containing the documents from forty or so court cases that his reindeer-herding family have fought against the Swedish state over the past fifty years. The first five paintings and archive units address one decade each, beginning in 1971, while the sixth unit, made as Sunna's vision of the future, is presented as burnt remains, the artist having set fire to it beforehand. Five sonic dioaramas, combining courtroom proceedings, field recordings, interviews and voice overs accessed as QR codes in the paintings, immerse the viewer into the world of trauma and resilience narrated by the paintings.

Sunna has often described himself as a stateless person battling against 'a massive superior force'.[2] His paintings express this eloquently: gigantic men in Nazi uniforms emblazoned with the Swedish or Norrbotten's coat of arms on their armbands, hover over the land and against a backdrop of decapitated reindeer, skeletons and gallows. In this way, the paintings evoke Sunna's experience of colonialism in Sápmi as totalitarian occupation and brutal slaughter; they also convey a tenacious will to stand up against that brutality through clever acts of subversion.

Rendering darkness is a survival strategy, where rage and fury are orchestrated into sombre visuality, in the form of paintings, murals and installations. Born into a community where many reindeer herders are unable to withstand the pressures under which they are placed by measures imposed by the state, and where and suicide

1 Anders Sunna, statement during 'Museums on Fire!' at Office for Contemporary Art in April, 2017.

2 STRUGGLE #1, interview by STRUGGLE, a web-documentary by Simon Maraud, 9 June 2018 https://youtu.be/owKXQGztVx0, accessed 15 September 2021.

rates are tragically high, learning the skill of channelling anger for art production is literally life saving.[3] The rage in Sunna's case is generated by the injustices that his family has endured for generations while fighting for their customary right to continue reindeer herding in their ancestral Sámi area, a fight that has earned them a reputation as outlaws, trouble-makers, forest-pirates and guerilla herders by the Swedish state, by their non-Sámi neighbours and even by some Sámi peers.

Consider the words of Sámi artist and poet Nils-Aslak Valkeapää, also known as Áilloháš, a legendary figure greatly respected by Sunna:

They come to me
And show books
Law books
That they have written themselves
This is the law and it applies to you too
See here

But I do not see brother
I do not see sister
I cannot
I say nothing
I only show them the tundra[4]

Since the 1700s, the Swedish state has regulated various laws affecting the Sámi people. In parallel, the intensive settling in Sápmi by southerners, the closing of borders previously open to reindeer migrations, and the forced dislocation of reindeer-herding families to new areas are further examples of state-enforced policies that have had a dramatic effect on Sámi communities; not to mention the impact of christianisation, taxation, damming and mining in Sámi areas on Sámi livelihoods, spirituality, economy and health.

3
In a completely different context, the American writer Audre Lorde spoke about the need to orchestrate rage to survive in her 1981 keynote talk 'Uses of Anger: Women Responding to Racism' at the Women's Studies Association Conference, Sturrs, Connecticut. Available in Audre Lorde, Sister Outsider: Essays & Speeches by Audre Lorde (Berkeley: Crossing Press, 2007), 124–33. We borrow her words for the context of this essay with deep respect and understanding of the fact that they were originally uttered to describe anger from an intersectional black feminist point of view. Borrowing her words here does not mean that we conflate the struggle of black women in the US and the struggle of Sámi people in the Nordic countries, but highlight their shared ground.

4
Nils Aslak Valkeapää, 'My Home is in my Heart' (excerpt), from *Trekways of the Wind*, translated by. Harald Gaski, Lars Nordström and Ralph Salisbury, (Guovdageaidnu: DAT, 1994).

5
Anders Sunna via email to OCA, November 2021.

When an unjust new reindeer-herding act came into effect in 1971, the Sunna family did not sit idly by. They were ordered to give up their customary rights as Sámi people to continue reindeer herding, and instead to apply on a year-to-year basis for permission to herd a limited number of reindeer, to a board largely composed of non-Sámi landowners of the area. Secondly, they were told they must herd, in addition to their own reindeer, those owned by the non-Sámi landowners, which greatly outnumbered their own reindeer, without receiving any compensation for this extra work. Thirdly, they were instructed to pay those same landowners a fee for the right to herd what was essentially their own reindeer on their own land. The next fifty years have been characterised by draining legal disputes, none of which have been won by the Sunna family; the situation has only escalated into absurd complexity. The Sunna family has been evicted from their own herding lands, the state has removed their earmark registration (which is needed to own reindeer and is handed down over generations) and although there are amendments to the law of 1971 indicating that the family may have been in the right, and that the state misinterpreted the law, no court or institution seems to have had to date the power to undo or compensate them for the malpractice.

Initiating the hexalogy *Illegal Spirits of Sápmi* is a painting that depicts the force of Sweden's officials in the 1971 courtroom, the first step in what Sunna explains as 'the persecution of us in order to take away our nourishment and culture … [so that the] Sámi would become slaves and Swedes lords over the Sámi.'[5] The painting is more than a mere documentation of the first court case, although it includes some documentary aspects (such as portraits of real people who were there): its strength lies in revealing the power asymmetry of the courtroom in simple, yet effective ways. In the top left, the Swedish law book comes thundering down from a stormy sky. This becomes the backdrop to the dominating figure of Norrbotten's governor, who throws a disdainful gaze down towards the lower right, where law books are crossed out and members of the Sunna family are placed against a forest background. Centre stage is the Sámi goavddis, the sacred drum, representing on the one hand Sámi ways of being, thinking and doing since immemorial times, and on the other, a microcosm of colonialism since the Sámi spirituality (in which the drum is central) was persecuted by the church and state. Swedish and Norwegian courtrooms have since the 1700s until today, persistently ostracised the Sámi drum, and hunted down the Sámi noaidit (spiritual leaders), who were in many instances sentenced to death by burning as part of a wave of witch hunts across Europe. While such sentences were not in use in the 1970s, the colonial domination was shockingly similar, and the tool to achieve this continues to be the book of law.

The above-cited poem by Valkeapää, as well as the 1971 painting by Sunna, go to the core of an issue with which many Indigenous peoples worldwide are all-too familiar: nation-states such as the Nordic countries uphold the legal system to protect their population, and consider law as one of their most important tools in advocating for global human rights to which they align as UN-friendly states. Yet, when a nation state such as Sweden is founded on Indigenous territory, and has interests in its natural resources, the legal framework, which is written by that nation state, serves that same nation state's interests better than it serves those of the Indigenous population. Sweden was one of the countries that advocated for the UN's Convention on Indigenous People (ILO 169) in the late 1980s but has still to ratify that Convention at home. This hypocrisy is exactly what Sunna targets by emphasising Sweden's totalitarian attitude when it comes to Sámi relations, currently and in the past. This dark

6 Anders Sunna in the film *The Sámi Pavilion*, by Egil Pedersen. Commissioned by OCA, 2021.

7 Anders Sunna in an email to OCA, November 2021.

chapter of Nordic history is still unresolved; there is no postcolonialism in Sweden. Sunna's paintings of his family's reality, echoed by similar stories all over Sápmi, destabilise the humanitarian image of Sweden and the other Nordic countries abroad, revealing the tragedy of current Sámi existence.

> Every authority you can imagine has been after us. During the day we are helping the reindeer in the forest, and during the evening we are sitting in the police station.[6]

In his painting depicting the 1980s, Sunna addresses two parallel injustices that personally affected his family and also serve as structural evidence of the political, social, legal and overall colonial terrors to which Sámi people are subjected when they insist on their right to maintain their world-views and ways of life. Part of the painting depicts his grandfather in intensive care with the authorities taking advantage of the situation to subpoena him to the courtroom while he was on his sickbed. On the other side, Sunna focuses on one of the most dramatic encounters between his family and the state, an event that took place in 1986. While the family were conducting their annual calf marking, one of the most meaningful parts of reindeer herding life, an uninvited delegation of policemen and local landowners arrived, 'with orders to forcibly relocate our reindeer and us', as Sunna recounts it, 'over 30 people against my dad and his three brothers'.[7] A 30 kilometre long fence was erected in order to keep the Sunna family's reindeers away from their traditional grazing grounds, and in the chaos of the eviction, the family's animals were stolen by those present. The event led to a massive loss of land, animals and community – essentially the factors that are needed to sustain a livelihood.

8
Anders Sunna in the film *The Sámi Pavilion*, by Egil Pedersen. Commissioned by OCA, 2021.

Two further archival elements compose Sunna's hexalogy. The first is a series of folders containing,

> 'The legal papers … from 1971 until today. All the cases about what has happened to our family … My father, my mum and my oldest son are copying the legal papers that will be part of the art piece … You can feel it, you can take it out, you can have a look at it … to see the amount of papers, text, and everything.'

The second, is a series of audio pieces, one per painting, relating aspects of the story of the family's conflict with the Swedish authorities. Excerpts from the family sound archive of the courtrooms, as well as new field recordings, are layered in a way that is reminiscent of Sunna's paintings. These sonic dioramas have been conceived and technically realised by Sunna in collaboration with dramaturgy advisor Gaby Hartel, writer, radio author and professor of sound art at Lind University and 'The Sámi Pavilion' curatorial group. The dioramas have served as the foundations to develop a radio play in collaboration and with the support of Prof. Hartel and Deutchlandfunk Berlin (one of the most prestigious and long-standing radio play specialists internationally). The play was aired in Germany to coincide with the launch of 'The Sámi Pavilion'.

The installation *Illegal Spirits of Sápmi* concludes with an act of renewal. Its sixth painting, made by Sunna to depict his vision for the 10 years to come, was burnt at his home as a powerful ceremonial act. By laying the ashes on the ground of 'The Sámi Pavilion', next to the last depicted decade, Sunna effectively rises with his family from those ashes like a phoenix. This act is as much a punctuation marking the end to 50 years of struggle, as a for a call of conviction for a new and truly postcolonial, Indigenised future. When the legal system fails, where does one turn

9 Anders Sunna's statement for 'NIRIN', the 22nd Biennale of Sydney, in which he participated in 2020 https://www.biennaleofsydney.art/participants/anders-sunna/, accessed 15 September 2021.

as the last resort? In Sunna's case, his artistic career has become a way to to unite his family and to relate their story to an audience much greater and wider-reaching than that of the courtroom. Following the Sámi custom of respecting Elder voices and fostering the transmission of knowledge in the community across generations, Sunna has benefited from dialogues with Ánde Somby, Sámi Professor of law, noaidi and juoigi (practioner of juoigan the Sámi musical practice) who has provided his knowledge regarding the complexity of this legal history, within the context of colonial law. Intent on exploring these narratives through his artistic practice, as Sunna puts it: 'Imagine being able to speak all the world's languages without saying a sound. To reach people's hearts first and then their consciousness. The anger you are carrying suddenly finds a way to emerge but in a more creative form, stronger than iron. Art is that.'[9]

Illegal Spirits of Sápmi is an artistic project fronted by Sunna, in which his family has been involved every step of the way. It is a testimony, and living archive that would not exist without the memories that his father, mother, uncles and older siblings have shared with him, handed down over generations and narrated as detailed stories told during family visits. His brothers built the wooden archive units holding the hexalogy of paintings, with wood from trees felled in their area; Sunna's children and parents helped him gather, organise and photocopy the court files and sound recordings for inclusion in the installation. *Illegal Spirits of Sápmi* is more than a painting installation: it is the magnum opus of the Sunna family's collective efforts, a work that empowers their stories, with tenacity and resilience.

For Sunna, art is survival but it is also healing. Being present in the Venice Biennial, standing shoulder to shoulder with his family, is an opportunity to amplify the Sunna family's call for justice through the global stage of this event. It is also a moment of fortification and renewal;

it is a moment of Sámification and of advocacy for Sámi worldviews. As Sunna noted when he spoke the words of a poem (presented in full in this section of the book) composed specially for the launch of 'The Sámi Pavilion' project in The Sámi Parliament of Norway in October 2021:

'Your future is not for me.
And not really for you either.
Follow me instead, I said.'

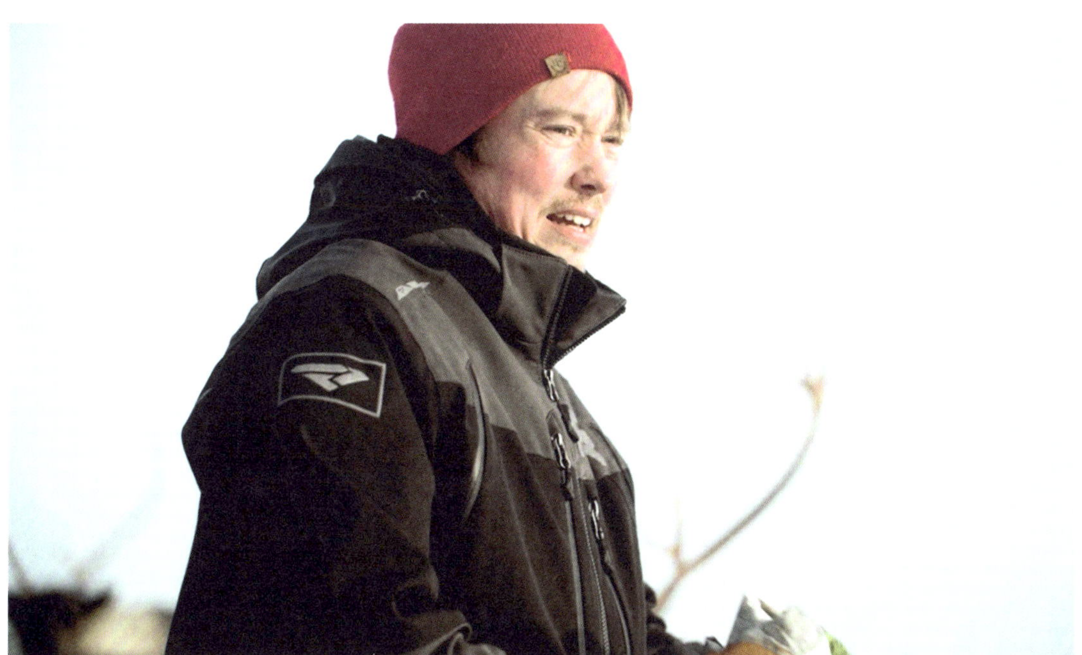

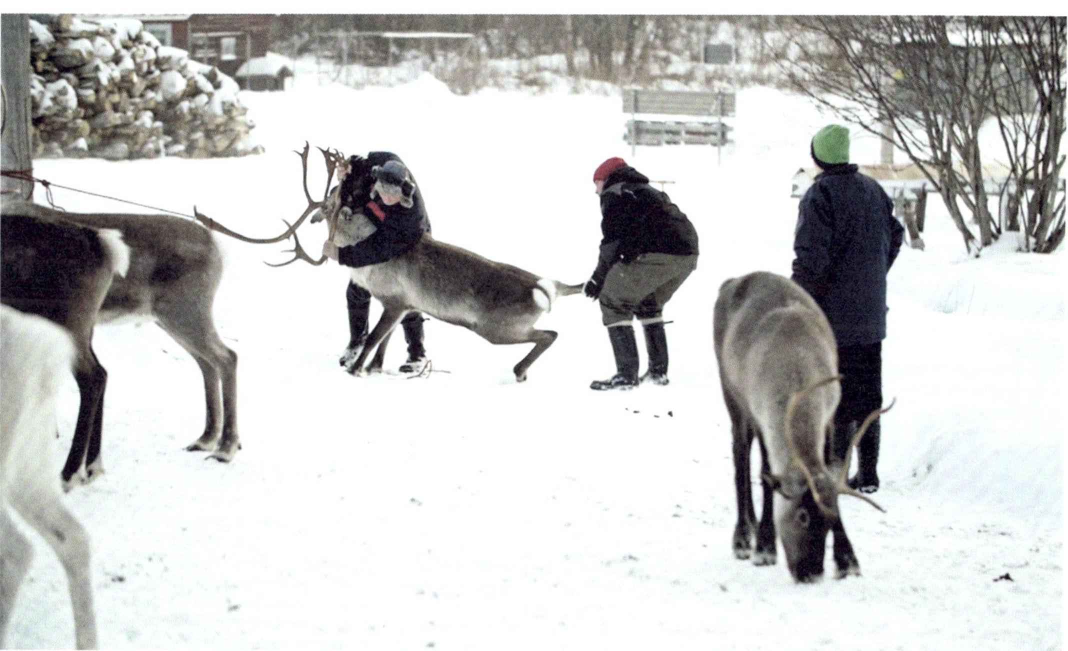

Top: Anders Sunna Bottom: Anders Sunna and family members.
Stills: Egil Pedersen, 2021

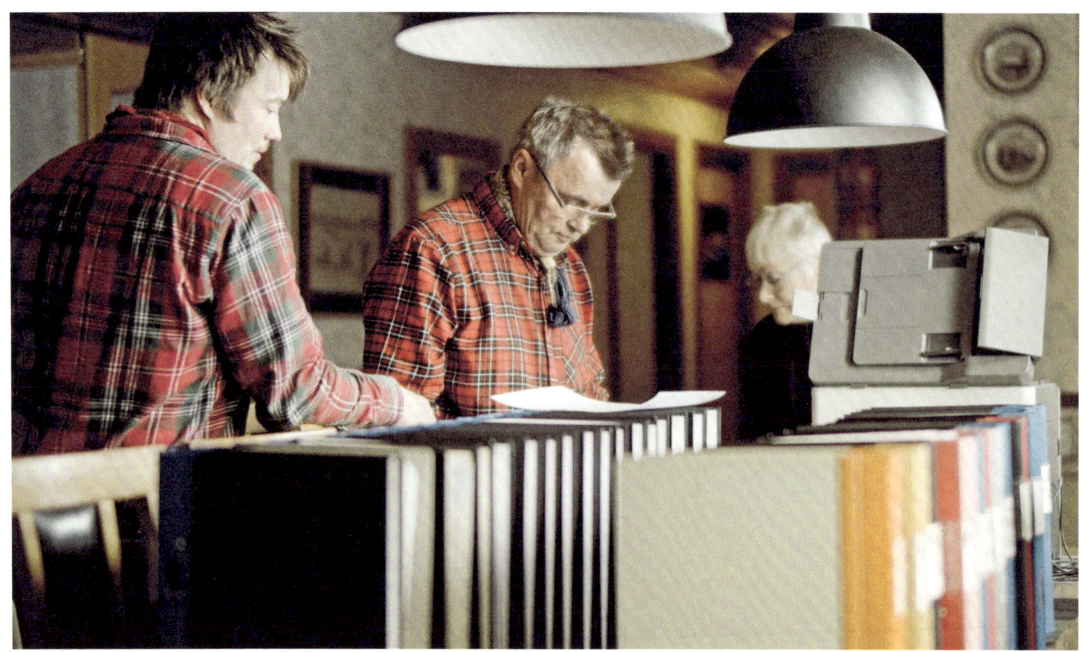

Anders, Bo (his father) and Britt-Inger (his mother) Sunna

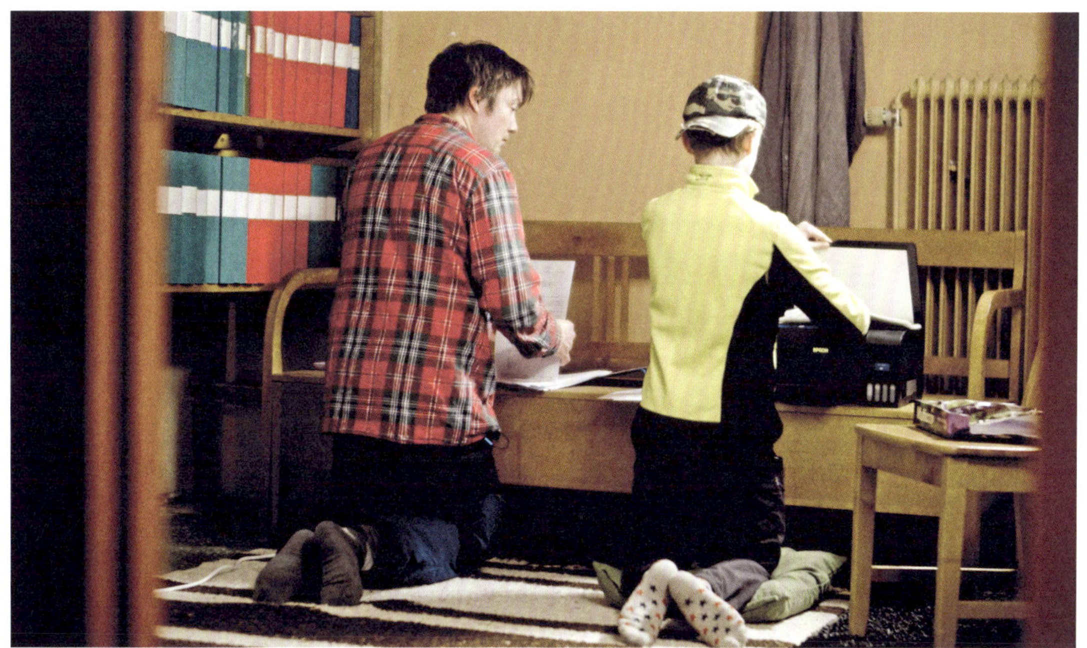

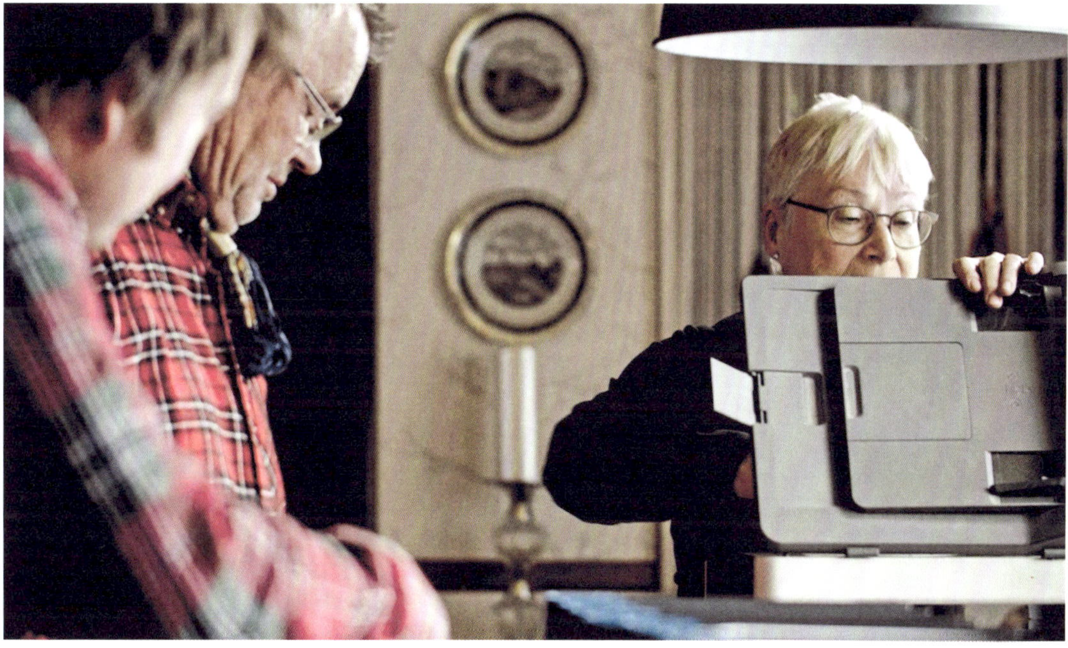

Top: Anders and one of his sons. Bottom: Anders and Britt-Inger Sunna.
Stills: Egil Pedersen, 2021

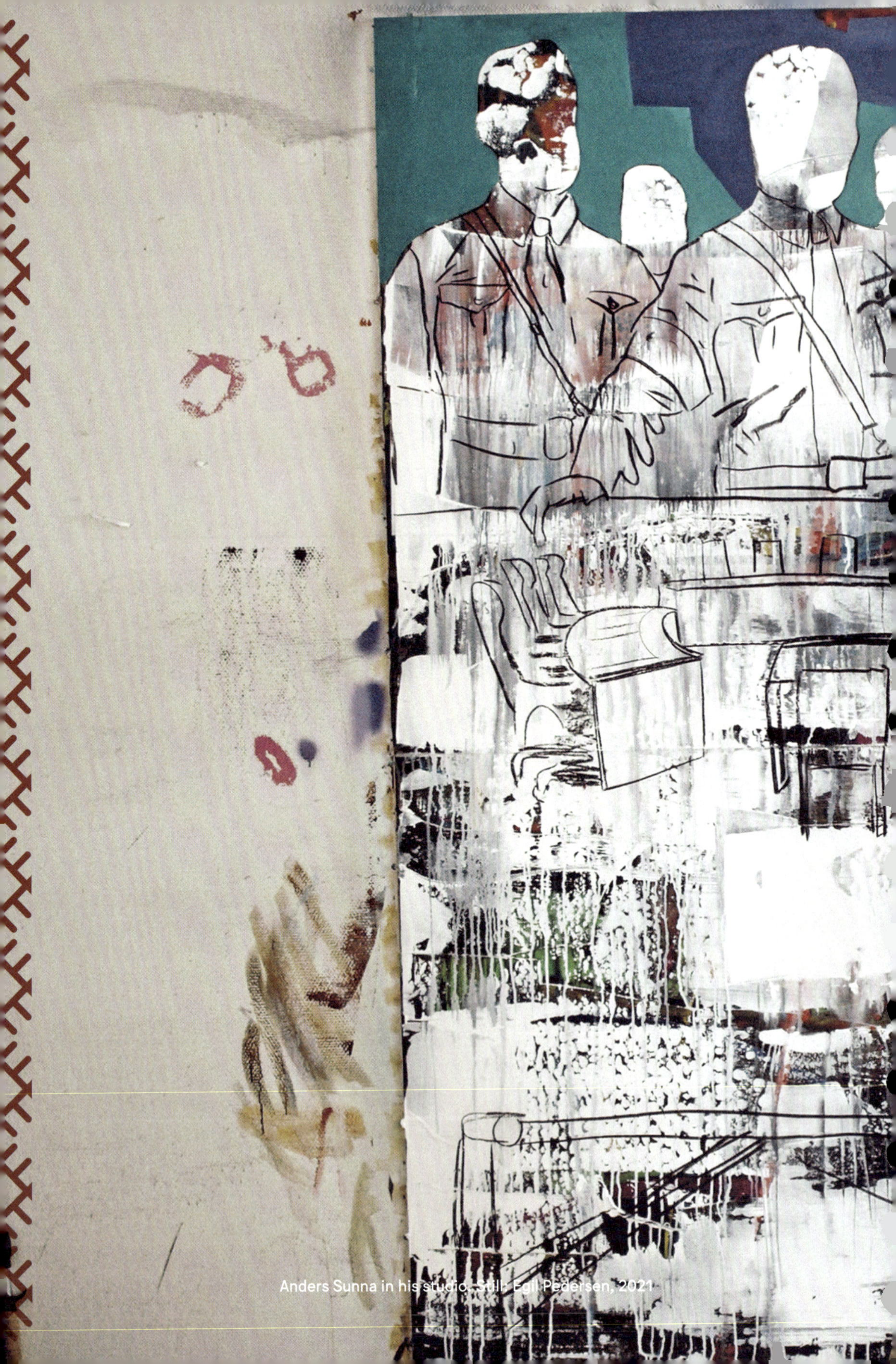

Anders Sunna in his studio. Still: Egil Pedersen, 2021

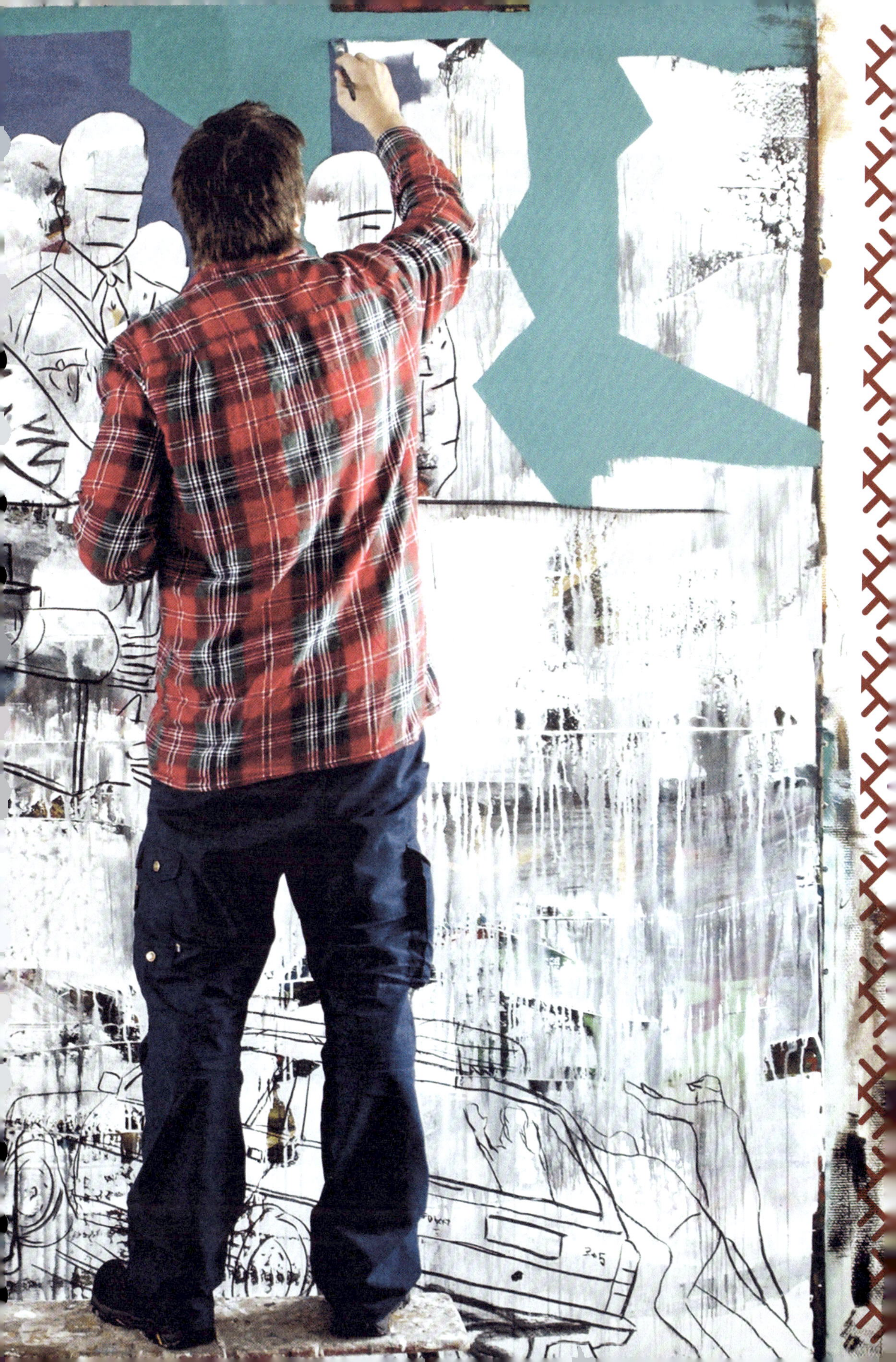

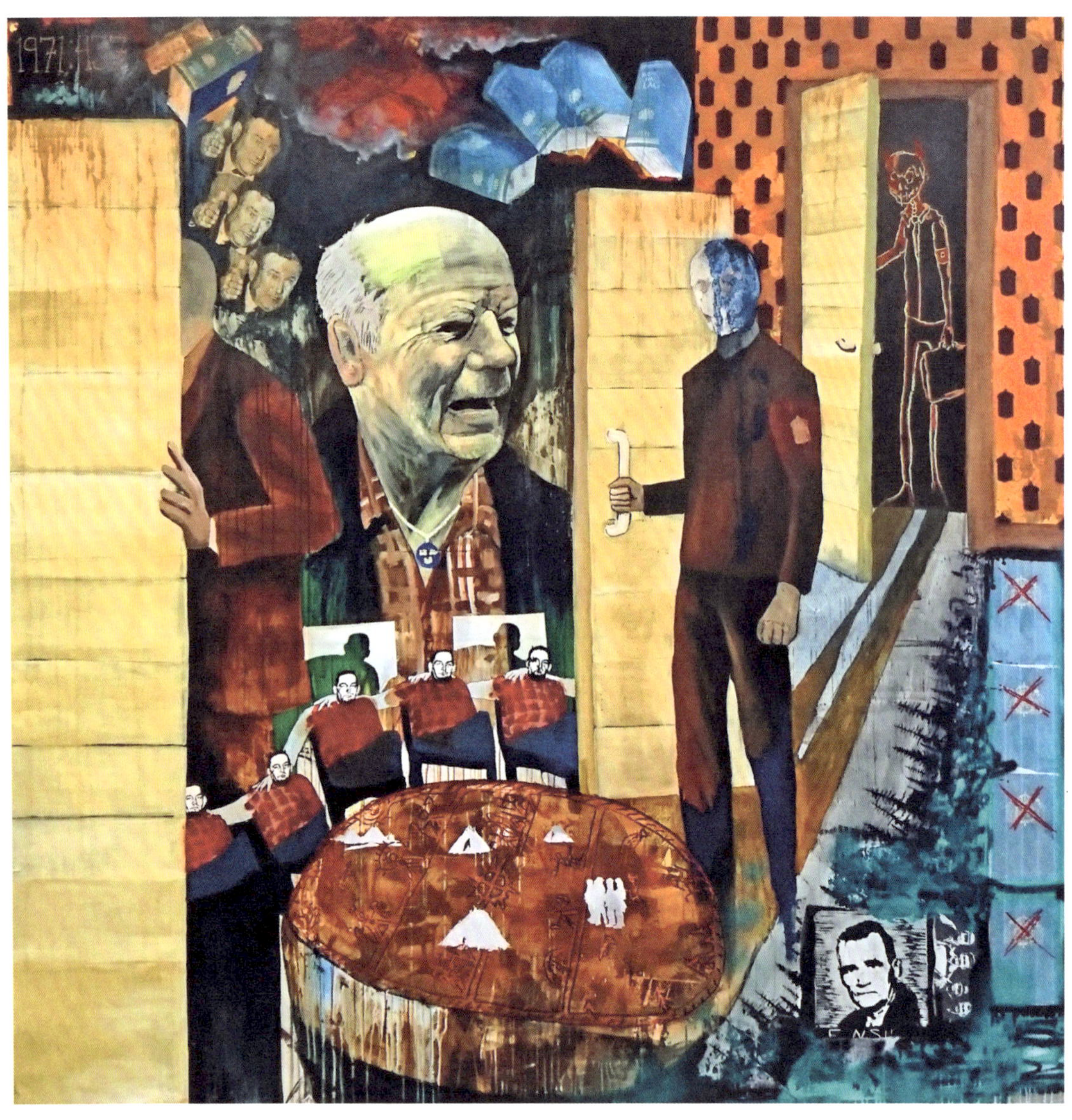
1971:4

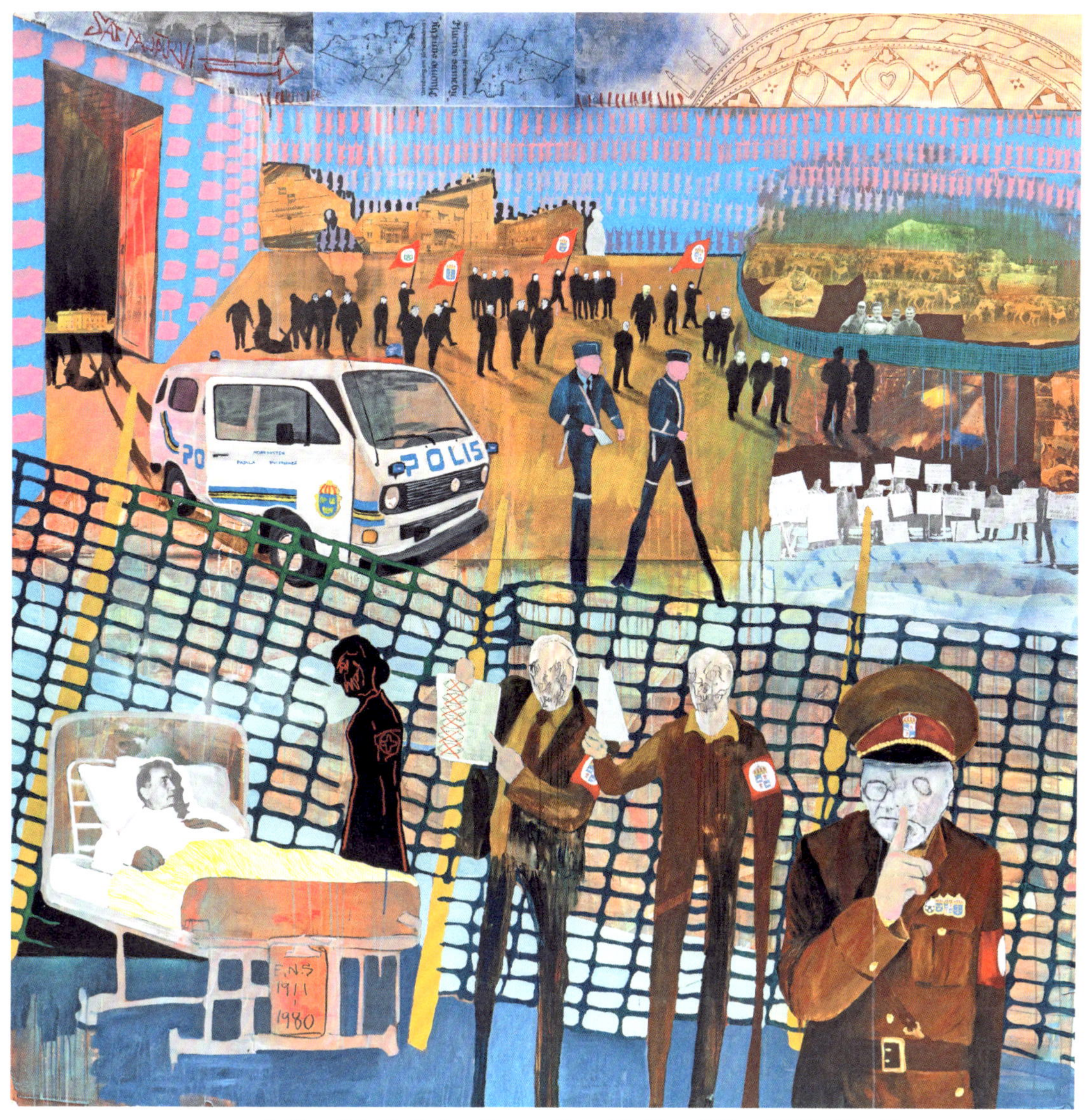

Left and right: Anders Sunna, *Illegal Spirits of Sápmi*, 2022 (detail).
Photo: Piera Niilá Stålka. Courtesy and © of the artist

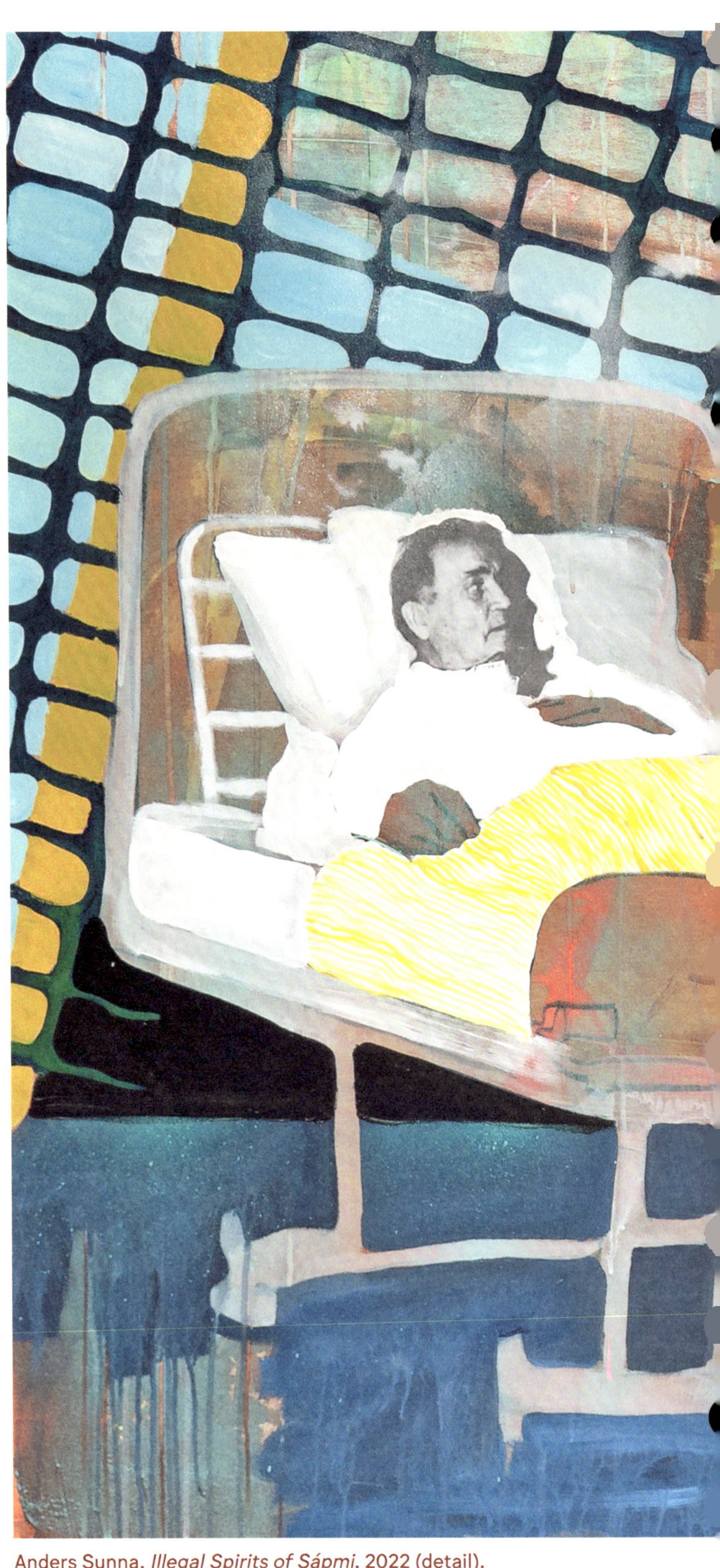

Anders Sunna, *Illegal Spirits of Sápmi*, 2022 (detail).
Photo: Piera Niilá Stålka. Courtesy and © of the artist

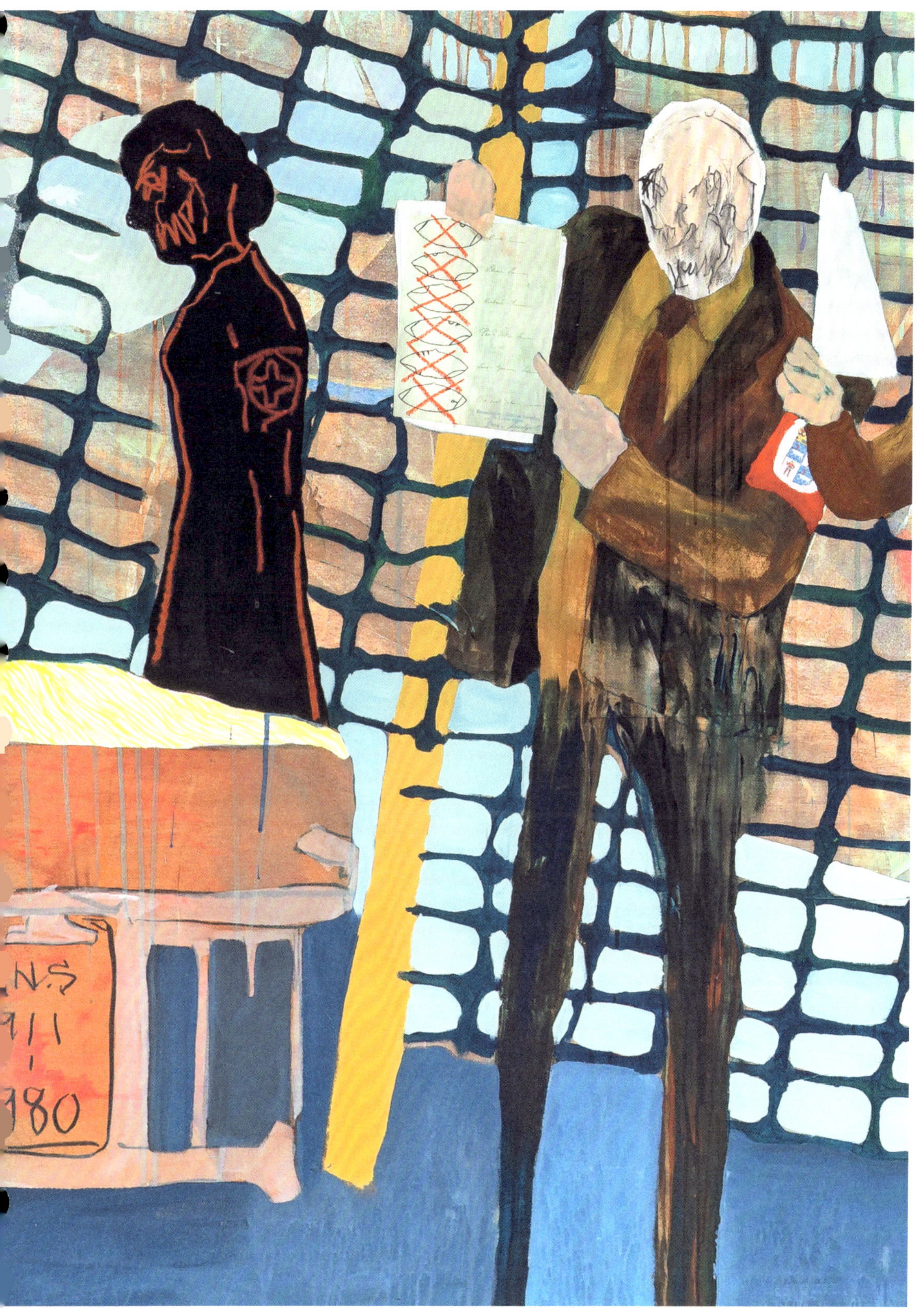
N.S

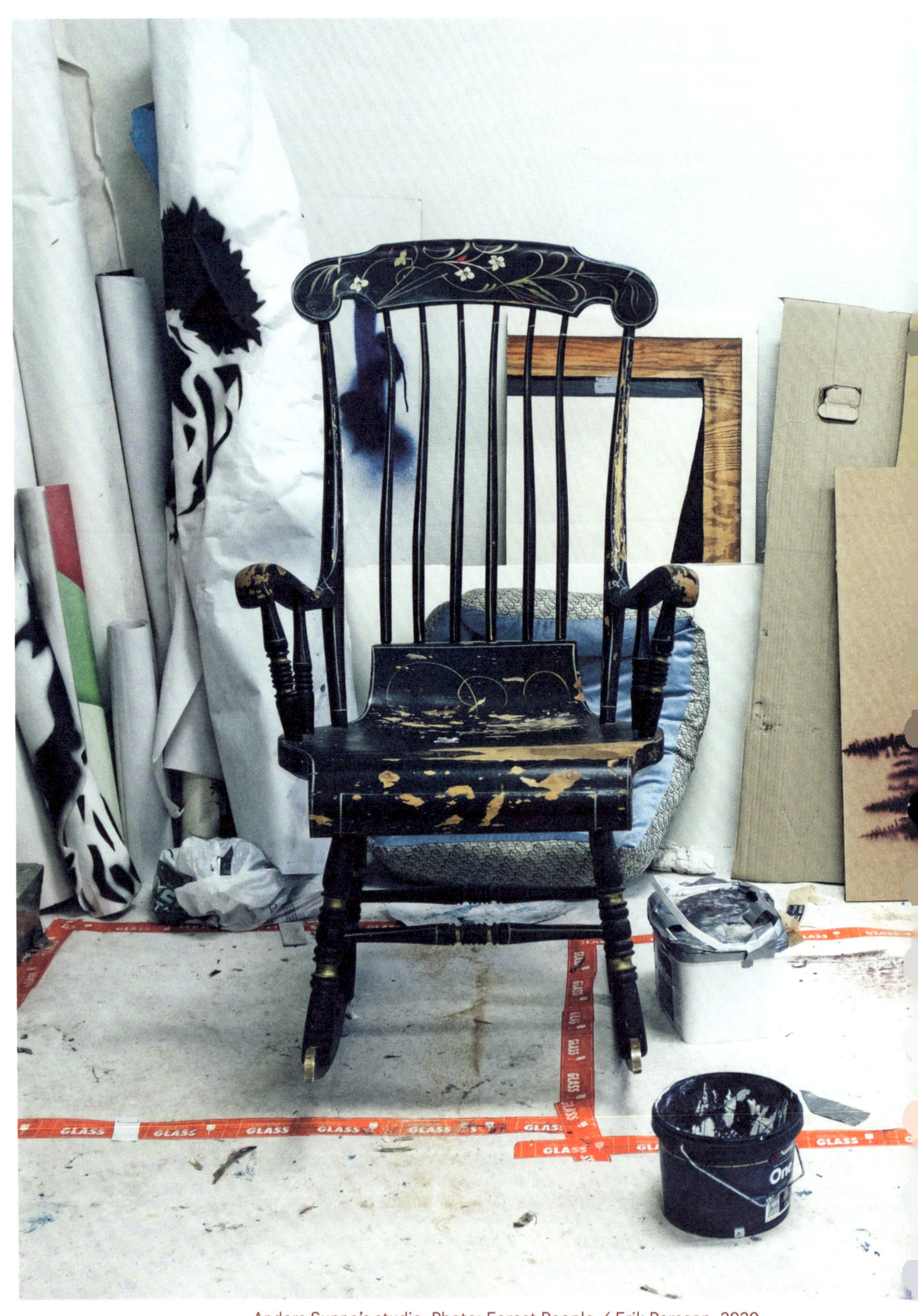

Anders Sunna's studio. Photo: Forest People / Erik Persson, 2020

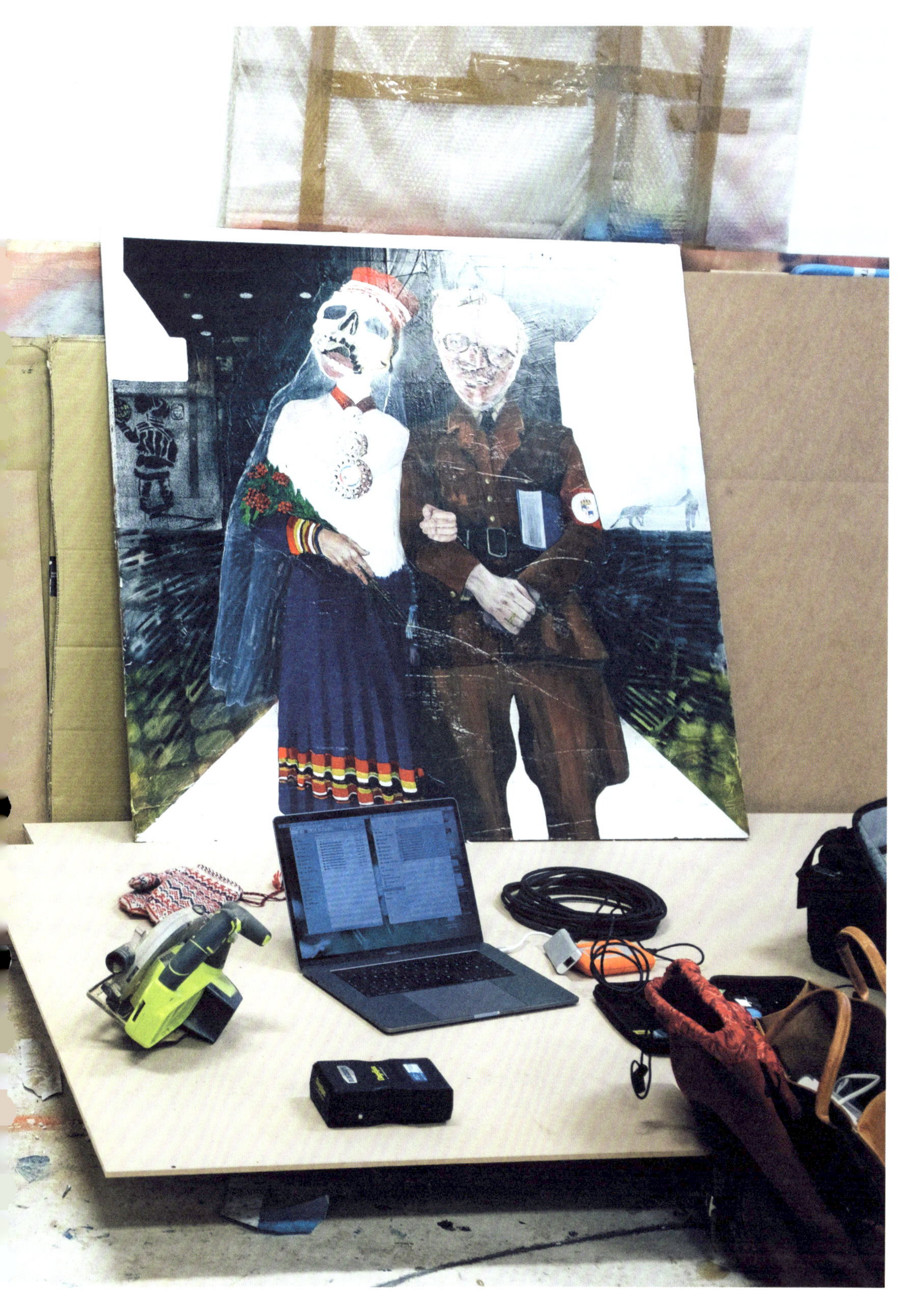

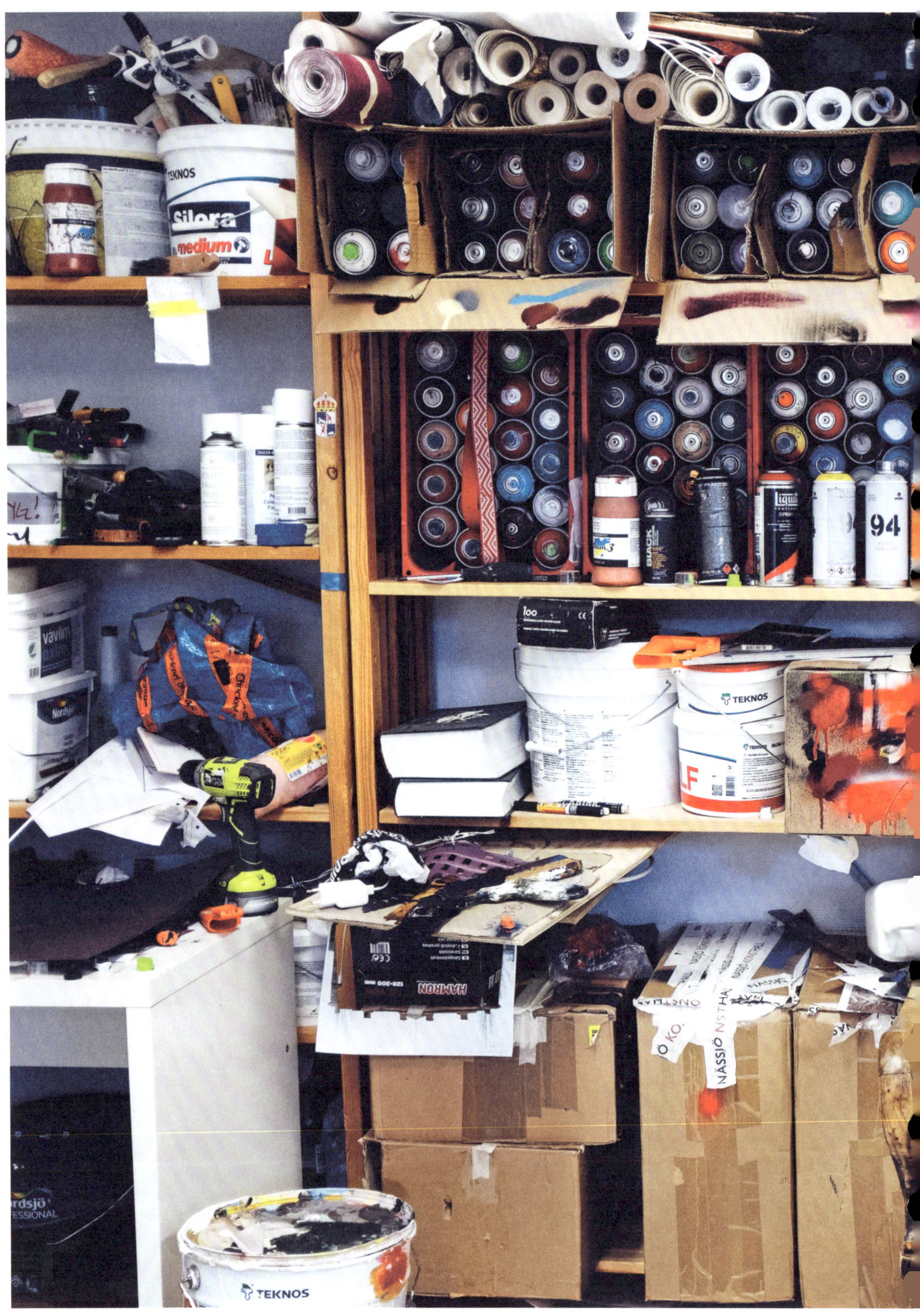

Anders Sunna's studio. Photo: Forest People / Erik Persson, 2020

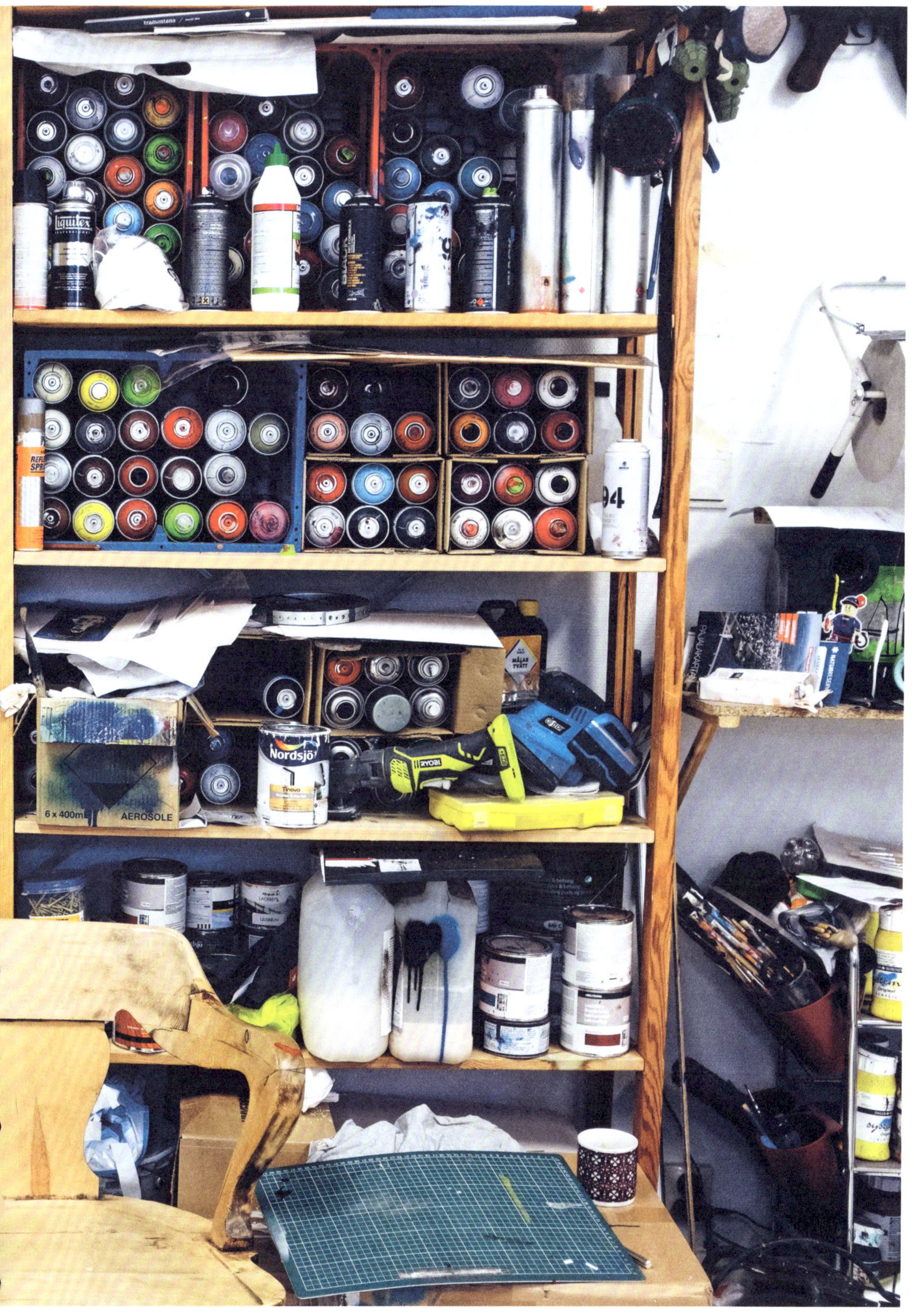
tramontana
liquitex
94
Nordsjö
RYOBI
6 x 400ml
AEROSOLE

Image selection by Anders Sunna

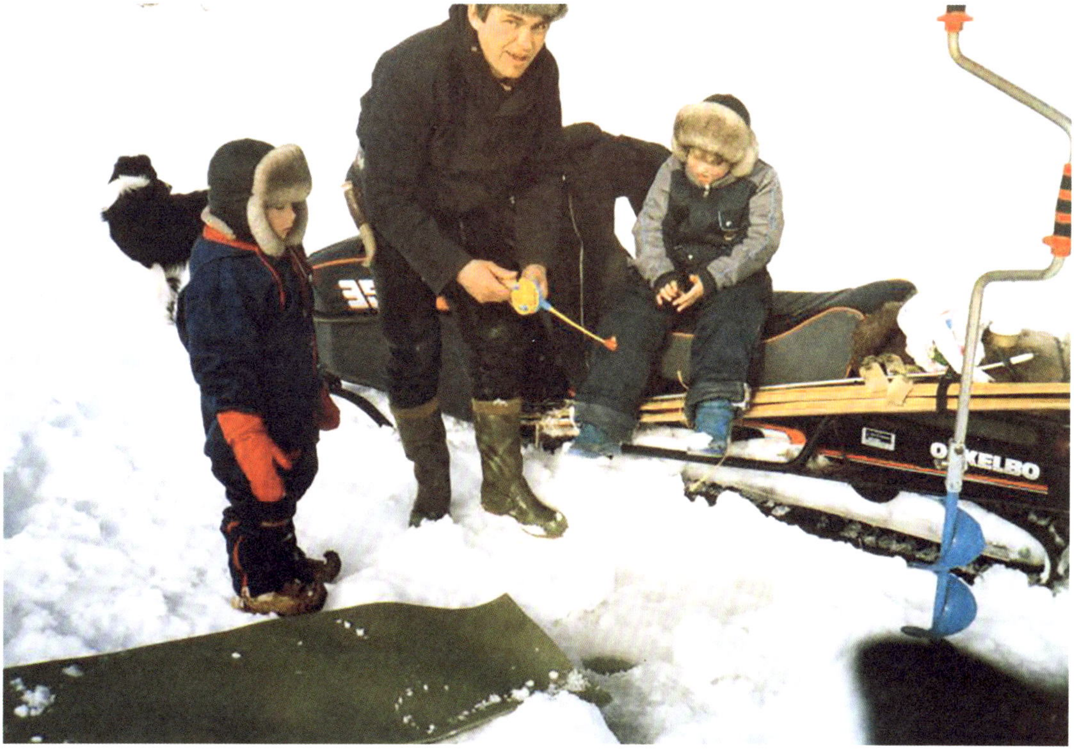

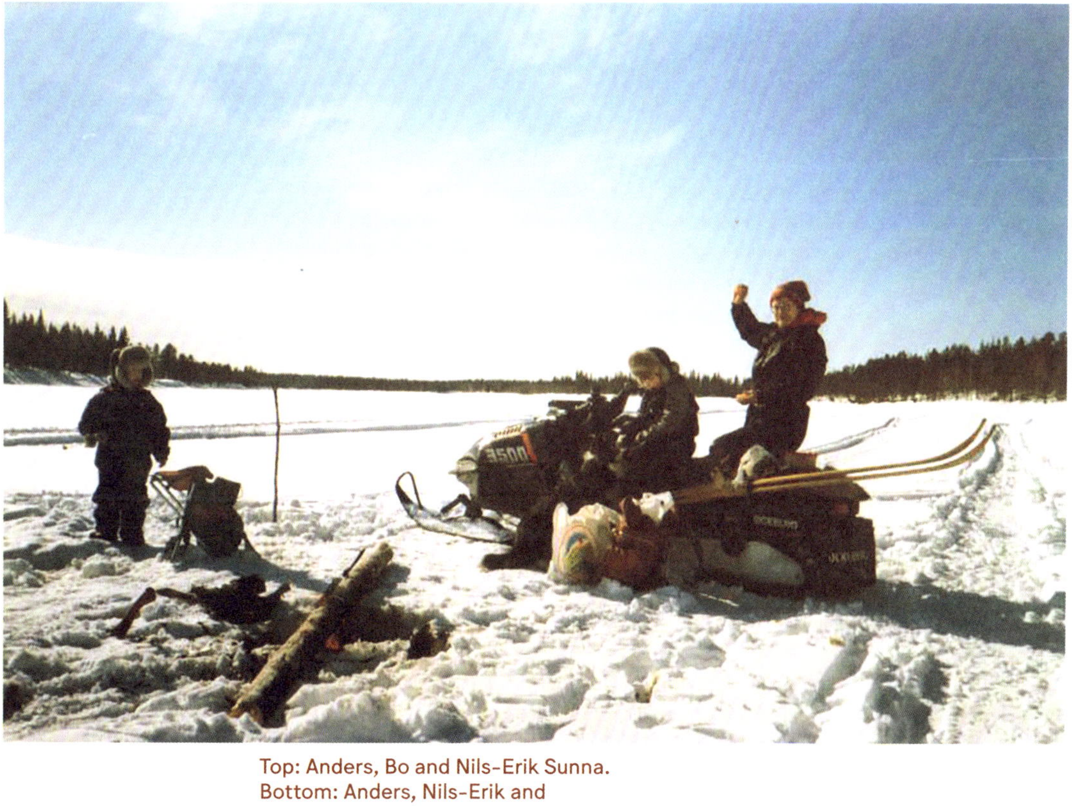

Top: Anders, Bo and Nils-Erik Sunna.
Bottom: Anders, Nils-Erik and
Britt-Inger Sunna. Photos: Britt-Inger Sunna, 1990

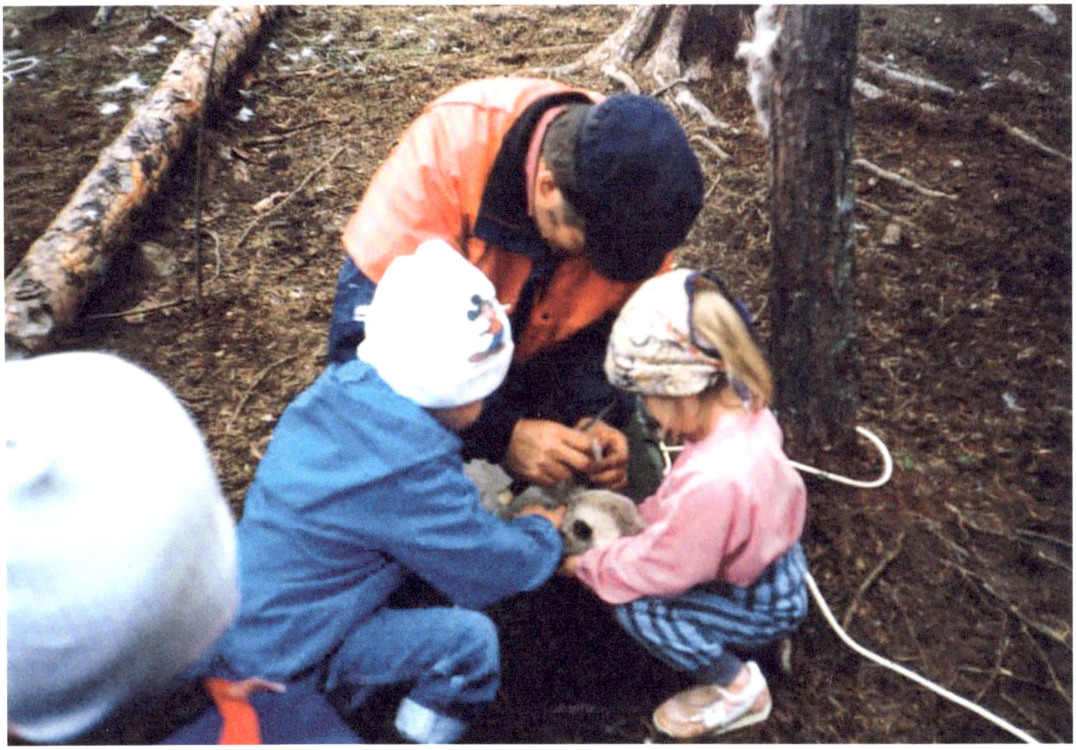

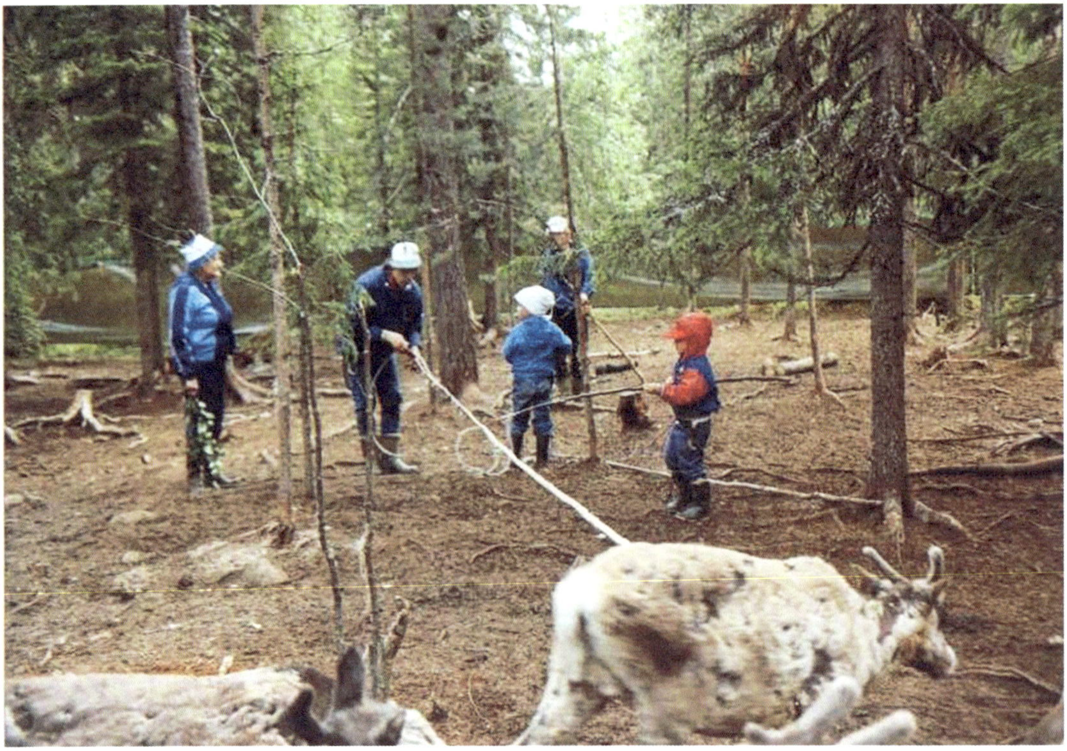

Top: Anders, Nils-Erik, Herbert and Carolina Sunna. Photo: unidentified, late 1980s
Bottom: Ann-Mari (Anders' grandmother), unidentified, Nils-Erik and Anders Sunna
Photo: Börje Sunna (Anders' grandfather), late 1980s

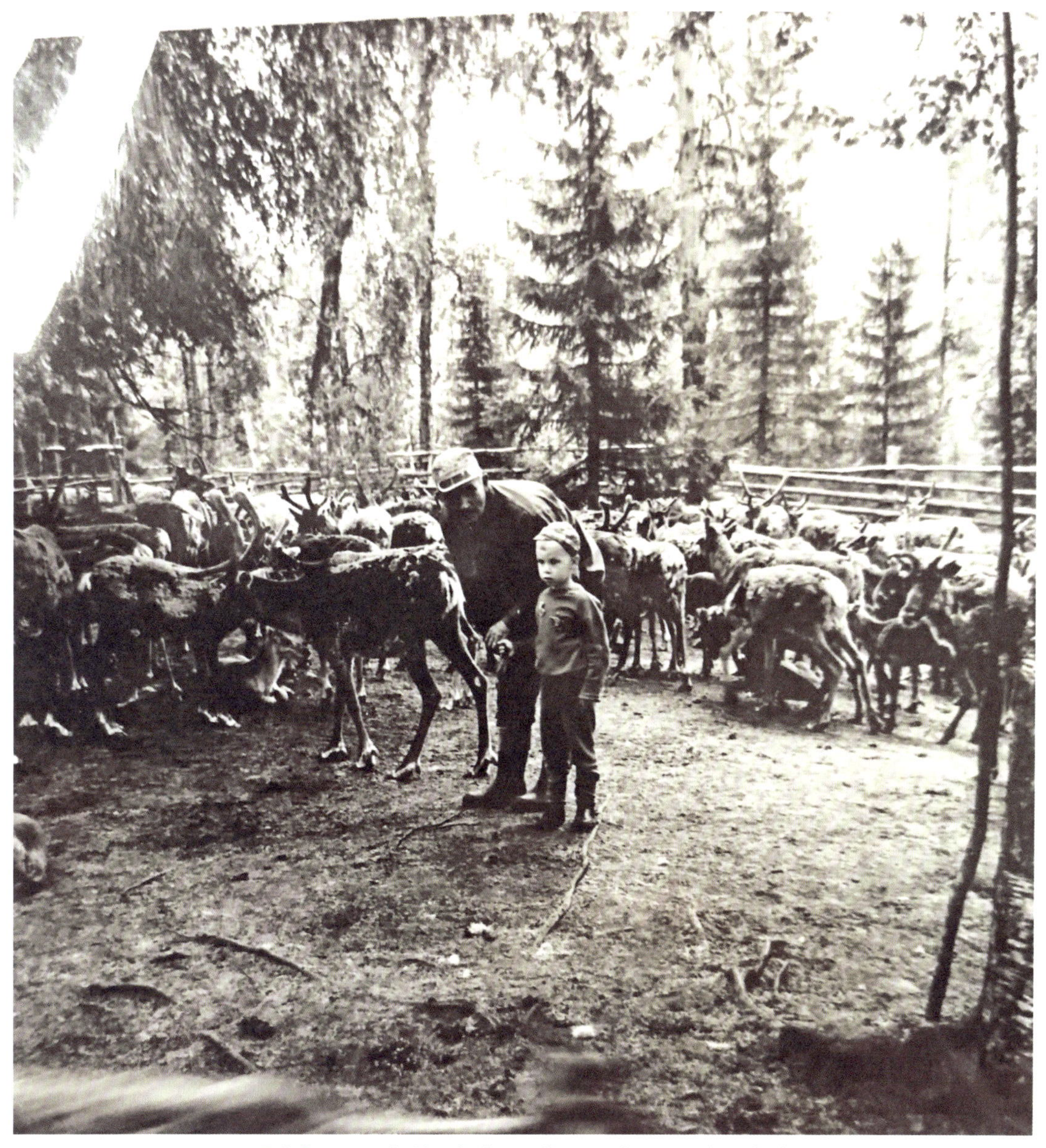

Erik Sunna and Mikael Vikman Sunna. Photo: unidentified, 1960s

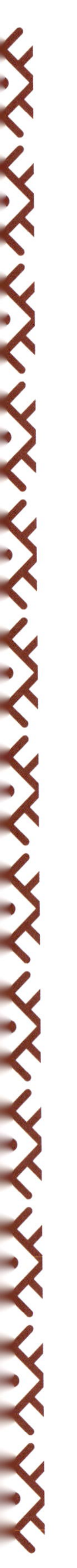

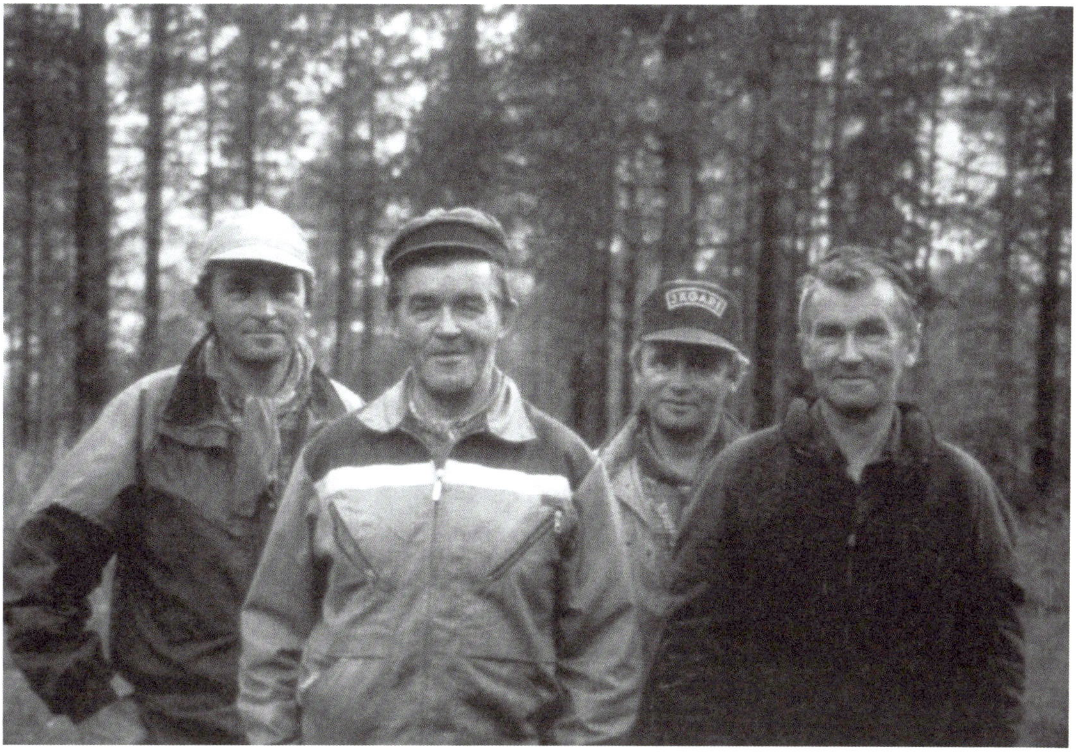

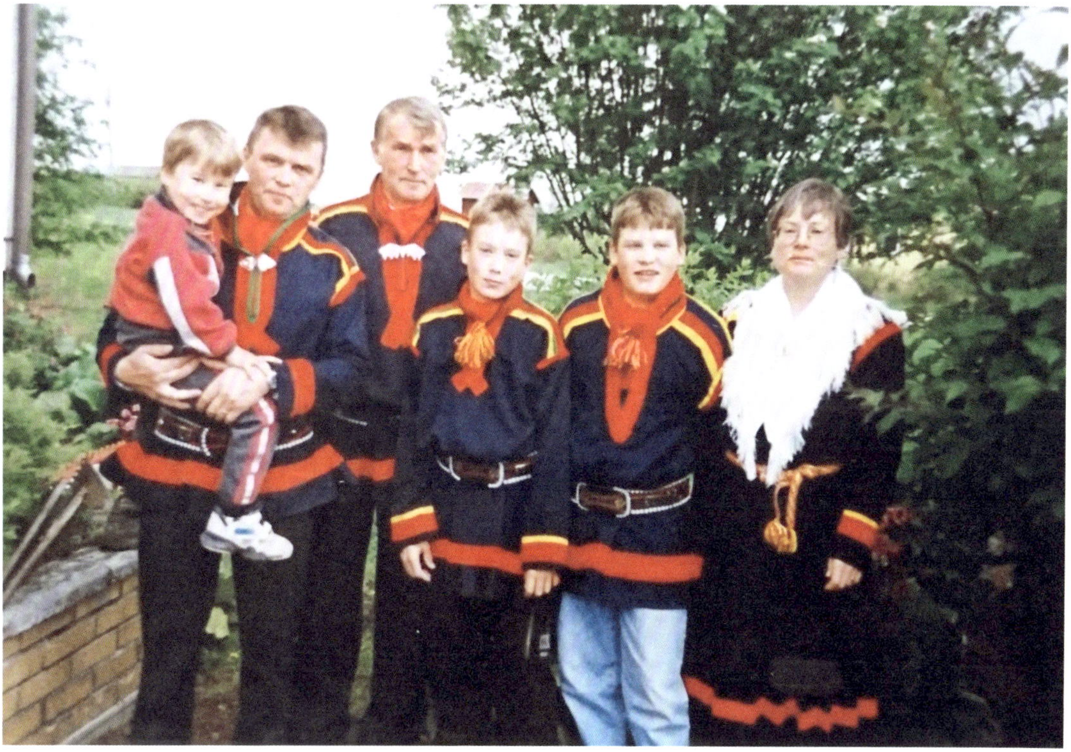

Top: Per-Åke, Herbert, Bo and Lars-Göran Sunna, Photo: Roland Snell, 1991
Bottom: Per-Olof, Bo, Lars-Göran, Anders, Nils-Erik and Britt-Inger Sunna.
Photo: unidentified, 1996

Andra skäl måste finnas, det enda jag kan finna är, som sagt var, min rastillhörighet.

Det är mycket vanligt att jag diskrimineras på grund av min rastillhörighet.

I detta mål åberopas bl.a. rennäringslagen (1971:437) och två företrädare för tillsynsmyndigheten är kallade som vittnen.

För c:a tre månader sedan anmälde vi hos DO (Ombudsmannen mot etnisk diskriminering) Peter Nobel, att rennäringslagen (1971:437) och tillsynsmyndigheterna idgar uppenbar rasdiskriminering mot oss koncessionssamer i klar strid mot bl.a. Europakonventionen och FN-konventionen om politiska och medborgerliga rättigheter, i vilken minoriteter ges ett särskilt skydd.

Vi kunde utförligt specifiera och motivera anmälan.

DO kunde konstatera att anmälan var befogat.

Han vidtalade docent Göran Melander vid Lunds universitet under vars ledning utreds spörsmålet och upprättas en uppsats-avhandling.

Vi har fått utse en av opponenterna, naturligtvis har vi utsett en koncessionssame. Vem kan bättre känna till om diskriminering än den utsatte ?

Därefter prövar DO vår anmälan.

Enl. min uppfattning, förstärker Ni med Eder vidtagna ståndpunkt, att jag är utsatt för en ytterst hänsynslös diskriminering.

Genom mitt skriftliga yttrande till Eder av den 27.11 1986 framgår det, att grundorsaken i detta mål utgöres av

att tillsynsmyndigheten, lantbruksnämndens rennäringsdelegation, utfärdar mig ett koncessionstillstånd i Muonio och ålägger mig att föra mina renar dit,

att enl. Rnl:s 70 § måste samebyn utskilja mina renar för att jag kan föra mina renar till det nya tillståndsområdet. Men samebyn gör ej detta trots att 3 1/2 år gått sedan tillståndet utfärdats.

Jag har därmed förlorat minst 1.500 renar,

att jag efter 3 1/2 år inser att jag förlorar alla mina renar = mitt levebröd och försöker tillvarataga min lilla rest, så blir jag åtalad för egenmäktighet.

Inser Ni ej att min situation är utomordentligt prekär ?

Hur skulle jag ha agerat ?

Låtit stjäla alla mina återstående renar också.

Då hade min hustru, mina barn och jag själv förlorat allt vi ägt och förlorat vårt levebröd.

Då hade jag varit en "laglydig" medborgare.

Inser Ni ej att fråga är om min och min familjs levnadsexistens.

Min egen existens är jag villig att tappa OM man kan garantera att min hustru och mina barn får behålla sina.

Ytterligare en omständighet.

Mina fyra medåtalade har också rätt till sina egna offentliga försvarare.

Länsåklagaren i Norrbottens län,
Box 718,
951 27 LULEÅ.

Anmälan om mordhot.

Lördagen den 28.8 1982, vid pass kl. 22.oo på bilparkeringen vid Tärendöholmens festplats i Tärendö, hotade █████, Anttis, Pajala, att skjuta mig och mina tre bröder.

Han yttrade ungefär i följande ordalag till mig:

"Under älgjakten skall vi skjuta alla Sunnas renar. När du ser korparna flyga så vet du att edra renar är skjutna.

Därefter skall jag skjuta dig och dina bröder. Lagen och myndigheterna är på vår sida, vi får göra vad vi vill. Och i vilket fall som helst får jag högst 12 års fängelse.

I Anttis har tidigare också skjutits en man."

Närvarande vittnen:

Harry Jatkos hustru Marianne, Bengt Jatko, Anttis, som försökte tysta ner Harry Jatko, och min sammanboende Inga Sevä, Kangosfors.

Då jag tager hotet på allvar och är införstått på att han säkert kommer att fullfölja uttalade hotet, vädjar jag om Edert omedelbara ingripande.

Jag vågar ej ensam utföra renskötselarbete längre trots att det är högsäsong f.n.

Postlåda 5492, 970 40 PAJALA den 30.8 1982,

Herbert Sunna.

Polischefen i Haparanda polisdt,
Box 83,

953 00 HAPARANDA.

Anhållan om förundersökning.

För en tid sedan blev jag uppringd av ███████, Pajala, ███. i Sattajärvi sameby.

███ hotade med, att han skulle skjuta mig och min broder Lars-Göran Sunna.

Vidare uppgav ███, att ███████, Pajala, skjutit våra två vallhundar vårvintern -82.

███ hade även sagt åt ███████, Pajala, var våra två skjutna vallhundar fanns,

Bevisning: Inför två Övertorneåpoliser, namnuppgifter saknas, påstod ███████ den 5.6 -82 i Paskarova, att han skulle "SKJUTA ALLA".

För red. Gunnar Vagerstam, Sveriges Radio, uppgav ███████ hotelsen, att han skulle skjuta "ALLA". Påståendet är TV-inspelad.
VAD ███ avser framgår av TV-inspelningen.

Även för ███████, Tärendö, har ███████ uttalat hotelsen, att han skulle skjuta.
Vem/vilka torde utredningen avslöja.

Emotser Eder utredning, samt att till mig tillställes kopia av förundersökningsprotokollet.

Pl 5492, 970 40 PAJALA den 20.7 -82,

Herbert Sunna.

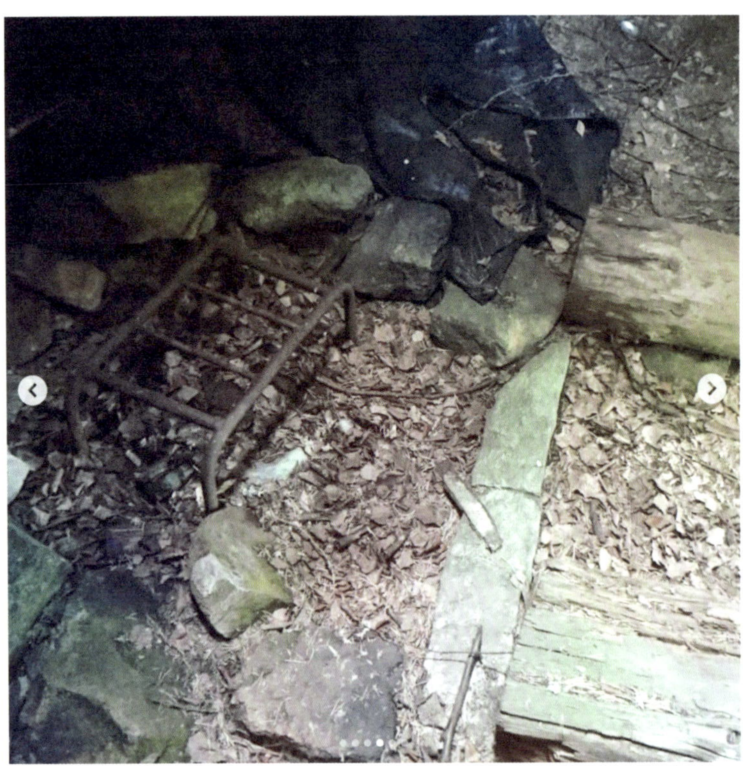

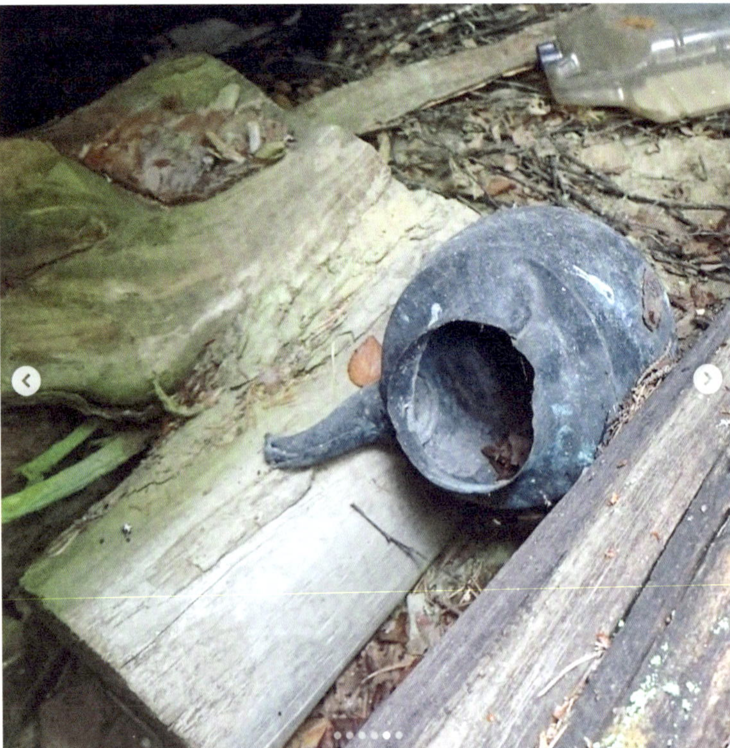

The interior of our lávvu at the summer pasture, which we were forced to abandon in 1973 due to the conflict and haven't been able to use since. The photo was taken in the summer of 2019. My father Bo was 12 years old and his brother Lars-Göran 15 when they built it together

Anders Sunna
Without Looking

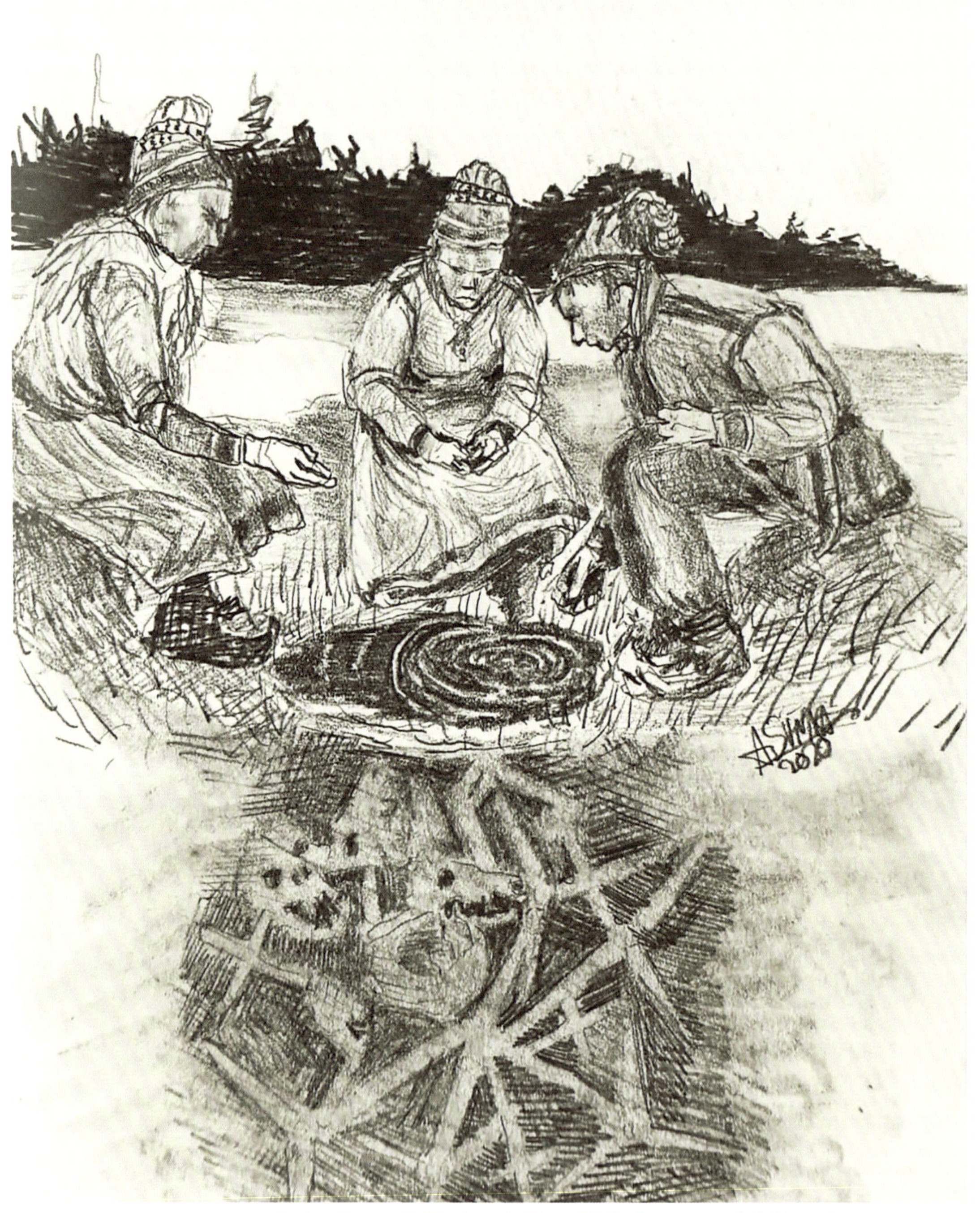

Anders Sunna, *Reflections in Time,* 2020. Courtesy and © the artist

Come on, they said.
Follow our religion, they said. Follow our comfortable development, they said.
Join and work in the industries and make lots of money, they said.
And follow I did.
The sound of chirping birds disappeared.
The scent of the flowers disappeared.
The sight of newborn reindeer calves disappeared.
In the future, you can buy what you want, they said.
I said.
– What I want has never been for sale.
What I want does not cost money.
Your future is not for me.
And not really for you either.
Follow me instead, I said.

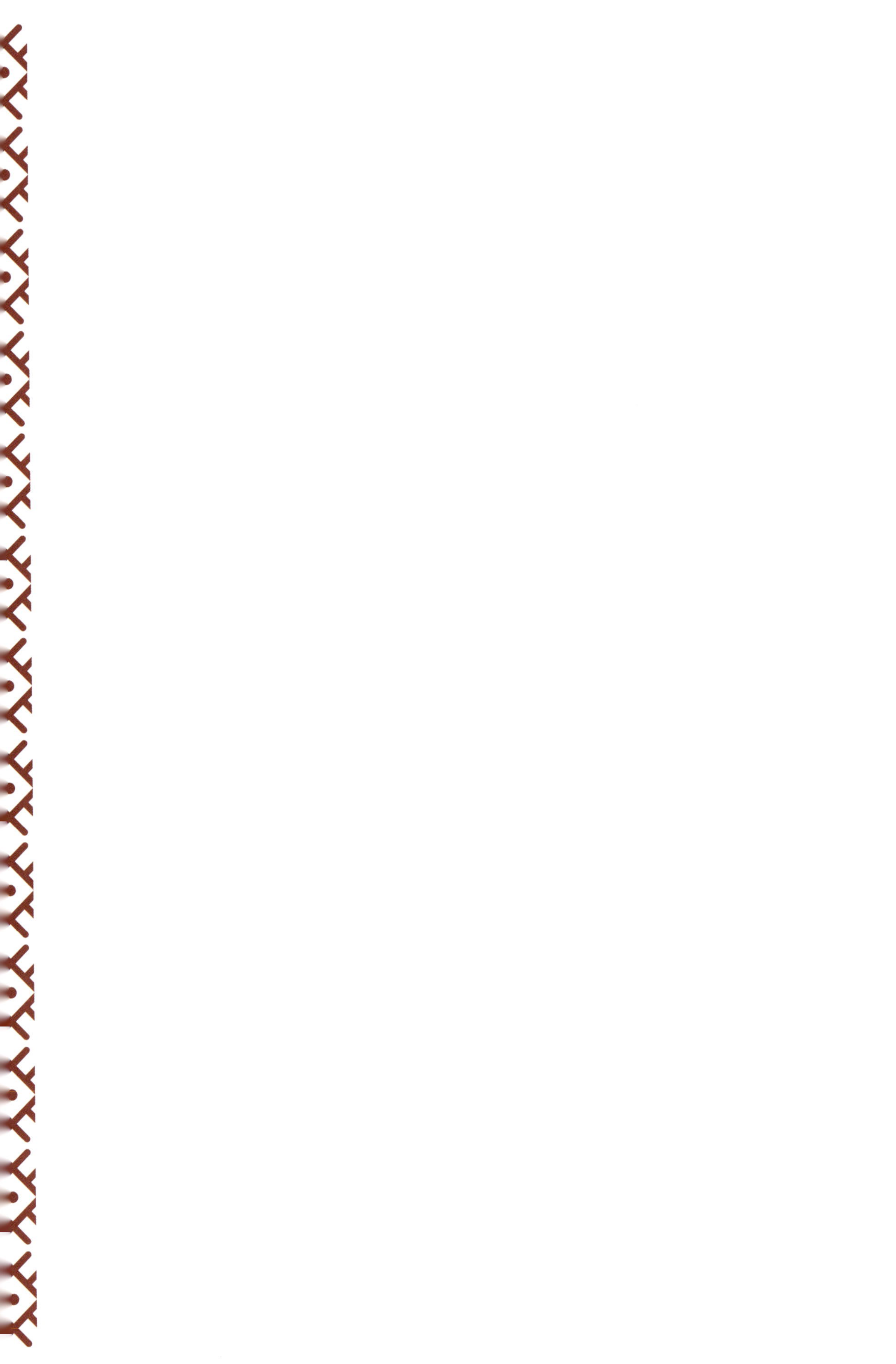

Máret Ánne Sara

Katya García-Antón
and Liv Brissach

When the Red Calves Arrive, the Hope Returns. Sámi Healing and Sensate Sovereignty in Máret Ánne Sara's Practice

1
Máret Ánne Sara in the film *Máret Ánne Sara Representing Sápmi at La Biennale di Venezia 2022*, by Forest People AS, 2020.
2
And extending into the Kola Peninsula (the whole is called the Fennoscandian peninsula).

> They had called us because our reindeer had been eating flowers in the city. I was a child, so I didn't fully understand the situation … What I do remember is how my father suddenly changed when he arrived at the station. Police officers were sitting there in their uniforms interrogating my father about the reindeer. My father's whole demeanour changed, and even his smell changed. That is something I never forgot.[1]

Colonialism in the Nordic region[2] is not a temporality that has passed; it is a far-reaching structure that persists. Its logic shapes how nations-states and the Sámi nation define life itself. It alters how Sámi people imagine the way their families and loved ones can behave and structure themselves, what they understand knowledge to be and how they sustain their spiritual beliefs. It forges the way Sámi people's languages come alive and thrive. It impedes how Sámi people know and form kinship with lands, waters, and other more-than-human beings, and how they can fulfil their obligations to those kinships within a colonial economy in which nature is capitalised and Sámi relations to land are penalised by colonial law. These are all-encompassing forms of dispossession. As the dispossessor of futures, colonialism today prevents Sámi people from imagining the future within their own ways of knowing, being, doing and thinking.

Based in Guovdageaidnu, in the Norwegian side of Sápmi, Máret Ánne Sara gained notoriety early on as a novelist whose narratives are based on Sámi cosmologies, and explore the tensions arising in the struggle to maintain Sámi worldviews in the face of the modern values of consumption. Coming from a reindeer-herding family, Sara has lived first-hand the struggles faced due to Norwegian and Nordic colonial law and their extractive economies,

3
Futurity is a concept explored in Mvskoke scholar Laura Harjo's most recent book, *Spiral to the Stars, Mvskoke Tools of Futurity* (Tucson: University of Arizona Press, 2019).

4
Borrowing its name from Pile o' Bones, the English translation of the Plains Cree name for Regina, Canada (Oskana ka-asas-tēki) and also referencing the photos of millions of buffalo heads that white settlers slaughtered in order to starve the Indigenous populations of North America.

including the cultural and spiritual loss experienced when reindeer herders are directly or indirectly forced to abandon their way of life. Teeming with energy, knowledge and spirit, Sara's creative practice sets out to spatialise and story-tell futurity for Sápmi.[3] She reflects upon how to emerge from the maelstrom of colonialism with works that reflect upon what Sámi people need in order to dream, imagine, speculate and activate the wishes of ancestors, contemporary kin and future relatives, and how they can sustain the interdependent continuum between people, lands, waters and other more-than-human beings.

One of her most ambitious works to date *Pile o'Sápmi* (2016–20),[4] presented at documenta 14, operates as a multi-part, time-extensive piece consisting of installations, festivals, screenings, debates, crowdfunding and performances, that drew attention to her brother (Jovsset Ante Sara's) fight against the Norwegian State's attempts to cull his herd so drastically that it would have brought him to bankruptcy and thus forced him and the Sara family away from their traditional lands, culture and way of life. The work spanned the length of three trials: her brother won in the district and regional courts during 2016–17 and was defeated in the Supreme Court in Oslo in December 2017. *Pile o'Sápmi*'s most emblematic component was a monumental hanging composed of 400 reindeer skulls, each with a bullet hole at its centre, indicative of colonially enforced reindeer slaughter, that gained legendary status when Sara hung it in the open air in front of the Norwegian Parliament in Oslo during the last of the trials. *Pile o'Sápmi*'s narration of the impact of colonial law on Sámi existence is explained further by the artist, who says:

> In Sámi and Indigenous people's philosophy and worldview everything is connected. What happens to animals happens to us. Humans are not the most important and supreme, as it is

5
Máret Ánne Sara in the film *The Sámi Pavilion,* by Egil Pedersen. Commissioned by OCA, 2021.

> defined in the Western world's understanding … What happens when laws and systems force you to break with your own ethics and morals; and when colonial world views criminalize your traditions and capitalize nature?[5]

As with the hundreds of similar cases faced by the Sámi today, whether reindeer herders, fisher-people, land defenders in the face of the so-called green ecology of wind farms, the corrosive process the Sara family has endured comes at a deep economic, physical, mental and emotional cost. Sara is thus deeply concerned with finding ways to heal the traumas inflicted by the colonial apparatus, repair the bonds of reciprocity with lands, waters, animals, and other entities, as well as resurrect Sámi knowledges and spiritual values. This has led her to reflect more deeply upon what happens to a people constantly worn down by such experiences, and what materials her practice could use in advocating for the right to Indigenous health and well-being, to Indigenous worldviews, and to a sovereign Sámi future. As she explains:

> After the long and hard struggle our family has been through against the Norwegian State to protect our reindeer against forced slaughtering while also fighting the same state against industrial ruining of our reindeer's lands, I have a strong need to seek and manifest hope … These exhausting experiences of constant fights within a structure of unbalanced and unjust power relations [… are] why I chose the stomach as an expressive material. It became central in telling the story of how we as beings react to colonialism and carry life experiences. Because the stomach is the seat of emotion and a deeper intellect, so it is a metaphor for the unseen and

non-verbal. How it affects you and ultimately how it affects your health and spirit. How something abstract eventually becomes physical … Imagine that feeling of your stomach turning for whatever reason. The tactile feeling of working with stomachs as a medium is meaningful, pulling on them and stretching them. Sometimes the stomach tears because it is fragile – just like our right to live healthily and in peace.[6]

Taking these thoughts as a starting point, Sara has made a new trio of works for 'The Sámi Pavilion' in which the reindeer and their stomachs play a central role poetically, spiritually and politically. The first element, titled *Gutted – Gávogálši*,[7] is an expansive sculptural installation, a constellation of forms made from reindeer stomachs where some are reversed, some torn and sown up again, all shaped and suspended in space. Flexible yet fragile, like her Indigenous heritage, people and land, and like life itself, each form has an existential register, as well as highlighting the sensate power of stomachs as first receptors of events in the world.

The second work, titled *Ale suova sielu sáiget*,[8] is a monumental hanging sculpture composed of dead and cured reindeer calves, cotton grass (which represents hope to Sara) and birch branches (representing ancestral knowledge). A carousel of death and re-birth, fear and comfort, the installation mourns the dystopian future faced by reindeer and life in Sápmi, as much as it rejoices in the power of each new calf to bring life and faith back to the land and the people. Sara was inspired to work with the red calf (newborn calves are born with red fur) in this specific way after speaking to a reindeer herder following a particularly harsh winter. He told her that despite legal trials and an expensive, long-lasting and exhausting battle

6
Ibid.

7
In Northern Sámi, 'gálši' means stronghearted while 'gávagit' means to bend or to lie down on one's back.

8
In Northern Sámi this translates as 'Don't let it wear out the soul'.

in which the reindeer-herders had to feed thousands of starving reindeer (because of climate change) far out in the tundra, everything was forgotten with the sight of the first newborn red calf. To hear this testimony in this particularly challenging time was a powerful experience for Sara, and prompted her to work at the intersection of the healing hope the red calf symbolises and the trauma of the massacre of baby calves by predator species.[9] Because eagles and wolverines are red-listed by Norwegian environmental laws, the reindeer herders are not allowed to kill them to protect their calves; this causes the loss of almost half of the newborn calves in Sara's area, while further south some herders are experiencing a decline in their herd year by year.[10] A cycle of trauma, healing and re-trauma thus ensues annually. *Ale suova sielu sáiget* is shaped like a giant baby mobile that spirals gently mid-air. It was made while Sara was carrying her firstborn and speaks of the fear of bringing another being into the colonially traumatised world in which she lives.

Last but not least, the most immaterial work in the trio is a duet of specially composed liquid smells titled *Du-šŝan-Ahttanušŝan*,[11] whose molecular arrangements create a complex sensorium of human and animal life. 'Western communication', Sara observes, 'takes place with a lot of words, with oral or written language, or with pictures', and in so doing, it undermines non-verbal communication.[12] Colonialism creates very specific situations in which non-verbal communication is pushed into crisis mode.[13] Washed across the white surfaces of reindeer sinew threads (Savo suotna and suotnagottur – the spine sinew and sinew from the legs), these smell clusters hanging at nose height act as powerful activators of perceptions that inhabit a deeper level in our bodies than the visuality that tends to dominate the Western art field.

9
Sara spent much time gaining access to the red calves, before starting to work with traditional methods in order to conserve the whole body of the calf. She herself was unable to collect the calves directly from the mountain since each calf belongs to a reindeer herder who must deliver it to the SNO (Statens Naturoppsyn) for autopsy (as evidence of prey kill) before claiming compensation for the loss.

10
According to the 2019–20 annual report on reindeer herding, around 40 % of newborn calves were lost in the Guovdageaidnu areas, and around 90 % of these losses were recorded as deaths caused by protected predators https://www.landbruksdirektoratet.no/nb/filarkiv/rapporter/Ressursregnskapet%20for%20reindriftsn%C3%A6ringen_2019-2020_ny%20versjon.pdf/_/attachment/inline/e0377ef7-bc0e-4538-b294-0b238f41a57e:7085e4f9664f4d9b6c4e028cb5c5659581c7c982/Ressursregnskapet%20for%20reindriftsn%C3%A6ringen_2019-2020_ny%20versjon.pdf, accessed 3 January 2022.

11
In Northern Sámi, 'duššat' means to die from unforeseen circumstances while 'ahttanuššat' is used to describe a thin, human or animal who is slowly rebuilding their health and strength.

12
Máret Ánne Sara in the film *The Sámi Pavilion*, by Egil Pedersen. Commissioned by OCA, 2021.

13 As the recollection of the artist at the beginning of this essay makes clear, the body, in this particular case her father's, speaks its own language when pushed to the edge. Sara recognises the same mechanisms and messages from the smell of distressed reindeer when they are rounded up in corrals for transport to the slaughter house.

By using reindeer, their stomachs and smells, Sara brings novel approaches to her practice. On the one hand she combines these elements to make a powerful case for the indivisibility of Sámi people and land, where land is defined by everything that constitutes it, in this case placing a particular focus on reindeer. In other words, what happens to reindeer happens to people. History tells us that one of the principal ways in which to eliminate Indigenous peoples is to target their spiritual values and their livelihood sources and interconnected knowledge systems. The practice of reindeer herding in Sápmi is being colonised almost to extinction, threatening the life of Sámi people. Absurd Nordic regulations, some of which are inspired by pig-farming methods in the European Union, are forcing the disintegration of reindeer herding; so-called environmental protection laws defend the rights of predators to the extent of endangering the lives of reindeer calves in their most fragile early days; ancestral forms of herding and slaughtering are criminalised; farmers are given rights that undermine nomadic herding practices. The cycle of life and death is at its most tangible in current Sámi existence, under the weight of Nordic colonialism. Sara's installations stand as a warning to the new Sámi generations of the deeply imbalanced world with which they must contend. As a new mother, the arrival of her own child in 2020 doubled her determination to shield new generations from colonial forces and to impart caution. In this sense, her works are also calls of conviction that hope is still to be found in Sápmi and in Sámi ways, and that one must nurture that hope however small and fragile it might be, to secure a vibrant sovereign future.

Sara's works in 'The Sámi Pavilion' highlight two ancestral and powerful structures that uphold forms of knowledge and communication at the core of Indigenous world views. One of these, symbolically represented in the use of reindeer stomachs and connecting humans and reindeer, is known as 'gamus dovdat' or 'čoalit dovdet' in Sámi (gut feeling in English). This describes the seat of a parallel intelligence in the human gut: the enteric nervous system (ENS), as it is scientifically known in Western perspectives, which is constituted by a thin layer of millions of nerve cells that line the stomach and intestines and which operate as a communication highway back and forth to the brain via the vagus nerve. The other is the olfactory sense invoked by the smell-duet in Sara's installation.

There is no sense in the human body more closely linked to memory, emotion and instinctive intellect than smell. The olfactory bulb, the organ responsible for handling smell information, is situated close to and has a direct connection to the limbic system and its amygdala, where emotions are processed, as well as to the hippocampus, which is responsible for memory. This explains why smell has the ability to trigger memories, knowledges and intense emotions in ways so powerful that they alter the interconnected systems of biology and mind. For the artist, smell is an elementary part of the non-verbal communication that happens between lifeforms and their surroundings. The smell duet takes you back to the corral, to the moment of fear and death when the animals are rounded up in a fence for slaughter selection. In direct contact with humans and capital industry, the animals are forced into a truck that will transport them to the slaughter house. Norwegian law prohibits traditional Sámi slaughter practices on-site, which would have spared the animals the stress of being pushed beyond their natural instincts. The smell is inspired by the fear chemicals expressed from the animals' glands in combination with the odour of stool and diesel from the truck. The hope-element of the duet is an interpretation of the smell of natural cleanness or a landscape that is undisturbed by industrial and colonial intrusion, mixed with the scent of reindeer milk and Sara's own

14
Máret Ánne Sara in the film *The Sámi Pavilion*, by Egil Pedersen. Commissioned by OCA, 2021.

breast milk. The artist aims in this way to subliminally relate to promises, care and commitment to new life within the lands of Sápmi, and this desire connects the smell work with the image of the red calf as a symbol of that new hope and life. *Ale suova sielu sáiget* was conceived by Sara with the advice of professional smell creator Nadjib Achaibou and Oswaldo Maciá, an artist with a long experience of olfactory installations.

These two specific forms of embodied knowledge – gut intelligence and smell memory – are central to both the conceptual and experiential ideas behind Sara's new installation in 'The Sámi Pavilion'. While they reflect Sámi ways of being and doing, they also invite visitors to generate their own embodied knowledge within the Indigenous frames presented by her. These works are advocates for an Indigenous sensate sovereignty that counters Western and modernist ways of perceiving the world; At a time in which the climate crisis is acknowledged globally as a direct consequence of the Western world's drive for modernisation, these Indigenous perspectives are of the utmost relevance. As Sara remarks:

> It seems that it is totally forgotten that we are all the time talking and communicating with everything around us. It is a communication that does not happen in words but via the body and instinct. As long as you are a human being on earth you are a part of it. These messages come to you too, whether you want it or not. With the situation the world is in today, I think it is becoming increasingly important to strengthen this form of communication.[14]

As always in Sara's work, ancestral Sámi knowledges and methodologies, spiritual and material, underpin the conception and realisation of these installations. Whether relating to the manner of preserving and manipulating reindeer materials, botanical elements and biological media, or story-telling the spiritual narratives they encompass, these Sámi knowledges and methodologies have evolved and been tested since time immemorial. The making of these works was thus accomplished with the invaluable guidance of Sámi Elder Gáren-Áhkku / Káren E. M. Utsi, in her transmission to Sara of deep knowledges not only of reindeer herding but of the material and spiritual knowledge employed in duodji. Duodji is the philosophy from which Sámi material culture and creative practices emerge. Often mistranslated as 'craft' by colonial agents of the arts, duodji encompasses a specifically Sámi and complex worldview of philosophy, including spiritual, material and environmental knowledge, concepts of beauty, utility and manual work that converge in the processes of making objects and in the objects themselves.

The newly made trio of works in 'The Sámi Pavilion' thus functions as a depository and activator of Sámi knowledges. They are testimonials of everyday hardships resulting from colonialism; they are wound healers and spiritual resurrectors. In Sámi culture, similarly to other Indigenous cultures that have transmitted memory and knowledge orally or through other means than the written word, stories are amongst the most important holders of knowledge and memory. In the Northern Sámi language, 'muitalus' means story, and 'muitaleaddji' stands for storyteller. Both are closely related to the verb for remembering, 'muitit'. The acts of narration in these works ensure that memories stay alive. Sara's ability to muitalit, to tell stories in each of her works, is powerful and important because they elevate Sámi experiences to a global level. Moreover, they bring attention to and strengthen the common ground shared with other Indigenous communities worldwide, and point to their relevance amongst non-Indigenous peoples today.

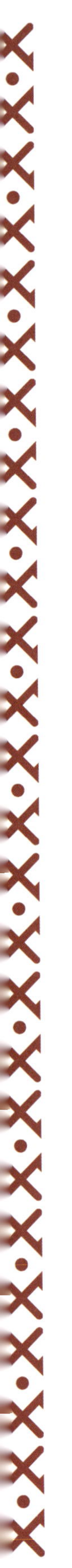

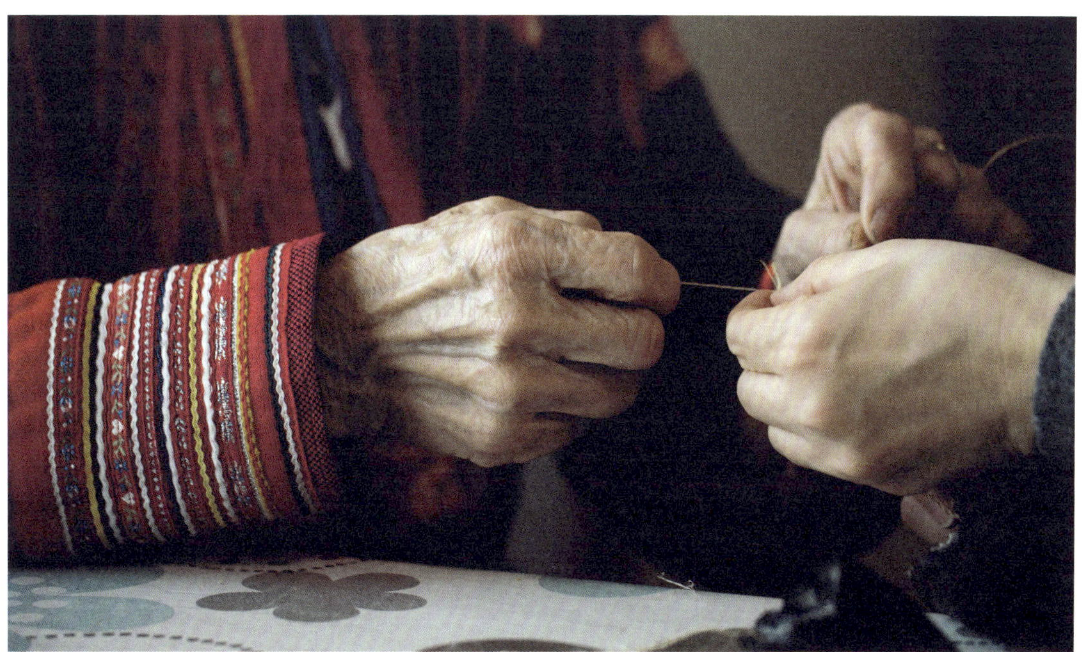

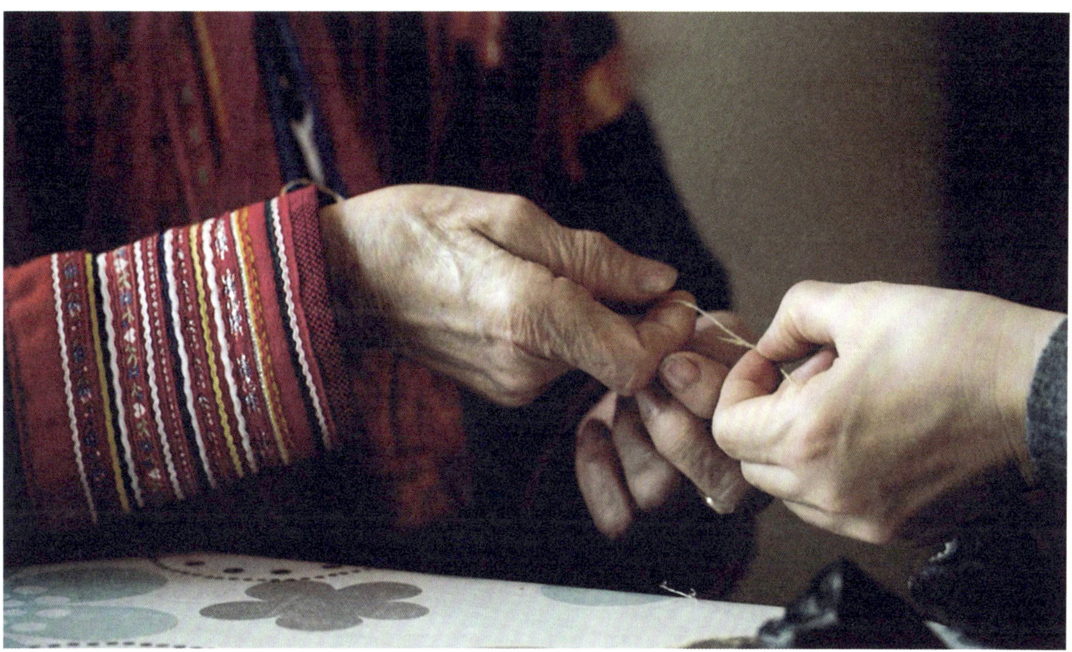

Máret Ánne Sara with Elder Karen E. M. Utsi. Still: Egil Pedersen, 2021

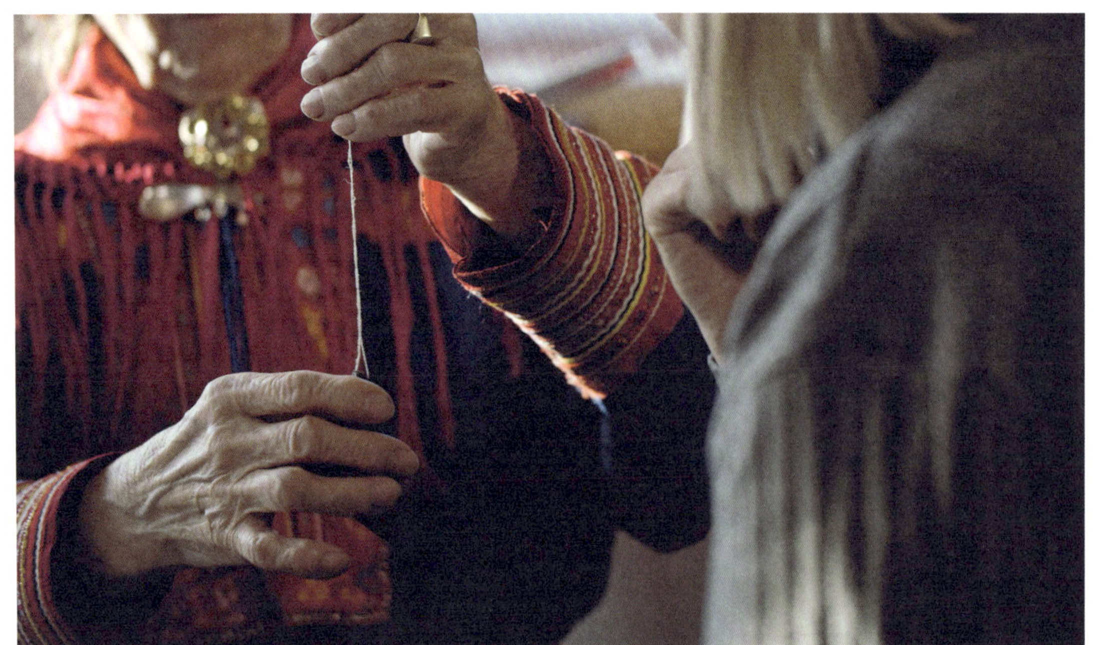

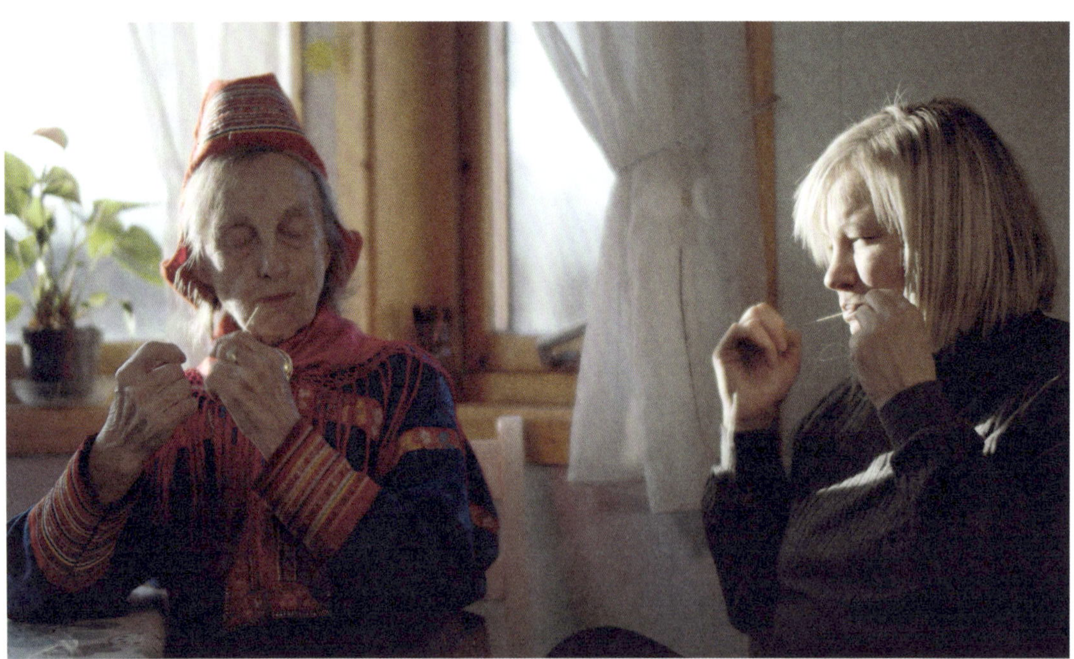

Máret Ánne Sara with Elder Karen E. M. Utsi. Stills: Egil Pedersen, 2021

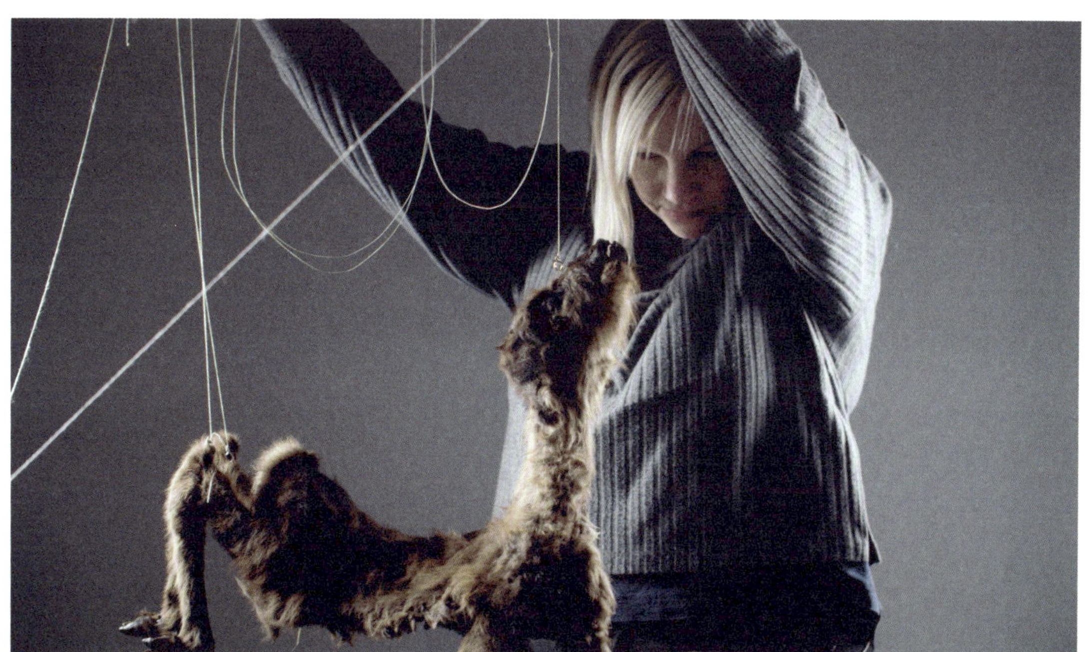

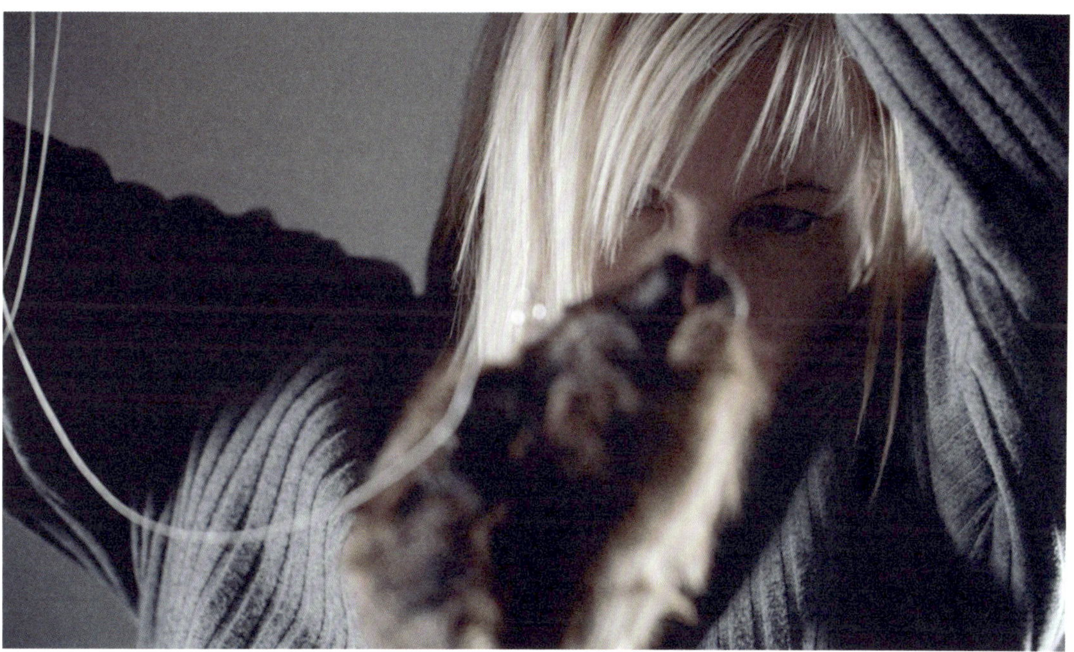

Stills: Egil Pedersen, 2021

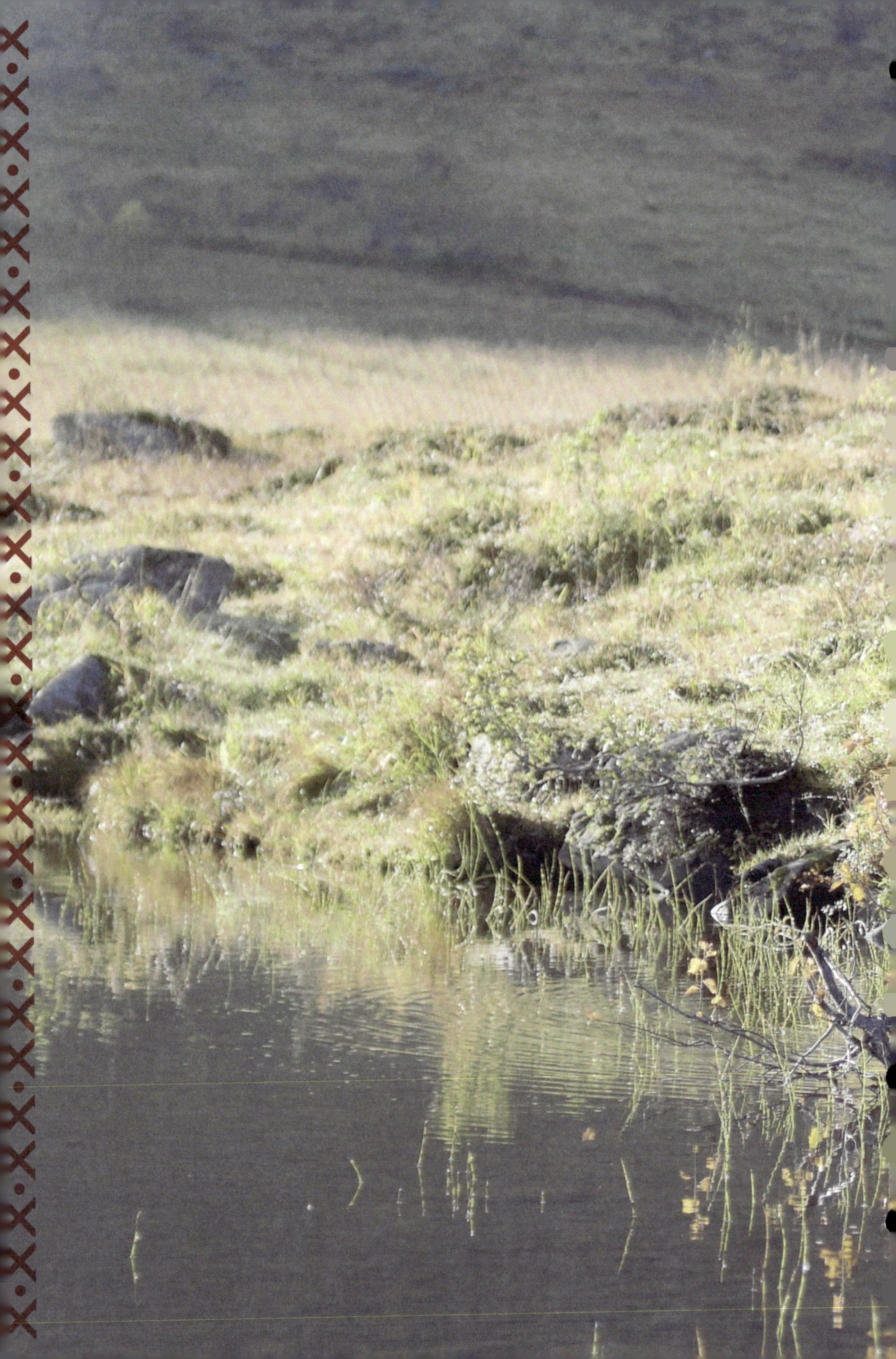

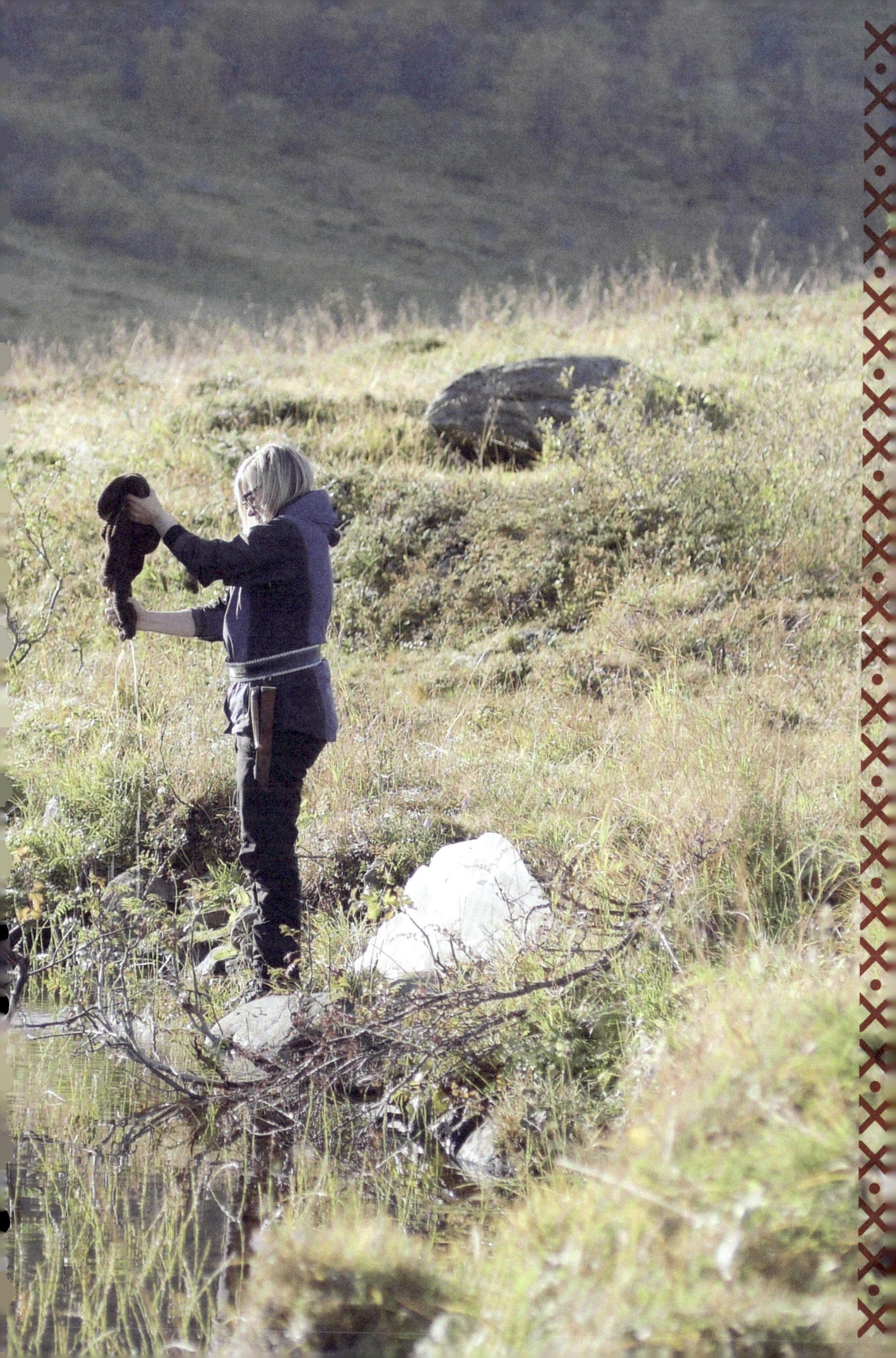

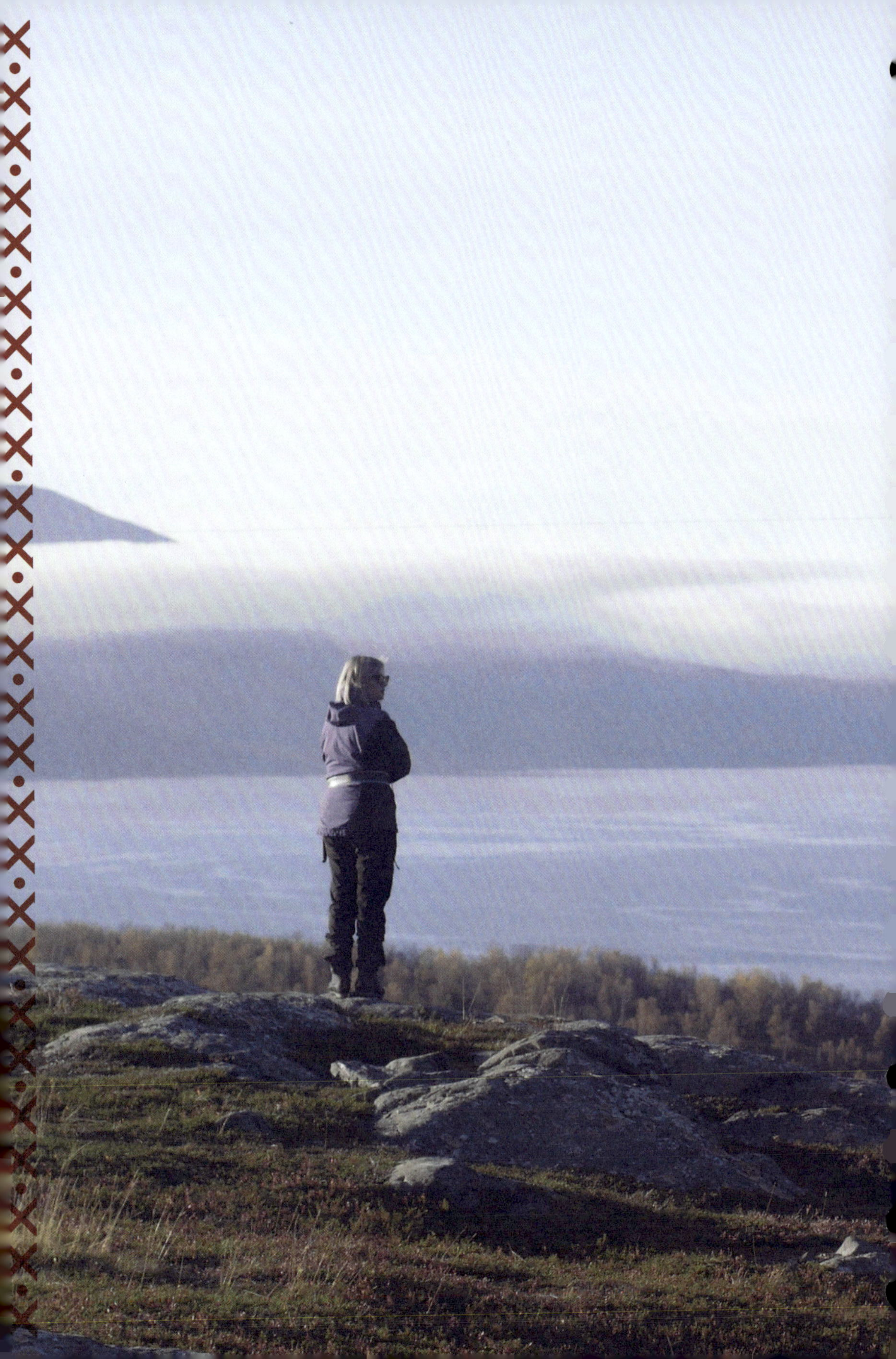

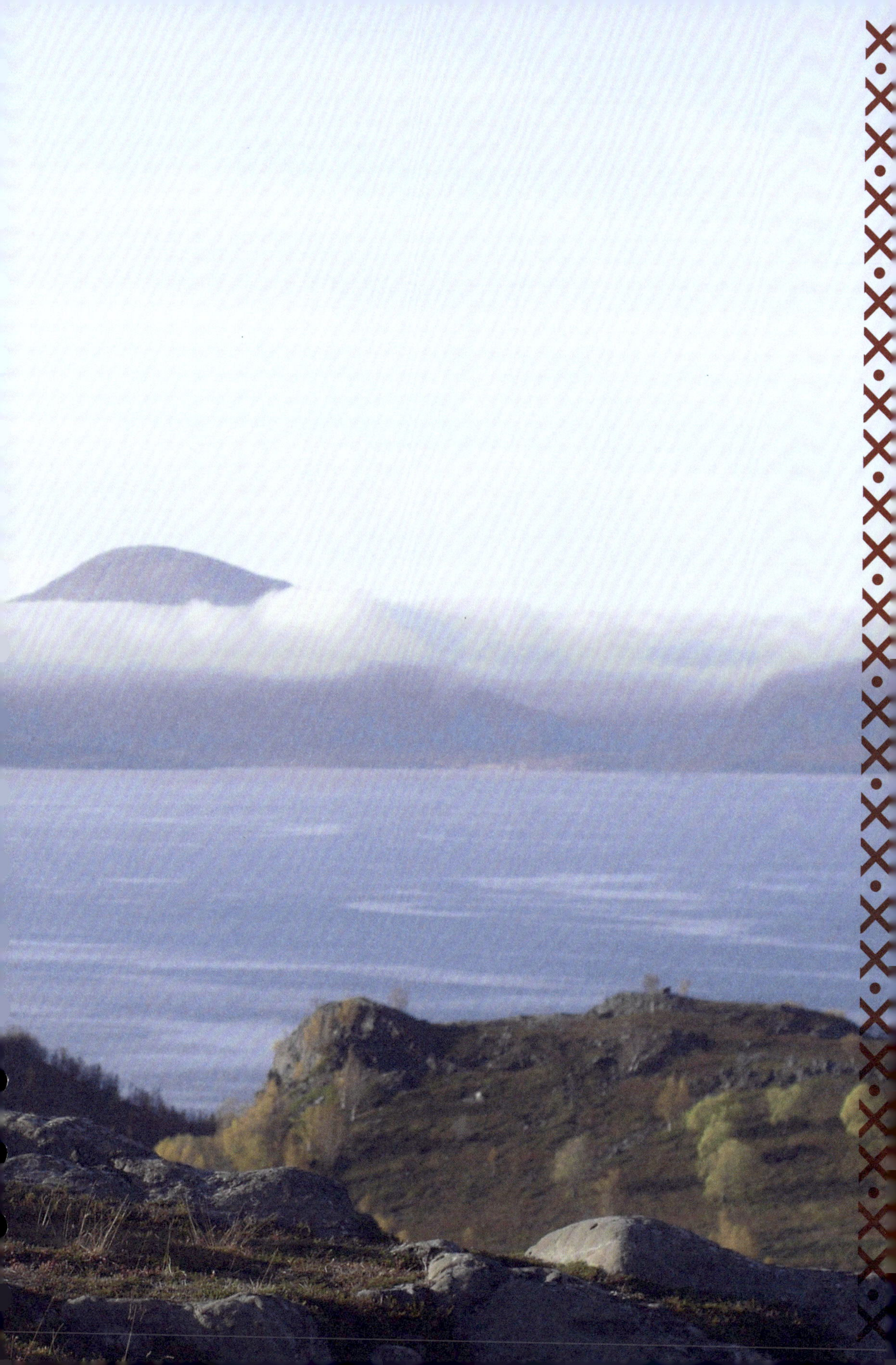

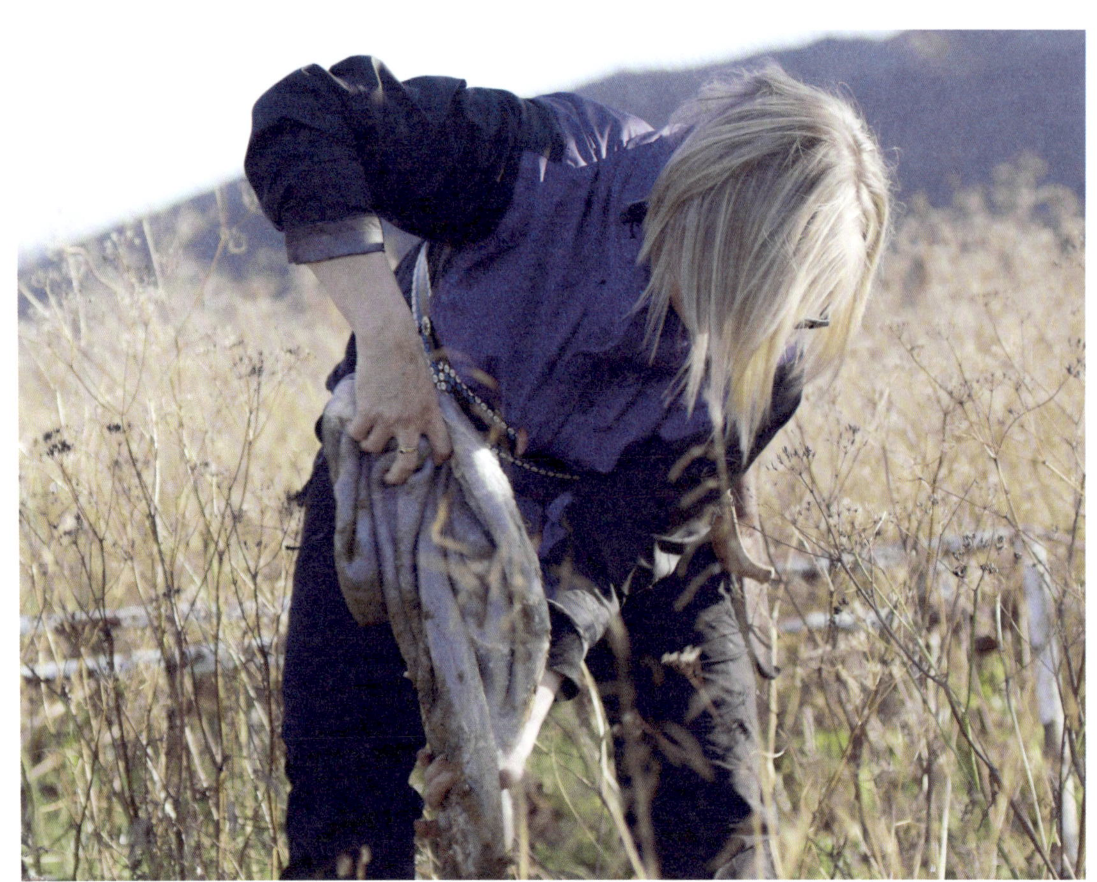

Stills pp. 98–103: Forest People / Per-Josef Idivuoma, 2020

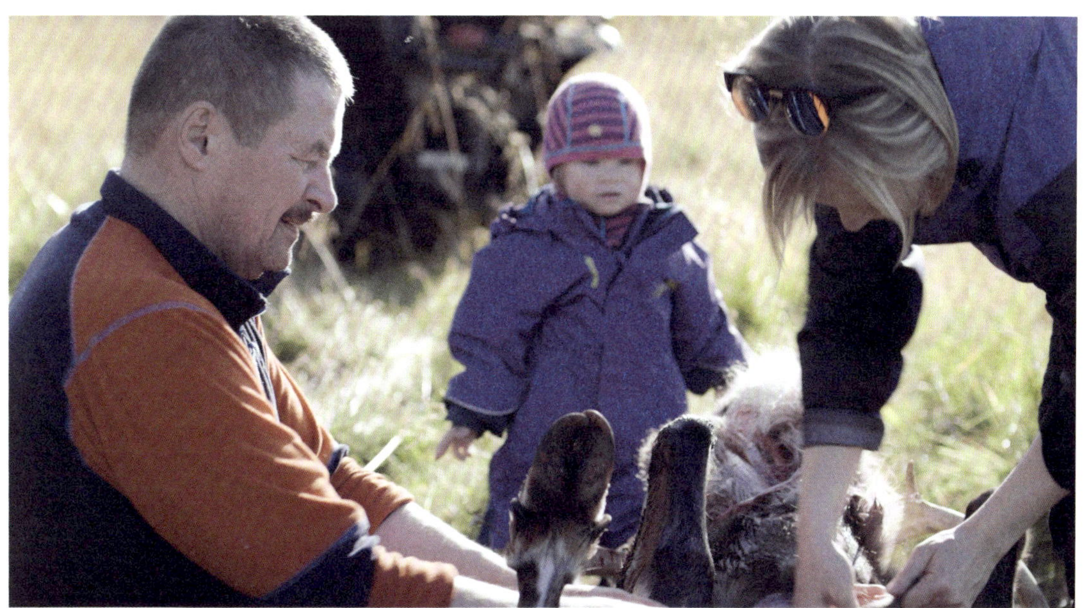

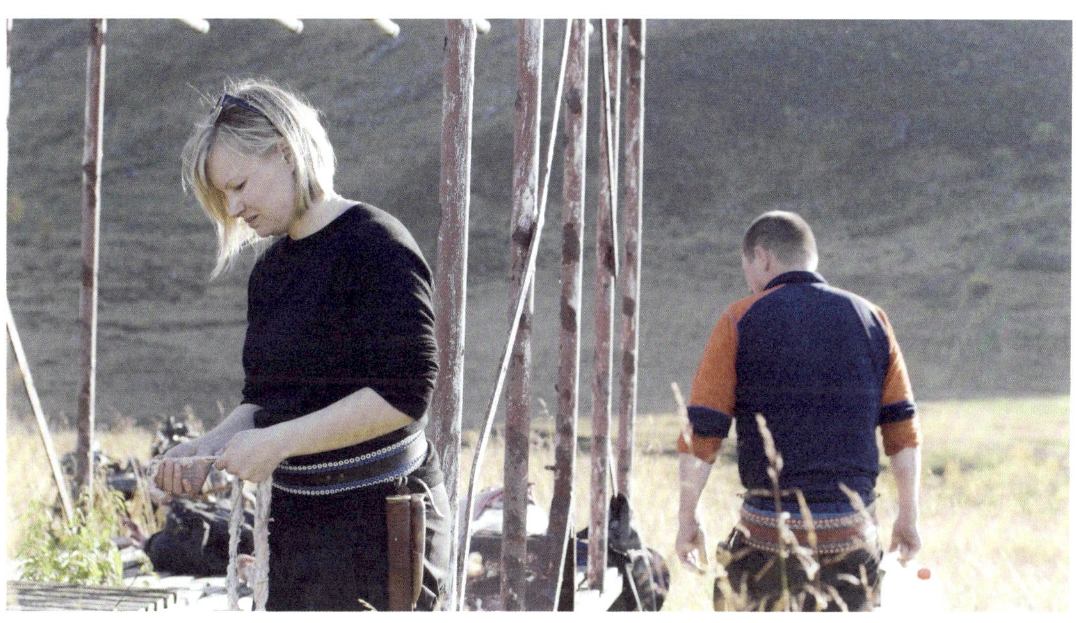

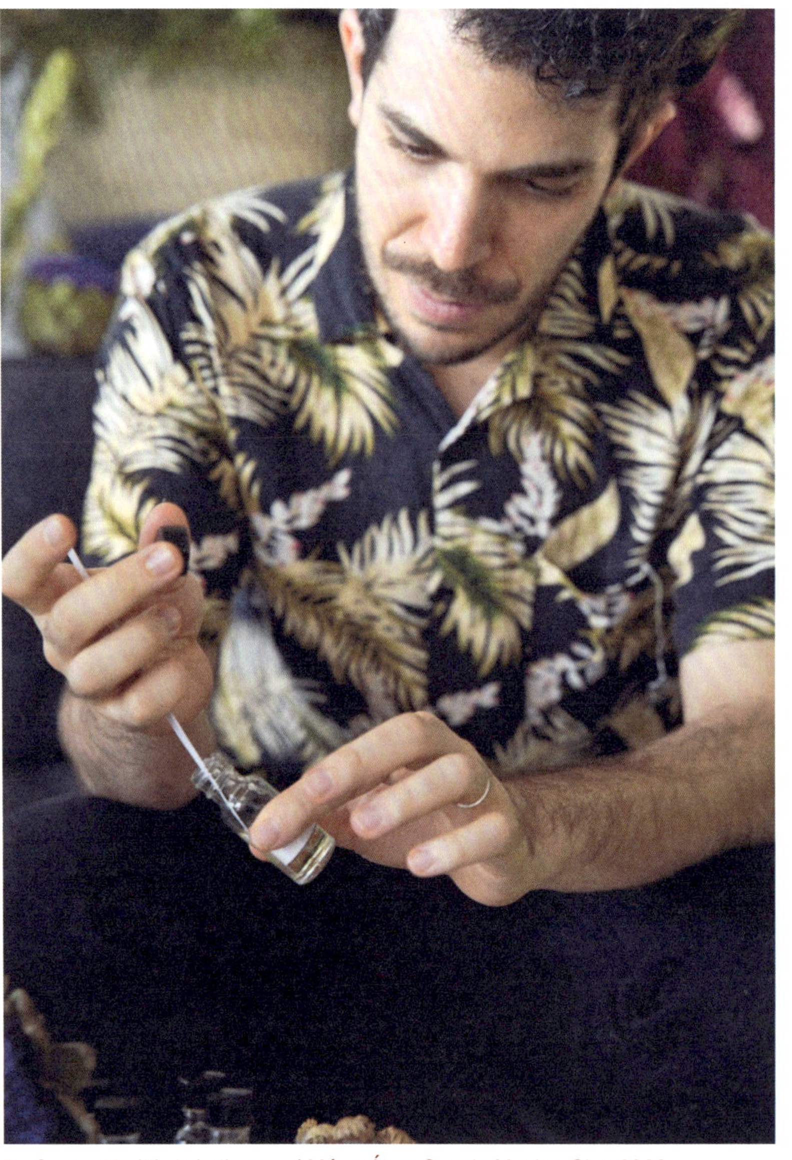

Perfumier Nadjib Achaibou and Máret Ánne Sara in Mexico City, 2020.
Photos: Karl Alfred Larsen, 2020

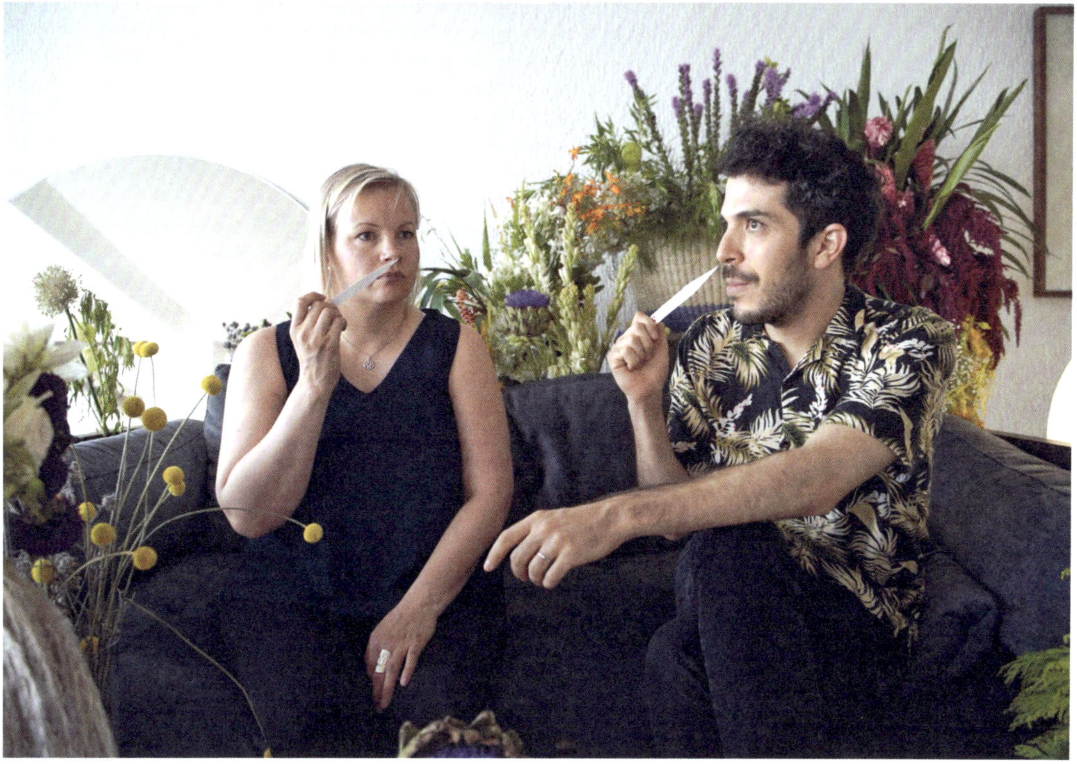

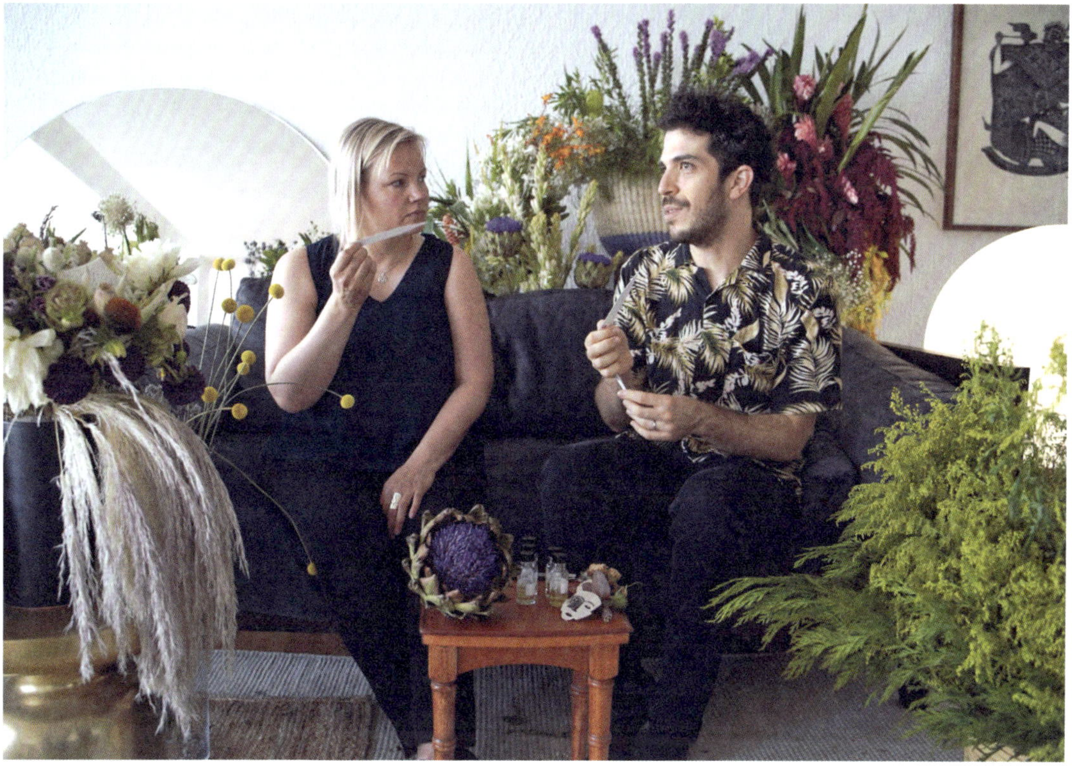

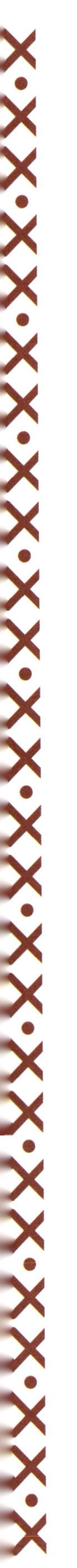

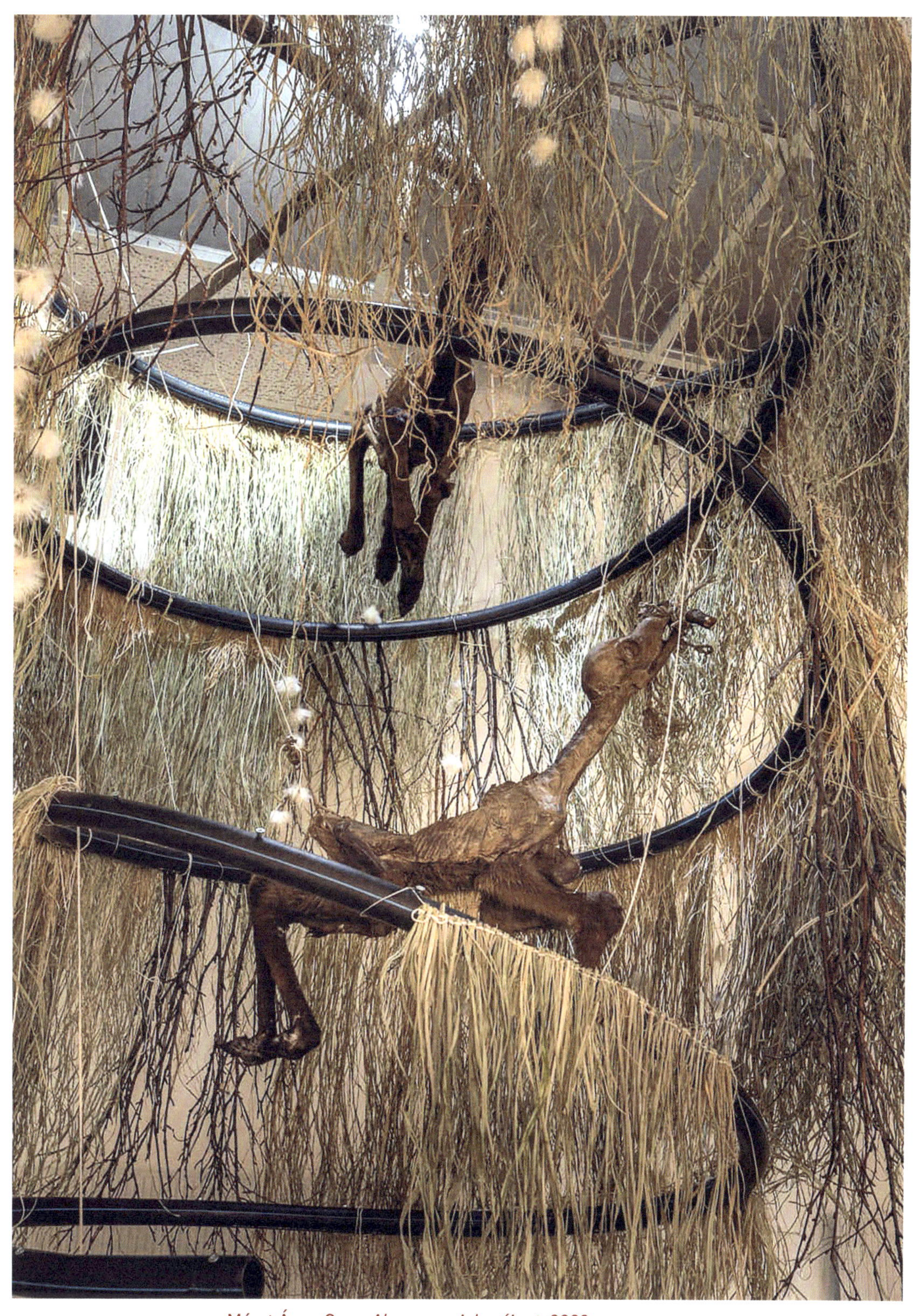

Máret Ánne Sara, *Ale suova sielu sáiget*, 2022.
Photo: Karl Alfred Larsen, courtesy and © of the artist

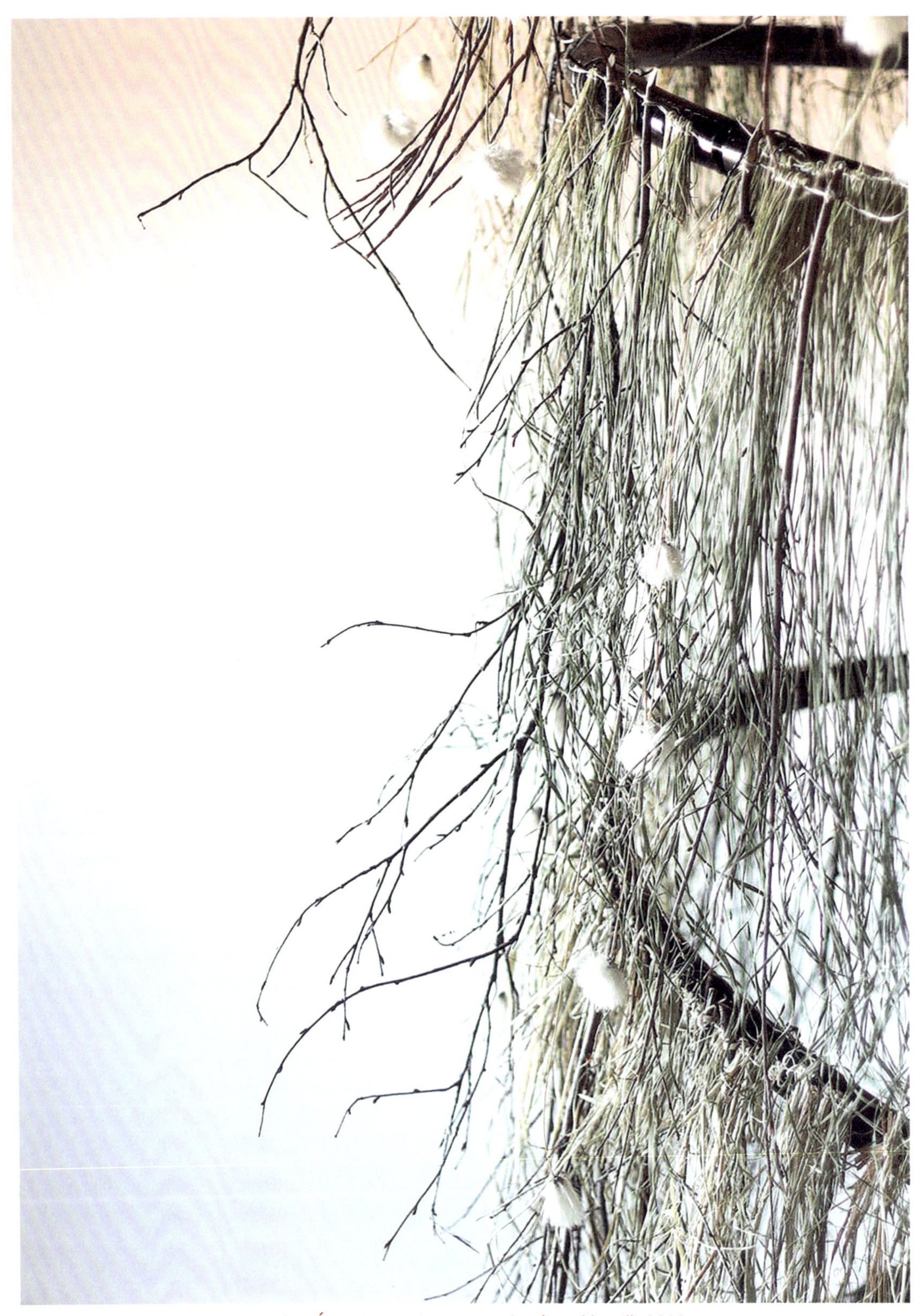

Máret Ánne Sara, *Ale suova sielu sáiget* (detail), 2022.
Photos: Karl Alfred Larsen, courtesy and © of the artist

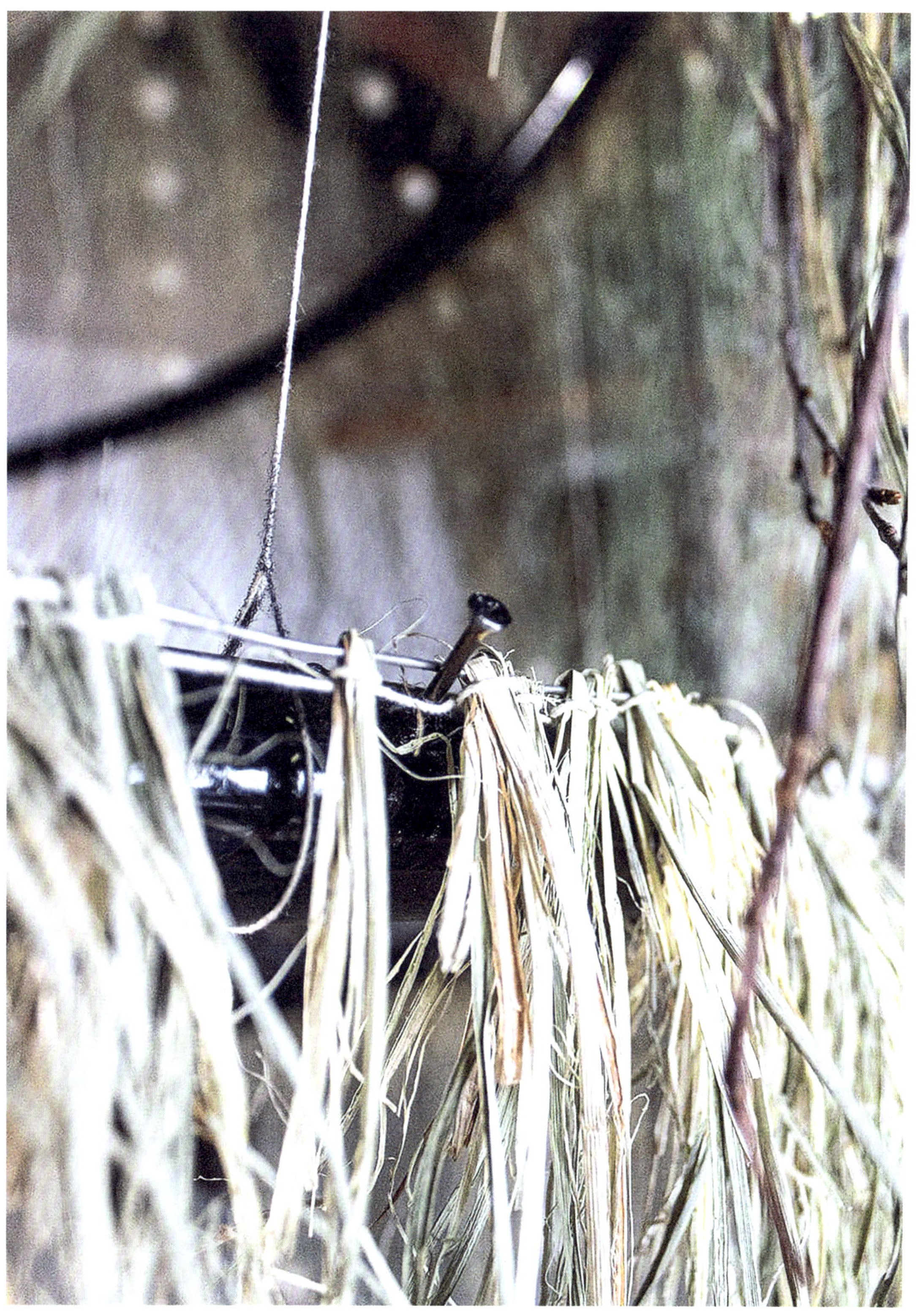

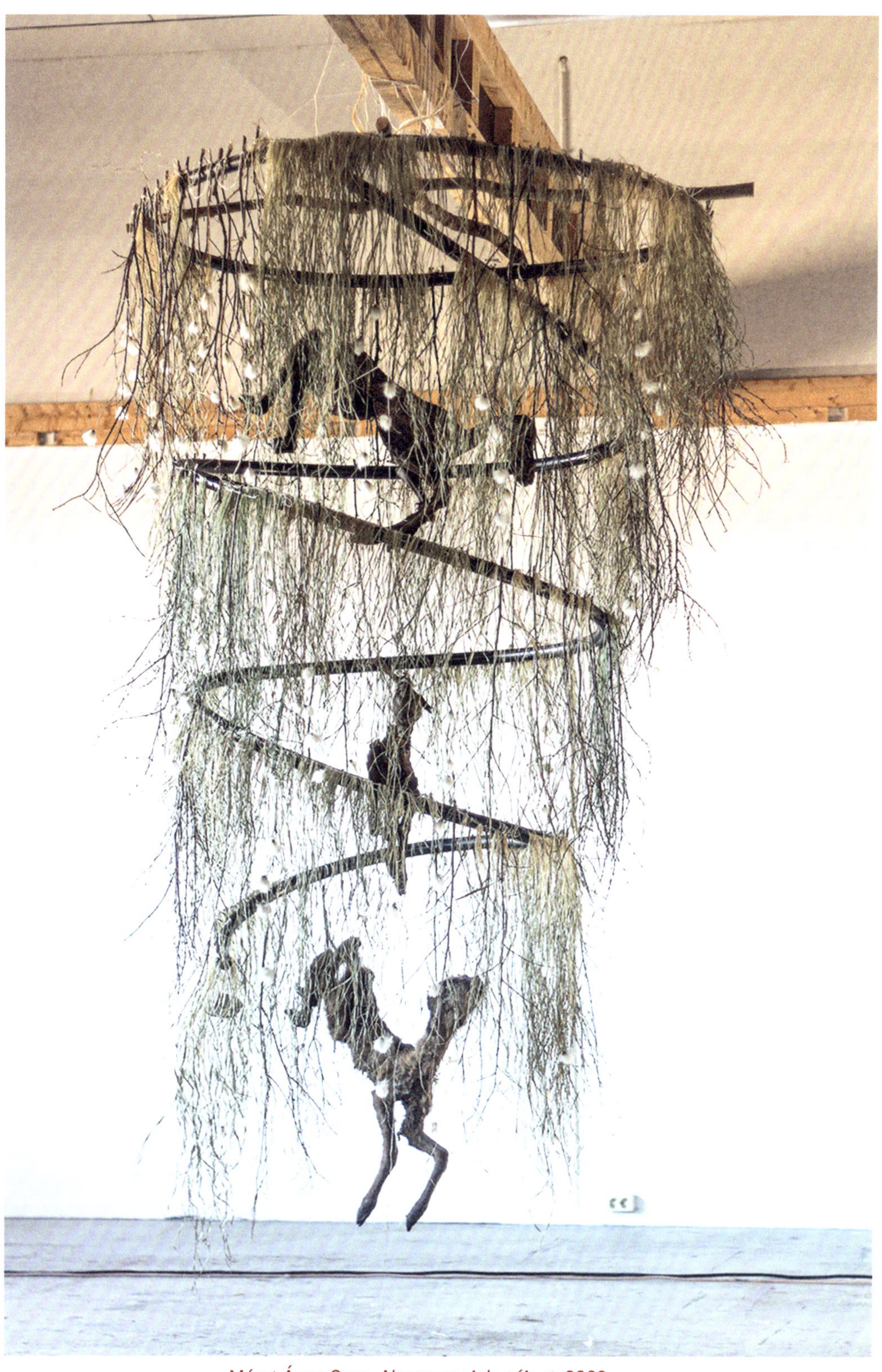

Máret Ánne Sara, *Ale suova sielu sáiget*, 2022.
Photo: Karl Alfred Larsen, courtesy and © of the artist

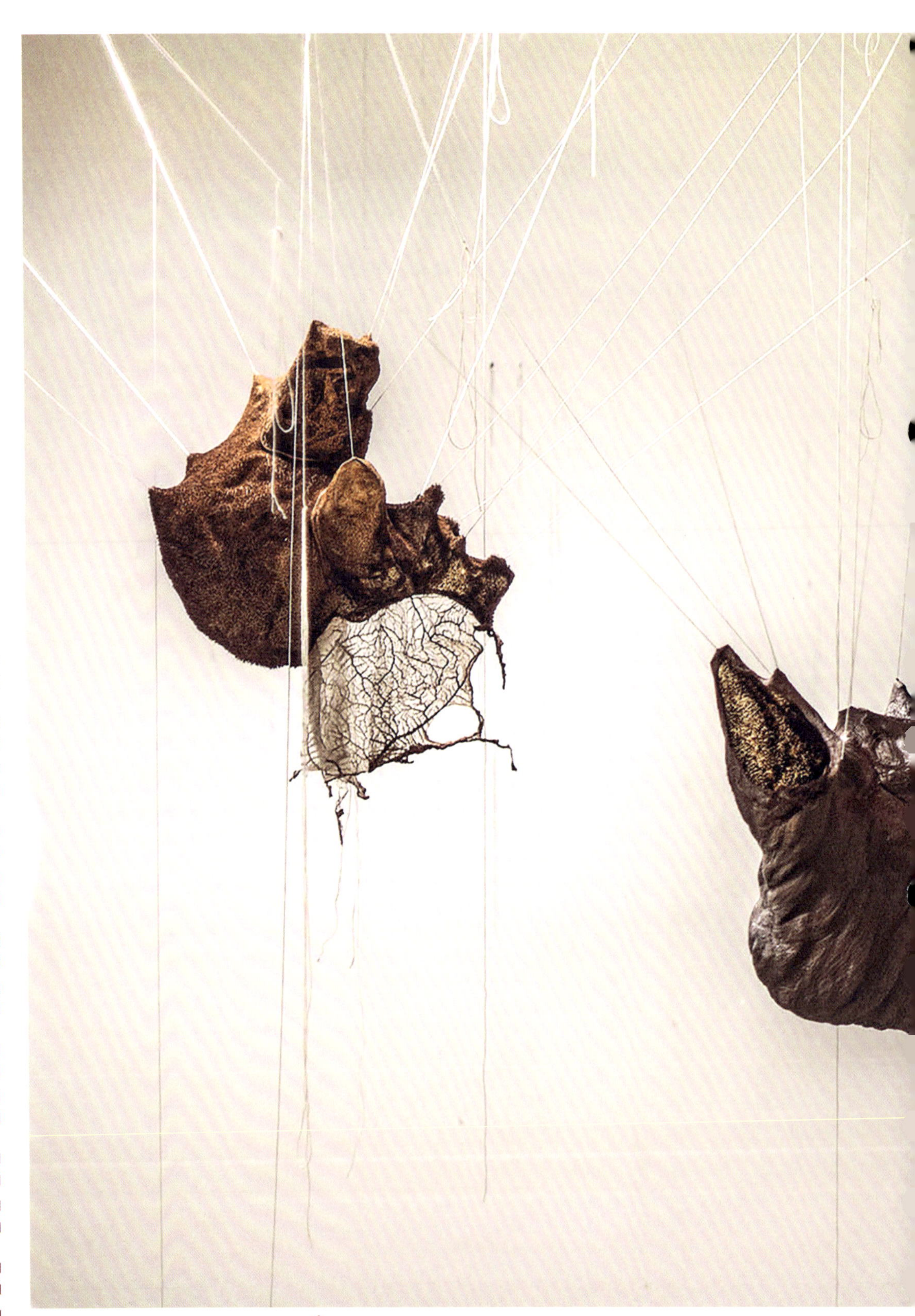

Máret Ánne Sara, *Gutted – Gávogálši* (detail), 2022.
Photo: Karl Alfred Larsen, courtesy and © of the artist

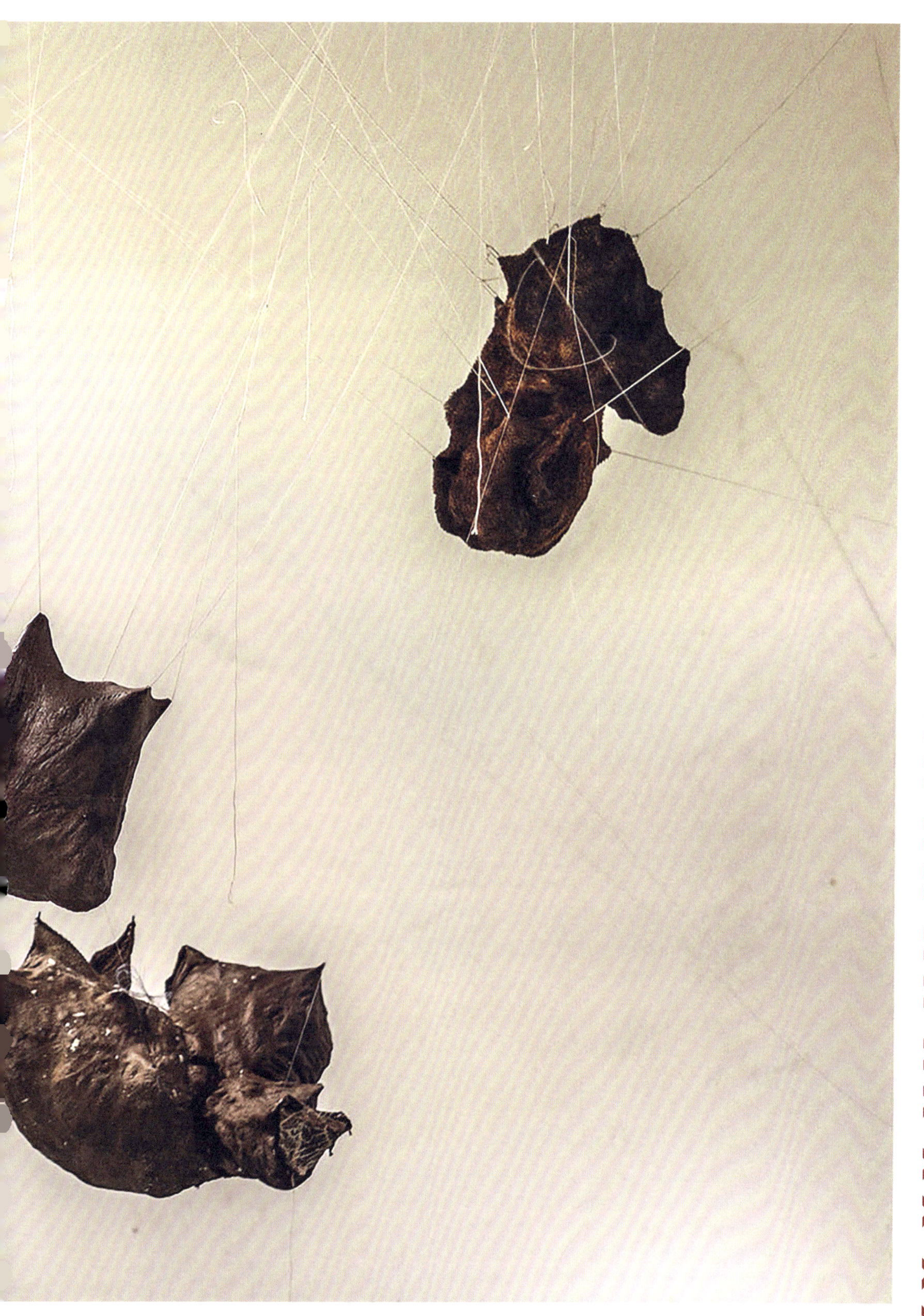

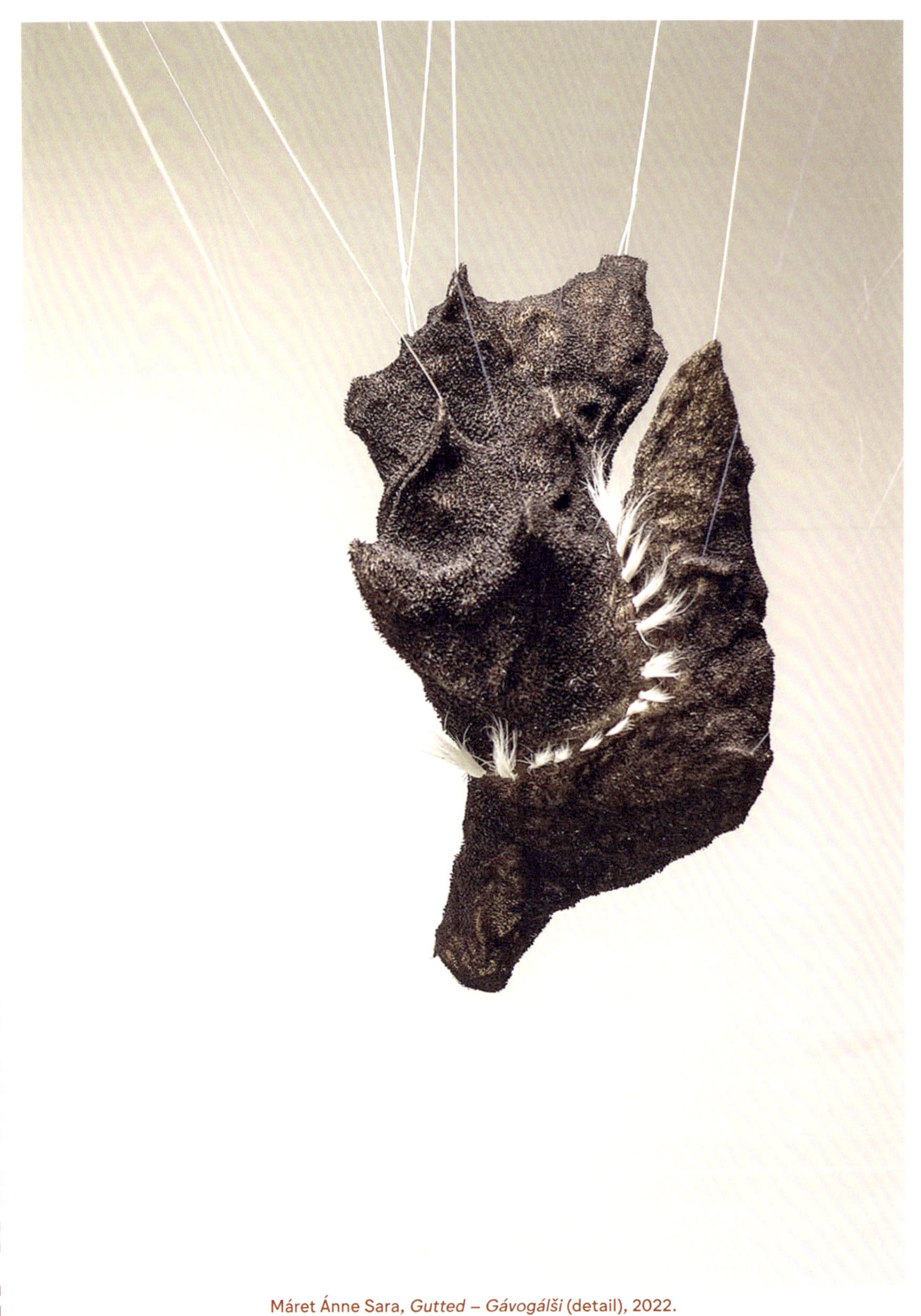

Máret Ánne Sara, *Gutted – Gávogálši* (detail), 2022.
Photo: Karl Alfred Larsen, courtesy and © of the artist

Máret Ánne Sara

Excerpt from ‘Indigenous Stories, Indigenous to Global Survival’

Excerpt from 'Indigenous Stories, Indigenous to Global Survival', in *Sovereign Words. Indigenous Art, Curation and Criticism*, ed. Katya García-Antón (OCA / Valiz, 2018).

There were numerous choices that led to my first novel, *Ilmmiid gaskkas* (In Between Worlds, 2013), many of them my own personal ones. I come from a traditional Sámi reindeer-herding society, and both sides of my family are reindeer herders. The tundra is our home, in addition to our life in Guovdageaidnu. As a child, following my father and the reindeer through the tundra, between the winter pastures in the south and the summer pastures on the northern coast, I learned to see nature and animals as an unquestioned and superior priority to our common existence.

As I became older, I gradually came to see a very different world once we reached our summer grazing lands in Fála/Kvaløya, where the city of Hammerfest is rapidly encroaching upon us due to the major oil and gas industry based in the area. While our reindeer grazed on the island of Fála, I followed my father to meetings with the police, the municipality and industries situated on our traditional summer-grazing lands, where reindeers and reindeer herders have become foreign and unwanted obstacles in the context of modern living and capitalistic/industrial expansion. These meetings gave me my first and deepest impression of the very different values and priorities of Western society compared to ours, and the deep conflicts that spring out of the collision of these two worlds. I witnessed from an early age the distress of these conflicts and the many intricate bureaucratic and political struggles for survival, the negative attitudes in the press and the population, leading to legal trials concerning our livelihood.

The Western society is still rapidly growing around us, and I still feel, as I did as a child, that my father and our people are being displaced by the language and power of bureaucracy. We are almost helpless against the political strategies, systems and forces that the Western democracy harnesses to reach its capitalistic aims. Coming back to the choices I made in order to begin the process of writing, I trained as a journalist basically to have a voice in crucial issues concerning a fragile Indigenous community that in most cases is neither heard nor understood. My later choice to leave journalism to pursue the arts came out of my realisation of the dimensions of our fights and the restrictions of the journalistic voice. The third choice, to adopt the narrative form used in traditional children's stories to deliver a strong political message, came instinctively.

When I started writing my first novel, I was mainly concerned about our many fights to protect our land against state and capitalistic interests. After finishing the novel, our fight had switched to an even more problematic one. An invisible battle was upon us, neither seen, understood nor debated by anyone outside the core reindeer Sámi community. Now, instead of addressing physical destruction, we were all of a sudden facing a powerful and faceless enemy. There has always been a conflict of interests regarding our lands: on the one hand my people need clean lands and waters in order to maintain our Sámi lifestyle of nomadic reindeer herding, fishing and small-scale farming; on the other hand, the state pursues capitalistic, large-scale industrial development in what it sees as vast and unused lands. To this end, the Norwegian state activated a forced culling of our reindeer herds. The official narrative was no longer about the destruction of the land through the implementation of their planned industries, but an accusation that Sámi people were destroying the land by herding too many reindeers. This one-sided official narrative offered a moral defence for the forced cullings. The state was then free to adjust the law to legally pursue the forced cullings that threaten not only our livelihoods but also the future of Sámi reindeer herding. Without having a voice in the public media, without anyone knowing your side of the story, how do you bring to the notice of an uninformed audience these manipulative political double standards? How do you bring about a serious discussion about systematic abuse in what is supposed to be a fair democracy? This is almost impossible in a nation coloured by political prejudice regarding its colonial history and an almost blind trust in the justice of the Scandinavian authorities. The immediate obstacles for my community are simple: to be heard, to be understood and to be believed.

Biographies

Pauliina Feodoroff is a Skolt Sámi theatre director, artist and nature guardian from Keväjäu′rr, in the Finnish part of Sápmi, and Suõ′nnjel, in the Russian part of Sápmi. Feodoroff has advocated for Sámi water and land rights in her previous role as President of the Saami Council and as an artist working to combine various fields of knowledge at the intersection of ecological conservation, theatre and film. In 2018 her cross-disciplinary project *What Form(s) Can an Atonement Take* used Sámi land-care practices, bringing together local and scientific knowledge to protect the waters and surrounding lands of the Njâuddam river in the Finnish part of Sápmi.

Anders Sunna is a Northern Sámi artist from Kieksiäisvaara, in the Swedish part of Sápmi. Sunna's politically charged artworks narrate the history of the oppression of the Sámi people and specifically address his family's five-decade long struggle for their land rights as forest reindeer herders. With powerful imagery and political satire, his paintings, graffiti, sculptures and installations depict how abuse of authority and power lead to the exploitation of land and natural resources, forced displacement and racial persecution of Sámi people. Sunna was recently commissioned to make a site-specific mural for the 22nd Biennale of Sydney, NIRIN, 2020.

Máret Ánne Sara is a Northern Sámi artist from Guovdageaidnu in the Norwegian part of Sápmi. She is known for experimenting with a range of materials and approaches that make visible the political and social issues affecting the Sámi people. Her works are often made from materials deriving from the sustainable practice of her reindeer-herding family, including reindeer bones, hides and intestines. Her installation *Pile o' Sápmi*, composed of 400 reindeer skulls and legal documents, was showcased at documenta 14 in Kassel, 2017. The installation was recently purchased by the National Museum of Norway in Oslo.

Liv Brissach is an art historian and writer based in Oslo who worked as Project Officer at the Office for Contemporary Art Norway (OCA) and curatorial assistant to 'The Sámi Pavilion' until March 2022. Brissach graduated with a degree in Art History from the University of Oslo (MA) and University College London (BA), specialising in contemporary art. As a writer, Brissach has contributed texts for Munchmuseet on the Move, *Kunstkritikk, Billedkunst* and Fotogalleriet amongst others. Brissach is assistant editor of *Čatnosat. The Sámi Pavilion, Indigenous Art, Knowledge and Sovereignty* and was coordinator of OCA's publications in the period 2018–22. From March 2022 Brissach is curator of contemporary art at the Munch Museum in Oslo.

Katya García-Antón is director/chief curator of the Office for Contemporary Art Norway. She graduated as a biologist, and transitioned into the arts with a master's degree in nineteenth- and twentieth-century art from The Courtauld Institute of Art, London. She has worked at The Courtauld Institute of Art, Museo Nacional Reina Sofía Madrid, ICA London, IKON Birmingham, and the Centre d'Art Contemporain Genève. She curated the Nordic Pavilion, Venice Biennial in 2015 and the Spanish Pavilion in the Venice Biennial 2011. In OCA, García-Antón has generated significant Indigenising practices and programmes. In August 2022 she becomes director of the Northern Norway Art Museum (NNKM).

Acknowledgements

'The Sámi Pavilion' project marks a ground-breaking moment in the history of the Biennale Arte in Venice: the Indigenisation of the Nordic Pavilion. Commissioned by OCA, with the support of co-commissioners Moderna Museet and Museum of Contemporary Art Kiasma, it also represents a pivotal moment in OCA's eight-year journey to advocate for institutional decolonisation. As a multi-layered initiative that has sought to centre Sámi perspectives every step of the way, the project has involved many collaborators over many years, all of whom we wish to honour in this acknowledgement.

First and foremost, we are deeply grateful to the artists whose dedication and creative thinking we deeply admire: Pauliina Feodoroff, Máret Ánne Sara and Anders Sunna. We express our thanks and we honour the artists' families and their ancestors. In addition we thank Hanna Parry, Outi Pieski, Eséte Eshetu Sutinen, Katja Haarla, Birit Haarla, Satu Herrala, Terike Haapoja, Marja Helander (collaborators in Feodoroff's project); Alexandra Harald (assistant to Sara), as well as Nadjib Achaibou, Symrise and Oswaldo Maciá (advisors for the smell duet in Sara's installation); Gaby Hartel (dramaturgy advisor for the sonic elements in Sunna's installation) and the Sunna family members who contributed to the production of the installation: Britt-Inger Sunna, Bo Sunna, Nils-Erik Sunna, Per-Olof Sydfeldt Sunna, Lars-Göran Sunna, Jon-Isak Sunna, Aino Strand Sunna, Conny Strand, Elena Sunna and Michiel Brouwer. We also thank Elder and the pavilion's Guest Book-maker Elle Hánsa / Keviselie / Hans Ragnar Mathisen.

Máret Ánne Sara also extends a special thanks to Fimben Áillo Ánte (Anders Aslaksen Siri). Pauliina Feodoroff thanks Sarakka Gaup, Elina Israelsson, Mio Negga, Anna-Stina Svakko, Jan Saijets, Osmo Seurujärvi, Esko Aikio, Kevin Francett, Jarmo Pyykkö, Jouni S. Laiti, Kaisu Mustonen, the 'What Form(s) can an Atonement

Take' project, Mary Beth Jäger, Amy Juan, Shawna Larson, Noor Johnson and Eero and Rita Murtomäki.

OCA extends a heartfelt thank you to members of the curatorial group Beaska Niillas, Liisa-Rávná Finbog and Katya García-Antón; and assistant curators Raisa Porsanger (2020–21), Liv Brissach (2020–22) and Martina Petrelli (2022), as well as the Elders Asta M. Balto, Ánde Somby and Karen E.M. Utsi, who were dialogue partners with the artists. In addition, we thank the International Indigenous Advisers to the project Brook Garru Andrew and Wanda Nanibush, as well as Harald Gaski and Beaska Niillas, members of the project's Language Group, for their collaboration.

We offer our very special gratitude to the inspiring collaborators in 'The Sámi Pavilion' project's extended programme: Poet in Residence Timimie Gassko Märak; ÁRRAN 360's filmmakers and artists Elle Márjá Eira, Marja Helander, Ann Holmgren, Hans Pieski, Siljá Somby and Liselotte Wajstedt, as well as ISFI Director Anne Lajla Utsi and project manager Maria Utsi, ISFI colleagues Morten Pettersen and Liisa Holmberg, and NFI Director Kjesti Mo and colleagues Nedin Mutic and Stine Oppegaard; for the special 2022 edition of aabaakwad, which comes to Venice under the auspices of 'The Sámi Pavilion', we thank founder Wanda Nanibush, the aabaakwad curatorial team and all participants (too numerous to name here); and for the collaboration with the TBA–21 Academy's Indigenous edition of their Ocean Fellowship Programme we thank mentors Harald Gaski and Rebecca Belmore, the Fellows Matti Aikio, Liryc Dela Cruz, Ursula A. Johnson, Fernanda Olivares Molina and aqui Thami, and collaborators Wanda Nanibush, Markus Reymann, Niall Smith, Mareike Dittmer, María Montero Sierra, Graziano Meneghin, Chus Martínez and Barbara Casavecchia (with input from Brook Garru Andrew and Megan Tamati-Quenell).

OCA is deeply grateful to the editors of *Čatnosat. The Sámi Pavilion, Indigenous Art, Knowledge and Sovereignty* Liisa-Rávná Finbog, Katya García-Antón and Beaska Niillas (and assistant editor Liv Brissach). This publication is the fruit of an intensive journey of reflection, asking the question 'what does it mean today to make a book from a Sámi perspective, given the colonial repressive legacy of book making and the written word?'. We are forever thankful to the authors: Brook Garru Andrew, Asta Mitkijá Balto, Liv Brissach, Pauliina Feodoroff, Liisa-Rávná Finbog, Katya García-Antón, Harald Gaski, Timimie Gassko Märak, Beaska Niillas, Máret Ánne Sara, Sigbjørn Skåden, Ánde Somby and Anders Sunna. We are also humbled by the powerful insights of the participants of the two Collective Jurddabádji (online gatherings) that set the conceptual ground for the making of this publication: Anna Afanasyeva, Katarina Barruk, Liv Brissach, Tanya Busse, Pauliina Feodoroff, Liisa-Rávná Finbog, Katya García-Antón, Harald Gaski, Eeva Kristiina Harlin, Elle Hánsa / Keviselie / Hans Ragnar Mathisen, Beaska Niillas, Taqralik Partridge, Outi Pieski, Fredrik Prost, Inga-Wiktoria Påve, Máret Ánne Sara, Sigbjørn Skåden, Katarina Skår Lisa and Anders Sunna. Finally we also warmly thank Tiina-Sanila Aikio, Aleksi Koponen, Christina Hætta, Harald Gaski and Siljá Somby for their advice on the publication, and the network of people who helped translate the book's dedication into eight Sámi languages: Mikkel Rasmus Logje and Siljá Somby (Northern Sámi), Pauliina Feodoroff (Skolt Sámi), Jørgen Kintel (Lule Sámi), Katarina Barruk (Ume Sámi), Inger Fjällås and Peter Steggo (Pite Sámi), Domna Khomyuk (Kildin Sámi), Joseph Fjellgren (Southern Sámi), Henna Lehtola (Anár Sámi) and facilitators: Natalia Vaskova – Saami Council; Anita Kitok – Sámi Parliament in Sweden; Risten Länsman and Per-Martin Israelsson – Sámi Parliament Norway and Giellatekno Apertium – UiT The Arctic University of Norway.

We are particularly delighted with the pioneering collaboration generating the project's visual identity and publication design, between designer Hans Gremmen and Sámi duojárs Inga-Wiktoria Påve and Fredrik Prost.

We extend our deepest thanks to the the OCA team for their commitment to the project and we offer our warmest thanks to the following collaborators and friends: from the Sámi University of Applied Sciences: Lena Susanne Gaup, Laila Susanne Vars, and the Pathfinders; from Riddu Riđđu Festival: Sandra Márjá West and musicians Hildá Länsmann, Emil Karlsen and Lávre; Deutchlandfunk; Art Gallery of Ontario; from The Oslo School of Architecture and Design: Kai Reaver; from Valiz, Amsterdam: Astrid Vorstermans; Forest People AS; Egil Pedersen; Mette Henriette; Dáiddadállu Artist Collective; Aili Keskitalo; Siljá Somby; Magne Svineng; Tiina Sanila-Aikio; David Garneau and Elin Már Øyen Vister.

We are deeply grateful to Sarah Greenberg and her team at Evergreen Arts for the international communication and events work for this project; as well as to Anna Clark, Valeria Gemelli and to the Palazzo Nani Bernardi.

We offer our thanks to the following project supporters: The Norwegian Ministry of Culture and Equality, The Norwegian Ministry of Foreign Affairs, Nordic Culture Point, Fritt Ord – the Freedom of Expression Foundation, The Sámi Parliament in Norway, in Sweden and in Finland, The Sámi Parliamentary Council (SPC), The Norwegian Film Institute and Canada Council for the Arts.

We remember the Sámi artist Aage Gaup, due to exhibit in Biennale Arte 2022's central exhibition, who passed unexpectedly and whose presence in the celebration of this historic project will be deeply missed.

Finally, we thank the numerous Sámi peers who gave invaluable advice and support along the way.

'The Sámi Pavilion' in the Nordic Pavilion at the 59th International Art Exhibition, La Biennale di Venezia, 23 April – 27 November 2022

Co-commissioners
Katya García-Antón (Office for Contemporary Art, Norway)
Gitte Ørskou (Moderna Museet, Stockholm)
Leevi Haapala (Museum of Contemporary Art Kiasma, Helsinki)

Artists
Pauliina Feodoroff, Máret Ánne Sara and Anders Sunna

Elders
Ánde Somby, Asta Mitkijá Balto, Karen E. M. Utsi

'The Sámi Pavilion' Guest Book-maker
Elle Hánsa / Keviselie / Hans Ragnar Mathisen

Curatorial Group
Liisa-Rávná Finbog, Katya García-Antón and Beaska Niillas

Assistant Curators
Liv Brissach (2020–22), Martina Petrelli (2022) and Raisa Porsanger (2020–21)

Artists' assistants and collaborators
Gaby Hartel, Nadjib Achaibou, Symrise, Oswaldo Maciá, Snowchange Cooperative, Alexandra Harald, Britt-Inger Sunna, Bo Sunna, Nils-Erik Sunna, Per-Olof Sydfeldt Sunna, Lars-Göran Sunna, Jon-Isak Sunna, Aino Strand Sunna, Elena Sunna, Conny Strand and Michiel Brouwer, Hanna Parry, Outi Pieski, Eséte Eshetu Sutinen, Katja Haarla, Birit Haarla, Satu Herrala, Terike Haapoja, Marja Helander and the artists' families.

International Indigenous Advisers
Brook Garru Andrew and Wanda Nanibush

Language Group
Professor Harald Gaski and Beaska Niillas

Mediators
Pathfinders, Sámi allaskuvla / Sámi University of Applied Sciences

'The Sámi Pavilion' Extended Programme

Word Weaver (Poet in Residence)
Timimie Gassko Märak

ÁRRAN 360° – a collaboration between International Sámi Film Institute (ISFI), Norwegian Film Institute (NFI) and Office for Contemporary Art Norway (OCA)

aabaakwad 2022 in Venice – an Indigenous-led conversation on Indigenous art by those who create, curate and write about it, over several days in Venice

TBA21–Academy Ocean Fellowship 2022 in collaboration with 'The Sámi Pavilion' at the 59th Biennale Arte in 2022, the Office for Contemporary Art Norway, aabaakwad, and Artis

Architectural supervision and production
M+B Studio

OCA Project Manager
Luba Kuzovnikova

Installation support in Venice
Biung Ismahasan and Chen Chun-Lun

OCA Communications
Karoline Trollvik
Michael Miller
Maria Elena Putz
Vilde Svineng Boberg

International Press Office
Evergreen Arts

Graphic designer visual identity
Hans Gremmen, in collaboration with Sámi duojárs Inga-Wiktoria Påve and Fredrik Prost

With the support of
The Norwegian Ministry of Culture and Equality
The Norwegian Ministry of Foreign Affairs
Nordic Culture Point
Fritt Ord – the Freedom of Expression Foundation
The Sámi Parliament in Norway
The Sámi Parliamentary Council (SPC)
The Norwegian Film Institute
Canada Council for the Arts

‘To all those who came before us,
and to those who will come after us’

‘Gájk dajda ma buhtin mija åvvdålin,
ja dajda ma buhti mija maŋŋelin’

‘Gájkijde giäh mïjjan uvddale bühten,
jah gájkijde giäh mïjjan miŋŋiele bühth’

Čatnosat (Northern Sámi) means connections, attachments or bonds. The dedication on this page is in the following languages: Pite Sámi and Ume Sámi.

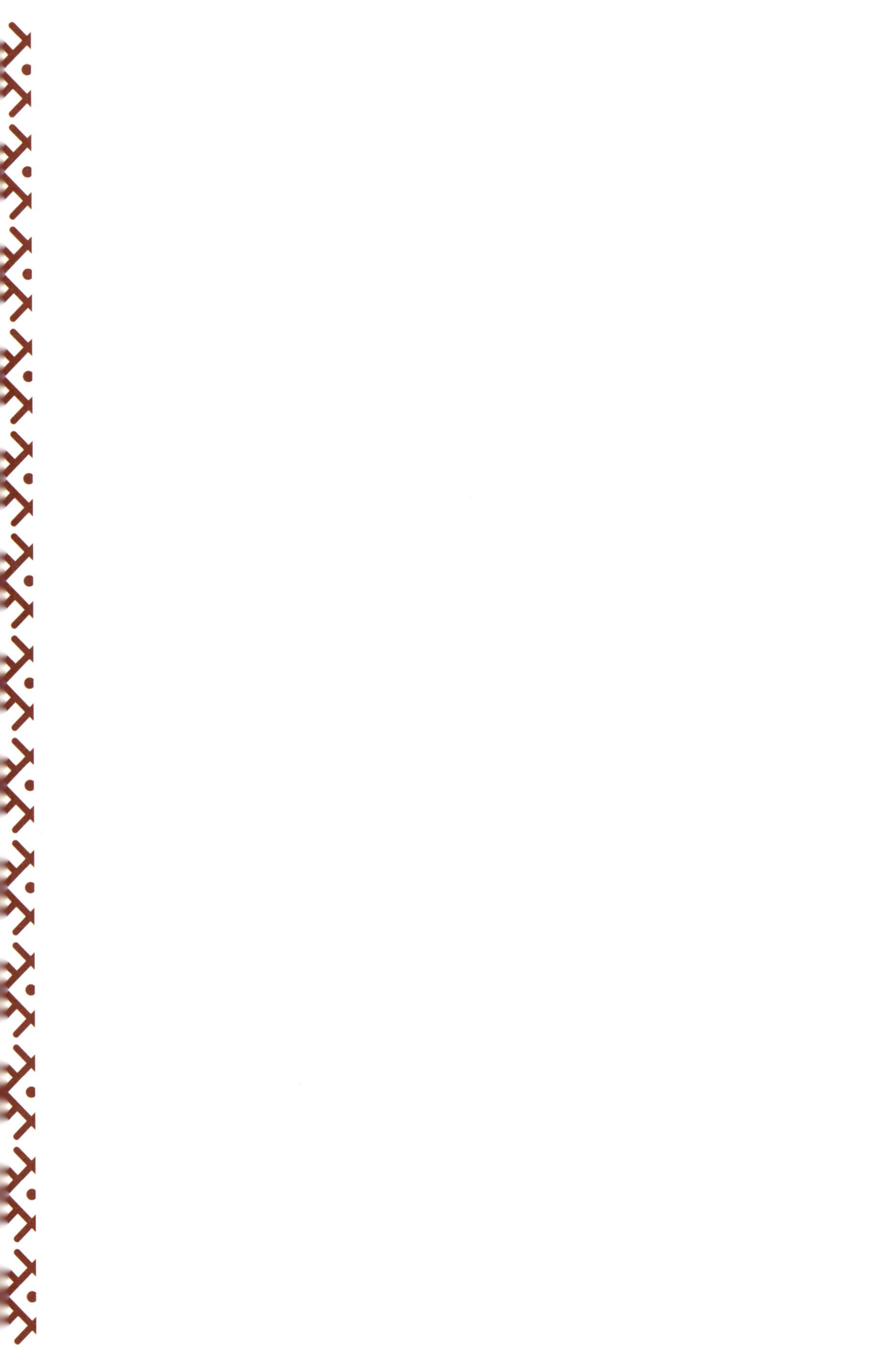

Liisa-Ràvnà Finbog
The Story of Terra Nullius. Variations on the Land(s) of Saepmie[1] that Nobody Owned

1 This is the Southern Saami spelling of the Saami homeland.

Liisa-Ràvnà Finbog's text 'The Story of Terra Nullius. Variations on the Land(s) of Saepmie that Nobody Owned' was first published in *Action Stories*, an online urban activist platform initiated in 2021 by Grow-lab Oslo and partners.

2
Kristin Jernsletten, 'The Hidden Children of Eve: Sámi Poetics: Guovtti ilmmi gaskkas' (Tromsø: University of Tromsø, 2011), p. 4.

3
I. N. Goduka, 'Indigenous Epistemologies – Ways of Knowing: Affirming a Legacy', *South African Journal of Higher Education* 13, No. 3 (1999): p. 26.

Introduction

> *'Listen, child of my child, to the stories I tell. All you see before you is now as it once was, and it is how it will continue to be long after you and I are gone from this place.'*

The last time I saw my grand-uncle, at a family gathering, he spoke to me of the land and how it had shaped our ancestors and how it continued to shape us. He made sure to teach those of us listening the names and places of his childhood, and he made sure we knew that these lessons came from his elders and their elders. Three months later, I received the news of his passing, and I realised then why he put such importance on teaching us that day: Indigneous worldviews, our ontologies, are shaped by our relationship to land. It is this relationship that defines our existence, because the land is where we are born from, remain attached to, and must one day return to in order to be united with our ancestors. When we are dispossessed of our homelands, it is this relationship that is at stake and with it, our sovereignty and our surety of our place in the world. No wonder, then, that one of the more favoured colonial strategies is to implement a language to bodily alienate the people from the land.[2] Instead of Saami, the people came to be known as the 'Lapps', a term that is today regarded as highly derogatory. No longer Saepmie, our homelands instead became Norway, Sweden, Finland, and Russia.

This alienation is not recent, nor is it a thing of the past. It is both then as well as now, and likely it is also in our future. From the time of 'first contact', the story of Indigenous peoples has far too often been one of 'no speak and no-voice. It has been a story of silence, of invisibility, of conquest, marginalization and powerlessness'.[3] As a consequence, Indigenous knowledge systems, as well as our world-views, perspectives, and values have been equally silenced and disregarded. This is a process of *epistemicide*: the deliberate destruction of the knowledge and cultures of Indigeous populations, of their memories and ancestral links and their manner of relating to others and to the land.[4] The Sámi scholar, Rauna Kuokkanen, has conceptualised this continued silencing as an *epistemic ignorance*,[5] which refers to the ways in which academic theories and practises ignore, marginalise and exclude non-dominant Western[6] epistemic and intellectual traditions.[7] The implications of this are many and serious, but none more so that than the continued enabling of alienation between land and people. 'How so', curious minds may ask. The answer is neither simple nor easy.

Most Indigenous worldviews recognise that the land is a living entity with a subjective will.[8] Still, law- and decision-makers, informed and governed by Western ideologies and ideas that enforce control and domination, disregard this subjectivity in their practice. The land on which we live is, to them, nothing more than an object for the taking. Something that may be claimed for selfish reasons in the pursuit of financial gain.[9] This reflects what might be termed an ontological conflict 'where encounters with different ways of knowing and living with the land are central'.[10] But to begin to understand this conflict, we need to take a step back and remove ourselves from an Indigenous context, traversing instead into the Age of Enlightenment that for so long has been considered the foundation of modern political and intellectual culture in the West.[11]

The Age of Enlightenment and the Lockean Principle of Property

Heavily influencing the avant-garde of Europe in the seventeenth and eighteenth centuries, the movement of Enlightenment that would come to dominate the realm

4
Boaventura de Sousa Santos, *Epistemologies of the South: Justice Against Epistemicide* (London: Routledge, 2014), p. 18.

5
I have also heard epistemic ignorance being referred to as an epistemic violence, which enables '*ways of knowing – and the disabling of others*' that legitimise or endorse the practises of dominance and subjugation (Eeva-Kristiina Harlin and Outi Pieski, *Ládjogahpir – Máttaráhkuid gábagahpir / Ládjogahpir – The Foremothers' Hat of Pride* (Davvi girji, 2020) p. 143). 'Epistemic injustice' is also used in literature, but more to refer to the harm that Indigenous peoples suffer on account of 'domestic' justice systems, whereby foreign values are made the norm by which they are judged (R. Tsosie, 'Indigenous People and Epistemic Injustice: Science, Ethics and Human Rights', *Washington Law Review* 4 (84) (2012): p. 1136).

6
Distinguished, not as a particular location or social group, but rather as a collective philosophical, moral and scientific doctrine that is widely accepted as being the dominant collective discourse.

7
Rauna Kuokkanen, 'What is Hospitality in the Academy? Epistemic Ignorance and the (Im)Possible Gift', *Review of Education, Pedagogy, and Cultural Studies* Vol. 30, No. 1 (2008): p. 60.

8
Shawn Wilson, *What Is an Indigenous Research Methodology?* Vol. 25. (2001): p. 176.
Jelena Porsanger, 'Indigenous Sámi religion: General Considerations about Relationship' (Gland: IUCN, cop. 2012), p. 38.

of ideas for centuries to come, promoted a sovereignty of reason, by that a marked preference for empiricism and rational thought was encouraged that fully embraced the idiom of 'seeing is believing'.[12] In Europe, where the religious disputes of previous centuries had all too often been the cause of political upheaval and armed conflicts, faith and with it, the Church, was soon believed to have corrupted Western civilisation.[13] The consequence of this was that the 'Age of Reason' not only advanced the often-cited ideals of liberty, technological progress and constitutional government; it also promoted the separation of state and church.[14] Born in 1632, the British empiricist John Locke was a leading advocate for the separation, and he is often remembered precisely as such.[15] But this was far from Locke's only memorable achievement. He also holds the somewhat dubious honour, from an Indigenous perspective at least, of having fathered the Lockean principles of property.[16]

The Lockean principles of property argue that any 'primitive' society, if they were nomadic, would be excluded from any property rights to the lands that they had lived on and used for times immemorial.[17] The cornerstone of his argument was the idea of *terra nullius*, or 'no-man's land', a principle often used in international law to justify claims to territories. Locke basically stated that the principle of *terra nullius* was eligible if the lands in question were populated by 'primitive' peoples. To put this into context, in the glory days of imperial enterprise and colonial expansion it was considered an established fact that Indigenous and other non-Western cultures were evolutionary dead ends. It naturally followed that the people in question were arrested in development.[18] The popular convention was that they lacked the biological imperative needed to thrive and advance; simple rejects of nature that were unable to advance past their present state of development and their nomadic lifestyle. In one fell swoop, Locke

9
E.g., Damien Short, 'Reconciliation, Assimilation, and the Indigenous Peoples of Australia', *International Political Science Review – INT POLIT SCI REV* 24 (2003): pp. 491–2. Amiria Henare, *Museums, Anthropology and Imperial Exchange* (Cambridge: Cambridge University Press, 2005), pp. 68–70.

10
Britt Kramvig and Margrethe Pettersen, 'Living Land – Below as Above', in *Living Earth – Field Notes from the Dark Ecology Project 2014–2016* (Amsterdam: Sonic Acts, 2016), p. 135.

11
Daniel Brewer, *The Enlightenment Past: Reconstructing Eighteenth-Century French Thought* (Cambridge: Cambridge University Press, 2008), p. 1.

12
David N. Livingstone and Charles W. J. Withers, *Geography and Enlightenment* (Chicago: University of Chicago Press, 1999). Tony Bennett, *Pasts Beyond Memory: Evolution Museums Colonialism* (London/New York: Routledge, 2004).

13
Margaret C. Jacob, *The Enlightenment: A Brief History with Documents* (London: Bedford/St. Martin's, 2001).

14
Dorinda Outram, *Panorama of the Enlightenment* (Los Angeles: J. Paul Getty Museum, 2006).

15
Noah Feldman, *Divided by God: America's Church-state Problem – and What We Should Do about it* (New York: Farrar, Straus and Giroux, 2005).

16
Julian W. Korab-Karpowicz, *A History of Political Philosophy: From Thucydides to Locke* (New York: Global Scholarly Publications, 2010).

and the Age of Enlightenment removed any moral obstacle to the annexing and dispossession of populated land, which allowed for a colonial advancement of, among others, the US, Canada, Australia, New Zealand and Norway/ Sweden.[19]

In the case of the latter, there is clear evidence in a statement from the well-known Norwegian historian, P. A. Munch. In 1852, Munch claimed that it made very little difference if 'Lapps' since were the original population in the Saami homelands it was 'only settled with the coming of our Ancestors. And it is the first settlement, with which the history of a Country truly begins'.[20] From his point-of-view, Saepmie was *terra nullius*, which according to the Lockean principle of ownership gave him the moral justification needed for the continued dispossession of the land.[21] From a Saami perspective, however, our homelands are unceded [22] beacuse '[w]e have never been conquered in war and we have never signed agreements with any state'.[23] And even if we had, how could we claim the land to sell it?

Vaapste – the Land That Nobody Owned.

The concept of land ownership is one of Western make. This notion of property embodies values and relationships informed by the great chain of being, a hierarchical structure of all matter and life that disregards the subjective will of non-human beings. Saami values and beliefs, on the other hand, promote a different perspective. Saami philosophy teaches us that the world is made of relations, 'constituted of an infinite web of relationships' that 'apply to everybody and everything, including the land', which is perceived as a living 'physical and spiritual entity'.[24] In a Saami 'world-in-relation', to borrow a term from the Martinique-born writer and thinker Édouard Glissant[25] subjective will is as such afforded to all: to the land, the rivers, our ancestors long passed, animals and other creatures or beings. [26] It might not be the selfhood so

17 Øyvind Ravna, 'Rettsvernet for samiske rettigheter fram til siste halvdel av 1700-tallet – og betydningen av dette i dag', *Kritisk Juss* 29: (2002).

18 Tony Bennett, *Pasts Beyond Memory: Evolution Museums Colonialism* (London: Routledge, 2004): p. 59.

19 A Short commentary on Land Claims in BC, Union of British Columbia Indian Chiefs. Robert J. Miller, Jacinta Ruru, Larissa Behrendt and Tracey Lindberg, *Discovering Indigenous Lands: the Doctrine of Discovery in the English colonies* (Oxford: Oxford University Press, 2010).

20 Peter Andreas Munch, *Det Norske Folks Historie* (Oslo: Christiania, 1852), p. 4. This perception on the Saami and Saepmie was not unique to Munch. Already in the border treaty of 1752 between Denmark-Norway and Sweden-Finland, 'Lappish Nations survival' was said to be dependent on reindeer herding. This reflects the dominant view that those of a 'Lappish origin' not associated with reindeer herding had degenerated and now found themselves on the brink of extinction. The authentic 'Lapp', without fail, was the reindeer herder.

21 John Aage Gjestrum, 'Utstilling av levende mennesker: ei historie om samisk kultur og fremmede blikk', *Dugnad* 21, nr. 1 (1995): p. 102.

22 I use 'unceded 'in the context of an international language of Indigenous rights, where the term reflects situations where land has never been ceded.

eloquently defined by Descartes' 'I think, therefore I am,'[27] but it is nonetheless there, present in what we might term 'other-than-human beings'.[28]

Within this understanding of the world, to own land is a completely foreign idea. Rather, the land and people exist interdependently in a close interaction of sustaining and renewing the balance of the world. This ensures the maintenance of a good life, socially, economically, spiritually and in respect to health. [29] This is the way of *bïerkenidh* taught to children from a young age, and maintained in our ways of knowing, being and doing. When I was a child, my summers would see me in Vaapste and the surrounding municipalities, in the home community of my *tjidtjie*,[30] under the guardianship of my *aahka*.[31] Back then, summer seemed almost endless, and my days were filled with playtime, running barefoot in the grass, playing with friends and cousins who, like me, spent much of their summer with aahka. And yet, I also have fond memories of sitting by aahka's kitchen table, listening to my elders speak of times passed and of people long gone. I also remember long walks with my cousins, guided by our aahka or aunties, where these stories came to life in the surrounding landscapes, and in the cemeteries with markers of lives lived, brought into being through the words of our guides. Young as we were, the feeling of taking our place in a shared history and the sense of finding home in a land where few of us lived full time, was profound. So much so that even decades after aahka's passing, we remember, and we pass on stories and experiences amongst ourselves and to the younger generation.

Vaapste, which is perhaps better known by its Norwegian name of Vefsn, is a municipality in the County of Nordland on the Norwegian side of the border. It is home to numerous South-Saami communities, amongst the kin of my tjidtjie. Each summer, aahka would introduce me to this land, and teach me that my will was not above that

23
Ole Henrik Magga, 'Sami Past and Present and the Sami Picture of the World', In *Awakened Voice: The Return of Sami Knowledge*, ed. Elina Helander (Guovdageaidnu: Nordic Sami Institute, 1996): p. 76.

24
Kuokkanen, Ruana, 'The Logic of the Gift: Reclaiming Indigenous Peoples' Philosophies', in *Re-Ethnicizing the Minds: Cultural Revival in Contemporary Thought*, ed. Thorsten Botz-Bornstein and Jürgen Hengelbrock, (Amsterdam & New York: Rodopi, 2006). p. 260, p. 258.

25
Édouard Glissant, *Une nouvelle région du monde* (Paris: Gallimard, 2006).

26
John Law, 'What's Wrong With a One-World World?', *Distinktion: Scandinavian Journal of Social Theory* 16 (2015).

27
Renè Descartes, *Principia Philosophia* (Amstelodami: Apud Ludovicum Elzevirum, 1644), p. 31.

28
Marisol de la Cadena & Mario Blaser, *A World of Many Worlds* (Durham: Duke University Press, 2018), p. 4.

29
Porsanger, 2012, p. 39.

30
This is the Southern Saami word for mother.

31
A Southern Saami word meaning grandmother. While most commonly used as such, it has also been used in the sense of 'old woman'.

of the land. 'If I listened to the land and the waters' she would say, 'I would always survive on them'. Living in this way, by way of bïerkenidh, we could ensure that 'all you see before you now, is as it once was, and it is how it will continue to be long after you and I are gone'.

As the years passed, I came to know the history of Vaapste. Not through any official records, which frankly say little about the Saami presence in the area.[32] Instead, I was taught a history compiled of stories that has been told for generations, found in the land itself; the rivers, the trees, the animals, and the ground we walked. For centuries, long before the Nations of Norway and Sweden were conceived of, my people made use of and lived on this land, though they did not own it. Sadly, this was not a perception shared by the colonising forces that from the eleventh century onward began to make great inroads into Saepmie.[33] The colonisers believed in owning the land. And so they laid claim to the land that the Saami did not believe could be owned.

In time the colonial expansion created a great change in Saepmie, and Saami values, beliefs, worldviews and livelihoods were forced to give way to those belonging to the new and self-titled landlords. Still, as Indigenous people have had to learn, adaptation is key.[34] For generations we made adaptation into a form of art, and despite the enforcement of colonial rules to govern the land, and contrary to the official policies meant to make the problem of a Saami people go away, the Saami communities of Saepmie, and of Vaapste persisted.[35] They continued to honour and acknowledge the subjectivity of the land, teaching their children and their children's children that if we only learnt to listen to the land and waters, we could continue to live off them. Nevertheless, the epistemic ignorance following colonisation continues to reign. Today, if I were to revisit the landscapes of my happy childhood, they would no longer be as they once were.

32
E.g. https://no.wikipedia.org/wiki/Vefsn, accessed 25 January 2022.

33
Neil Kent, *The Sami People of the North: a Social and Cultural History* (London: C. Hurst Limited, 2018).

34
Cathrine Baglo, *På ville veger? Levende utstillinger av samer i Europa og Amerika* (Tromsø: Universitetet i Tromsø / Orkana akademisk, 2011).

35
Not in the least the highly devastating assimilation policies of the eighteenth and nineteenth centuries.

36 https://www.nve.no/konsesjonssaker/, accessed 31 January 2021.

37 https://www.statkraft.com/what-we-do/wind-power/, accessed 20 October 2020.

Of course, change is inevitable and we are all subject to time and change. The change that has lately come upon Vaapste, however, is not of natural or arbitrary make. Like wounds scourged into the landscape, constructions, the purpose of which is to promote 'sustainable extractive industry', are now slowly appearing on the paths that aahka and I, alongside those who came before us and in the envisioned company of those who had yet to come, once walked. At Øyfjellet, where the Jillen Njaarke sijte, a unit comprised of several reindeer herding families, have their grazing land, such a wound has been inflicted. In 2019 the Norwegian government awarded Øyfjellet Wind, a subdivision of Eolus Wind, concessions to build and operate 75 windmills. For years now, the Jillen Njaarke sijte has been embroiled in a legal battle with Eolus Wind. But they are not alone.

In fact, a large part of the concessions granted to energy development in the last years continue to show disregard for the relationship between the Saami and Saepmie as large parts of the latter are being relinquished to industry.[36] The wounds that these concessions cause are deemed negligible because wind power, after all, is 'a renewable and emission-free energy source that is well suited for large-scale energy production'; a sacrifice deemed acceptable in the pursuit of 'a carbon free future', as articulated by Statkraft, a state-owned Norwegian enterprise. [37] For the Saami communities whose homelands are implicated by such development, however, the wounds caused are abhorrent. And yet, far too often we are told that the good of the many outweighs the good of the few. It is not surprising to see who takes on the role of the latter. In my tjidtjie's homecommunity, in Vaapste, it is Jillen Njarke siijte.

It is all too easy to claim that the ontological conflict we see in Vaapste centres around abstract things – epistemologies and systems of knowledge, values and morals, worldviews and perspectives. But there is a more concerning aspect to such conflicts.

The UN's report on biodiversity of 2019 states that Indigenous peoples, numbering only 5 % of the global population, are responsible for 80 % of Earth's biodiversity.[38] Environmental change and this threat of destructive extinction has

> been less severe or avoided in areas held or managed by Indigenous Peoples and Local Communities […] Nature managed by Indigenous Peoples and Local Communities is under increasing pressure but is generally declining less rapidly than in other lands.[39]

In other words, the issue of ontological conflict might very well be one of survival. More and more, I think it is clear that how humanity interacts with land is not only a question of Indigenous sovereignty and justice after centuries of (ongoing) colonialism; it has also become an issue of our future. Where do we see ourselves moving in the next 50, 30 or even 10 years? We stand at a crossroads where the Nation states of the world may continue the gross subjugation of the land and the abuse of resources, or we Indigenise how we interact with our surroundings, recognising

> '[…] the positive contributions of Indigenous peoples to sustainability such as their unique knowledge, innovations and practices, institutions and values … that often enhances their quality of life, as well as nature conservation, restoration and sustainable use, which is relevant to broader society.'[40]

Taking the latter path would allow us to leave behind a continued life for those that follow, where I one day might tell my child or my grandchild, as my aahka once told me 'All you see before you is now as it once was, and how it will continue to be after you are gone from this realm'.

38 https://ipbes.net/news/Media-Release-Global-Assessment, accessed 31 January 2021.

39 Ibid.

40 Ibid.

Brook Garru Andrew
The matter of murungidyal healing

The following giilang story is a woven piece of writing inspired by separate conversations between Brook Garru Andrew and the artists Máret Ánne Sara, Pauliina Feodoroff and Anders Sunna. This giilang story is presented through Brook's Wiradjuri way of being in giilang-biyarra storytelling and is not a linear narrative in the Western sense of giilang-biyarra storytelling.

The matter of murungidyal healing,
murundhaany healers
waluwin healthy
dhaagun earth
wuriyabari mind
dyindha stomach
dhulubang spirit
guwanbarra blood
dyandyamba medicine,
is that maybe it is not yours to take.

Máret Ánne Sara (MA) The stomachs: I think this was the first piece where I really started to navigate the huge political debate about the individual, and mental-health issues in relation to that in our society. It's not only in Sámi but in Indigenous communities in general.

Anders Sunna (A) It's trying to build the whole picture of my family's struggle from '71 to now. I also included my family, doing different stuff in this project, copying the papers for the folders and building this shelf for the painting. Every member had some finger in the art piece. So everything is made by the family, and it's also about the family.

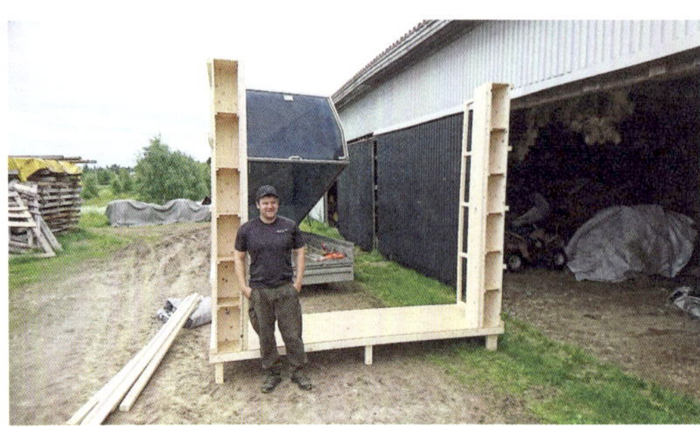

Brook Garru Andrew (B) Dyandyamba medicine isn't easy to take, to consume: it goes straight to the dyindha (stomach) and into the guwanbarra (blood stream) or through the dhulubang (spirit) and into the other worlds of the body. It may taste bitter or feel uncomfortable.

Pauliina Feodoroff (P) We've been working for so many years in order to be able to say, 'Okay. Let's start buying the land into security' and then two weeks ago comes this news that a Swedish mining company has set a huge reservation for a certain part of our area. You can really study the different structures of power use and misuse, and you can really study the science and have these logical and scientific arguments on your side, and you can gain this much, but then, when the empire wants to have something, they can just do it. Obviously you just need to pull your shit together and start working against that. But at the same time, it's so fucking depressing. These moments of rest or moments of joy are so short, but you just have to realise how precious it is to have such moments.

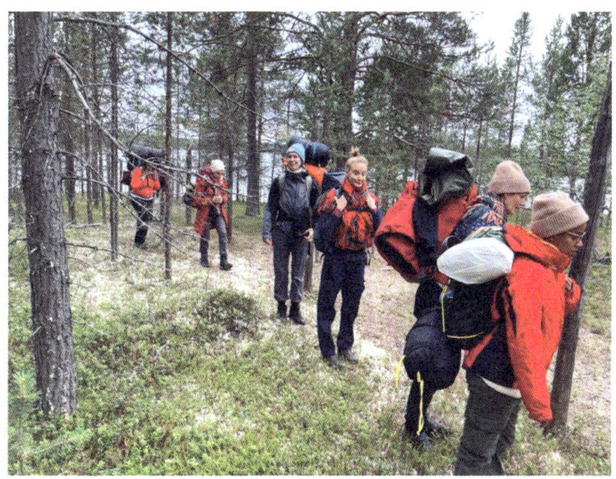

B It can be an inheritance, or a plant, the touch of the land or an animal, or an attitude and connection to an object or a feeling. Murungidyal (healing), murundhaany (healers), waluwin (healthy) can be invisible from a glance, and through spiritual guidance it can be a gift that is welcomed or seen as a threat. Its disguises can change and shift like shadows that entice love, rejection, fear or even curiosity and confusion.

A Last year in October, my uncle was threatened in the forest when he was looking for the reindeer. He was in his car, and it was getting really dark, and then another car came and just sat there, with its headlights shining on my uncle's car. And this was a really bad little road, a forest road. And then the man got out of the car and he had a knife in his hand and started yelling: 'You're on my land. This is my land. If I see you here again, I'll kill you!' And then my uncle closed his car door, and then the guy started to hit the window with the knife.

P That's the basic thing. We discussed these steps that you need to have for healing. What are the steps to healing that you have to do? You can't just go straight to the ceremony and then take that and leave. When you go, it's a lifelong commitment that you have. You can never get out of that.

B It may be in a group, or privately, in a letter, or smells, sounds, or secretly slipped to you, or hidden from many eyes and judgements, or it may be given freely in public. It can be culturally driven, or by age or gender or through customary law. Or it can be offered. But you think you know better, so you ignore it or think your dyandyamba medicine is better.

P Anybody's land. If they come up after this three-step procedure, we'll actually find out that there are 'materials enough that we want to mine here'. There's this legislation that gives the government the right to take one's property, to confiscate one's property and compensate them if the area has a larger societal importance.

A Yes. Yes, I think so. Especially with Máret Ánne, with this stomach of the reindeer, it's almost the same feeling, because she always has, in our conflict, a gut feeling. And you can't sense the smells in her work in the pictures. And so it's quite common that you can see connections between them. But also, with Pauliina's work with the forest that they're cutting down and destroying and her thing, where they're trying to buy the forest back: our family did that 50 years ago, I think. We started buying small plots of land because we knew that, 'Okay, this is going.' You have to organise and buy some land to protect it. We did it also to protect our reindeer, because then we know, 'Okay, this is our area. Nobody can take it from us.' My family had been very quietly thinking ahead: 'Okay, we need to do this.'

P Just showing the landscapes, telling the stories of each landscape but saying very straightforwardly that these are our areas, these are traditional areas. I'm showing the footage from the watershed restoration that we're doing. I'm showing the results of microplastics studies that we're doing. We put it all there. I want to do it so visibly. I'm begging you on my knees. And therefore I want to have a performance section there, a set with incredible, beautiful, strong Sámi dancers and actors and performers to come there and bring their gift. And we'll give them food and we'll give them … we're really baring our necks, saying, 'You have the power in this situation. You have the power. Please use it.' Then after this begging, I'm auctioning my works, even though I know that Venice is a non-commercial art event.

B Dyandyamba medicine can be bitter like an awkward truth. Dyandyamba medicine and murungidyal healing are not always compatible, but they exist mutually or connected somewhere along a path to somewhere.

P You need to have this basic set-up, where you have access to healthcare. Because my people don't. That's ridiculous: to think that we're living in Scandinavia in 2021, and there are still groups within Scandinavia that don't have access to healthcare! They have it on paper, but in practice, they don't get it if they don't have an advocate.

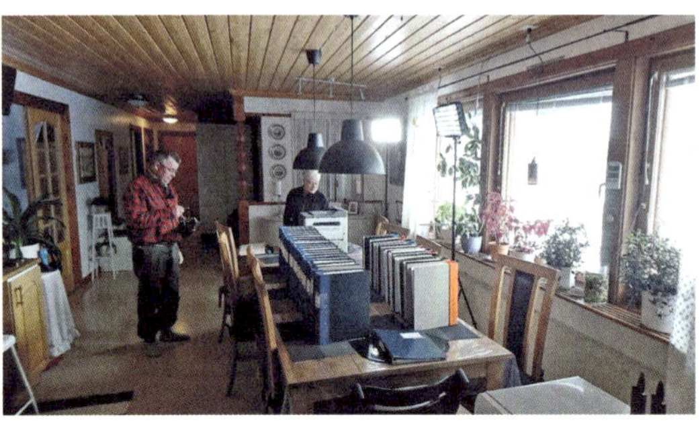

B When you're in a happy space, when life is what you dream it to be, it's hard to think that dyandyamba medicine can make it better, or that it's not someone else's truth. It's the same with those who aren't in a good space, but still refuse the dyandyamba medicine and the murungidyal healing. They're both a threat: the happy and the unhappy.

P Yes. Also, why I've been so slow myself in going to this last part, or even looking in the direction of ceremonies. I don't want to have anything to do with this New Age reinvented or self-invented ceremonious part. Let's heal the world's problems by just feeling nature.

A It's like a spiritual archive, because you see the folders, you see the paperwork and all this, but when you also see the paintings, like the spiritual handprint on the canvases, you're getting this emotional feeling as well. So if you read the papers – it's in Swedish – but if you read them, you can also see the pictures in your head.

B The renaming of the Nordic Pavilion as 'The Sámi Pavilion' is, for the West, a realignment of cultural and linguistic pragmatics. It's like introducing a Sámi way of being into contemporary life, also known as sámification, sámáidahttin and Indigenisation.

P Then there's this last layer and that's the hardest and at the same time, the most essential layer, the spiritual layer of healing: the work that we've been doing with reviving and restoration of the watersheds. First we take care of the physical damage and then at a very, very slow pace we have guests come and reflect with us: 'What do we do with this condemnation, and when this traditional ceremony has been cut, how do we start?' Their advice has been to just start by telling people about yourself and why you're here. The journey has been so slow, to get enough strength to go in that direction and then finally accept the fact that when the land responds to you in such an immediate way, your own head is ready to do it. Such an endless source of joy comes from that: that the land still responds to us. I think being in that place and being able to witness that and not just with yourself but with people around you, is a life-defining, life-changing thing. But at the same time, those other layers are still there. It's not like you've climbed up onto a second level and then you can stay there; you have to just bring everything that you've learned to the service of your community. But sometimes it's just so incredibly tiring.

B Regardless of who is who and where they are, in this arc of guwanbarra blood, there will always be new ways of seeing and being in the world.

P So that's also coming back to the healing within the siida (community or home). Obviously, I can't reply on behalf of the other Sámi tribes, but I know that within my tribe, the most important healing system was the annual migration, Ä'rbbmääddaid, vuu'did piâssad, when you visited the family shrines, you visited the family's sacred sites and you had this annual migration led by fishing, not by the reindeer – obviously you had the reindeer – but you followed the fish. I'll show you. This is my worktable. I've stuck different colour maps all over my computer's desktop. I'm surrounded by different kinds of maps, and in the last 15 years, I've mapped all the current families, traditional migration routes and where the family shrines are. That's been a heck of a puzzle to find out. Those places, those sacred sites are the places for renewal and rebirth. I know for my own self that going frequently within those sites, even though you don't have access to them in the current situation, when they're somebody else's lands, but visiting those sites is a crucial element for your mental and physical health.

B The threat of the other one on land you think is yours. Then there's the moment when you think you're doing everything you can to make a point of view clear. Then you realise it's upside down, and you can't understand it. The fire builds up inside you.

P There are plenty of Sámi warriors, for instance, and the example should be set. I think then it would start to roll, but somebody needs to throw the first punch. This is like this very rough thing, where I come and beg for money to buy our land back.

B Though only when the dyandyamba medicine or murungidyal murundhaany waluwin comes from a different hand does it breed contention and possible threat. Does being Sámi really matter?

MA I hope so.

A Sámi people have the power to make change or stop, but they just turn their backs and pretend not to see what's happening. So they're also in the picture.

MA When I was eighteen, I got into a really personal crisis because I didn't know what was real and true. Was it the Christian faith, or was it the traditional one? And you know, the first commandment is that there's no other God but God himself. And then we're on the mountains and you have this holy rock, and we're supposed to respect this rock and do no harm to it. And I was so confused. And then at one point, I decided I had to really test this, to know what's sincere and real. We were earmarking the reindeer calves in my mother's district where we're now based. And there's this one really big sacred rock on the way there, you pass it when you go back and forth from our cottage to the reindeer fence. And I'd had one of these talks with my grandmother the night before about God and Christianity. And she was really trying to convince me that this is the total truth and the only truth. The next day, I told her, 'Okay, we had this talk yesterday, and since we agreed that there is no other God and there's nothing else to believe in, I decided I'm going to take the money that's been sacrificed to this stone, because then it doesn't mean anything. I took it.' And her reaction was so scary. She was so mad at me and she was sincerely afraid of what was going to happen to me. And she commanded me to go straight back to that stone with my apologies and to give back everything that I'd taken from there, in the hopes of rescuing me from whatever was coming from disrespecting the holy place and taking what was given to the stone. So this was sort of my ultimate end to this discussion. There's equal belief in both embedded in our people.

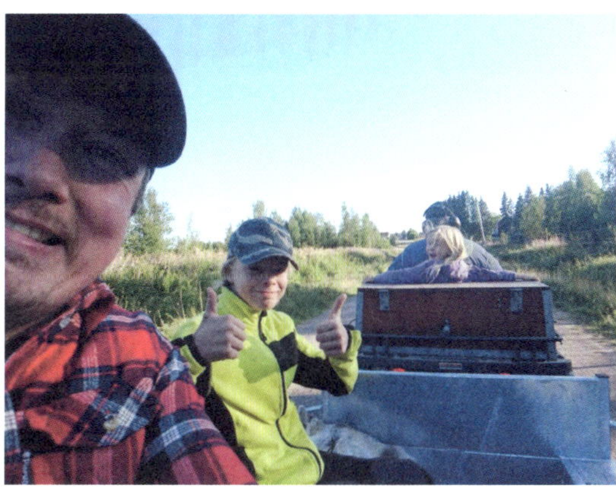

A And that's also like a healing process: that you're building something together and working with this conflict we've all been in. It's almost like a spiritual healing process, because you have to look back at what's been happening over all the decades, and copy it, paper by paper. And sometimes, when you see our text, you automatically start to read a little bit. And my oldest son copied some stuff, and my father, and my mum, and my wife and so on – everyone is part of it somehow. And my oldest brother is building this thing, taking the material, which he can, from our forest and so on. So we're trying to make as much as possible from what we have and what we can do.

B The arc of conjecture caught up in bureaucracy may not see the dyandyamba medicine nor the murungidyal healing. The maze only sees what it is, which is a maze. Self-denial and self-illusion only react, and exist as what they are: conjecture. If you're stuck in a box with mirrored walls, what then?

P That's the basic thing. We discussed these steps that you need to have: what are the steps to healing that you have to take? You can't just go straight to the ceremony and then take that and leave. When you go, it's a lifelong commitment that you have. You can never get out of that.

B Systems in place – they're in the body, though the guwanbarra blood.

P Čiŋlmõõvvâd tõõzz, mii mee′st õinn lij.

A I think for my family, it's been a joy. They're feeling that they're making progress or a change, or a resistance against the government, in a way where they don't have to be in the court where the government is the boss. Now, they're on their own permission, and they're doing what they can by hand. They're on their own permission, and not in the hands of the government or the court or the judges.

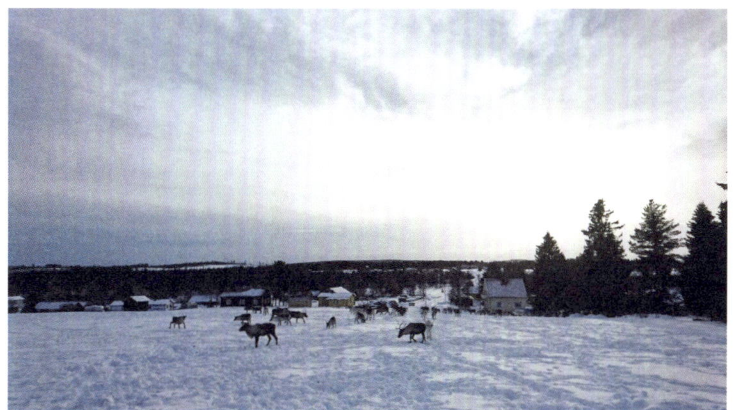

B The world is suddenly inverted again and when you look out, maybe there's a horizon that looks similar to how you see it in your own mind, in your life, and then you're at peace.

MA I was looking for this sort of manifesto for hope and positivism for the future after this horrible winter, when people were exhausted because, to feed the reindeer herds, they had to transport these heavy balls of grass and pellets miles and miles to the tundra. Eventually they got help from the government – which is the first time in history that they paid for a lot of helicopters to help them. But this help came in the last part of the spring, so the reindeer herders had already been doing this for several months. So this was costing them a lot of money and a lot of work – physical labour. So people were exhausted. And after this horrible winter, I was speaking to one reindeer herder who'd just seen the first reindeer calves. We call them the red calves because when they're born, they have this red colour in their fur.

A It's about the reindeer herding. Because the Sámi Parliament has forbidden our reindeer marks.[1] They're cuttings off our livelihood and our support to have a good economic situation. They're taking away not just my parents' rights,

1 Editorial note: The Sámi Parliament on the Swedish side, which is one of three Sámi Parliaments.

but my own and my children's rights as well. And when we talked to them through the media, they said, 'Oh, we didn't know anything.' But they're still making these decisions while saying that they don't know anything. And for the Sámi Parliament opening for this four-year period, they're also inviting the Swedish royal family and the head of the church and the Swedish government. It's a hypocritical party. So we want to show this, because it's really wrong.

B On an international stage, murungidyal murundhaany waluwin is a powerful state of mind. Some would say that murungidyal murundhaany waluwin is making slight changes to fix something that's out of alignment.

A I wish I had a good answer to that, but I think that the answer that's closest is that they're listening to what the government says and that the Sámi Parliament's afraid to go against it, because then, they'll lose money for their organisation – for the Sámi Parliament. And I think they're also afraid to lose the rights that they have. So what's wrong with the Sámi Parliament is that they're too afraid to act, because they're afraid to lose the little thing they have. If they'd been working as a people, they wouldn't be afraid of losing anything because the main thing is the Sámi people, not what I have as a person or my rights. The goal for the Sámi Parliament should be that we should work as one people together and not leave anybody behind.

B Hope – like a sudden breath of air on the face, a memory sparkling through time that you think is fresh and alive.

P Yes, this is really what I hoped for. Despite the grotesque traumas, we can start talking about hope. To have this is even very new for me. I'm always making these horrible pictures and it's about fighting and roaring. But to be able to present something this naked, poetic and positive, within all of this madness and grotesqueness, is really good. It feels good.

B The anonymity of hope is a line that you can draw in your mind – it drives. But in despair it travels and then decides to stop and disappear. And then it reappears again.

MA Relocated yes. Yes. And this was very difficult. Almost impossible, because there's been a parasite in the wild reindeer in the central south of Norway. And this parasite has caused the borders to close. They weren't allowed to take their live animals from Norway to Sweden, which meant that they had to slaughter their entire herd here and then buy themselves a new herd in Sweden. And since there's no existing market for selling and buying live reindeer, this was just a lucky coincidence for us. At this specific time, when we took the reindeer to exile with our uncle, we had six months before he would then have the same threats made to him: 'You have too many reindeer. Now we're going to fine you. And if you don't slaughter them we'll eventually come and slaughter your reindeer.' So we had these six months to figure things out. And within these six months there was all of a sudden this one person in Sweden who was selling live animals and he said, 'Welcome! You can buy as many as you want and you can pick whichever you want.' So this was like 'What?' You could go there and you could pick the best and youngest females, which would be able to produce from next season on. So this was like a godsend. And things worked out for both my uncle's family and for us. So this is how the struggle on a personal level was resolved. But it's still unresolved on the level of the principle regarding the rights of Sámi reindeer herders. After all of this, what happens? What happens when these are the conditions for individuals in our community? And not only singular individuals, but a community as a whole. These are my concerns based on my own experiences. And I'm not even the main person in this issue. I'm just sort of a spectator from the side.

B A bitter pill maybe. Even within this gift there are awkward complications within the Sámi and Nordic world view. These world views echo internationally throughout many nations that are labelled Indigenous or First Nations or colonised nations.

A When they forced us out in 1986, and when they were building this fence that was 30 kilometres long, they knew about it, but they didn't say anything about it. They kept it quiet.

MA His comment was … it was beautiful, and just so simple. He was saying that now that he sees the red calf, all of the struggles are forgotten. This was powerful. This just became like the clearest vision for me of hope. How can you build up hope again after this devastating winter when people are so down? Then this birth of the red calf lifts the spirits and you forget everything of these struggles. Just the reminder of how important the reindeer calf is for us to carry on with strength and positivism and hope began my obsession with preserving a reindeer calf. Because this has a connection to another debate: the State gives very strong protection to predators in this country, and the predators are increasing in number every year. And for the last, I would say, decade there's been a desperate campaign on social media from reindeer herders across Sámi lands, to gain attention and seek to solve the situation, because the predators are killing so many of these red calves that in some areas in Norway there's nothing to sell. There's no more reproduction in the herd. So then you know …

B Smelling death …

MA I don't want to focus entirely on death and fear, and all these things, but try to also bring along the hope factor, the positive aspects. The smell piece will be a dialogue between these two smells. We're trying to create a smell of hope. Don't ask what it smells like, but we're making something.

B Protection and being inside that protection when no one from the outside realises the importance of this action.

MA We'd been talking a lot about how babies represent new life and hope and the future and then the baby calves, the red calf. What I did last spring was to milk one of the female reindeer. This is no longer really being practised anywhere because there's so little milk from a reindeer. There was a long process of taming the female first for a full winter to get it adapted to humans. Then it had a calf. And then we milked it. The idea was to use the milk as a starting point. My own breast milk, the reindeer milk, and then our babies and a lot of things: it's like a treasure hunt for positivism and hope.

B The spirit drives our murungidyal healing and hope.

MA So the thing is that if you go to the extent of protecting your property and your calves and your herd, you've become the criminal. Then you're likely to be in prison very soon. This is how strong the protection is of these predators. Morally and spiritually, this is quite interesting, if you consider the heavy symbolism that your herd has for carrying on hope. That you're not allowed to protect this most important thing for a positive future is really bizarre in my head. So it became very important for me to work on this calf. My main piece for Venice is actually a huge baby mobile, where I have a range of calves in the centre. And the reason why it became a baby mobile is probably because I was pregnant. I was carrying my firstborn child and thinking about how to raise a child who has positive belief in the future. How do you maintain that for the coming generation?

A And my oldest son had been copying some stuff, and my father and my mum and my wife and so on – everyone is part of it somehow. And my oldest brother is building this thing, taking the material, which he can, from our forest and so on. We're trying to make as much as possible from what we have and what we can do.

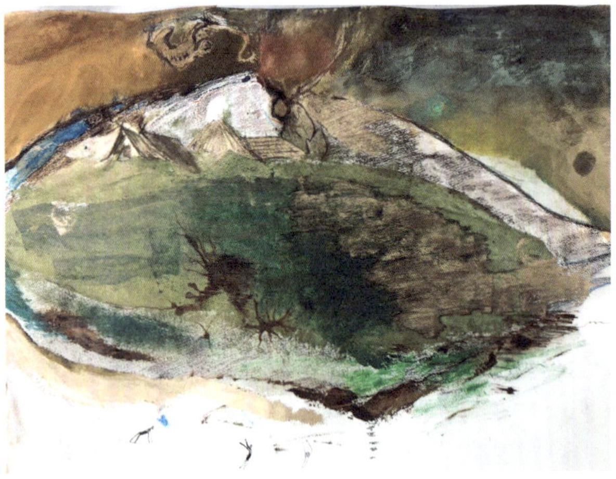

B The map is set – the mind and body are set. The spirit drives it.

P I really, really appreciate it because it's been such a slow process. Sometimes, I get so lost in my maps that I wonder what the heck I'm doing here. Mij jeä'p leäkku ni kuä'ss kuddnalla tiõrvtam kuei'meen. Åå'n lij muuttâsäi'ǧǧ.

MA This is really what I wished for: that despite the grotesque traumas, we can start talking about hope.

Timimie Gassko Märak

Sipping Coffee Motherhood

Sipping Coffee

Sipping coffee.
more than often

Women loving women
loving women and the land
Fighting for the right to breathe fresh air the
right to hold her hand the right to, for just
a while, feel one hundred percent safe

If you were to ask me to choose
between her and my culture
It would be like asking me to choose
between breathing or drinking water
I need both
Without any of them I am no longer me
Because what I am is not a choice so I cannot
choose to lose any part of myself

Coloniality
You hold functions because you don't fill one

Sipping coffee
more than often
but spilling tea

Gender benders beings beyond the binary
Decoloniality has always been a part of me
it is what we are
Sámi
I know you saw me
I know you know little to nothing about my
gábdde so don't come at me with your
questions and opinions about my identity

Coloniality
Having to pass to be able to pass people on
the streets without preparing to run

Sipping coffee
more than often
and we keep it salty

Manhood in the woods
in the mountains
in the middle of nowhere
and still you care
Out of all things, you choose the one thing
not connected to how
You act
I see friends act colonialy manly mainly
because of convenience
Your convenience
If not it is used as evidence when declaring
yet another war disguised as work
opportunity

Coloniality
You build roads and refuse us our ways

Sipping coffee

Decoloniality
Is feeling love for the land naturally

Decoloniality
Is to be you, present and connected
rather than do according to what ever has
effected our perception of perfect and
right

I'd rather do wrong
being me
than being right wing dividing human
beings.

Coloniality
Is not seeing that Indigenous starts with
I, with me. And ends with us.
And us includes u.

I cannot be without us

Women loving women
loving women and the land
If you were to ask me to choose
between her and my culture
It would be like asking me to choose
between breathing or drinking water
I need both

If you were to ask me to choose
I'd ask you to go first

Sipping Coffee by Timimie Gassko Märak was previously published by the Goethe-Institut in relation to the project *The Right to be Cold: Climate Justice for the Arctic* (July 2021).

Motherhood

She cries against my shoulder and I hold her
just as she had held me
She says
It's too hot
I can feel it
They cannot
Feel
Anything

She cries out in my hair that I grew out for
her as she grew it all for us
She says
It will all be over soon
My children don't hate me
They just cannot see
Anything

She brings herself together
Just as she brought us together
Says
Whether the weather will or won't change we
have to have faith
We cannot wait
Anymore
She is scarred but never complained
Sore

I’m scared but unafraid
I am scared but unafraid
I am scared but unafraid
I am scared

She burst out laughing
Because everything is different now
Nothing has changed though
Only those who want progress
Success
But squares are useless
Only circles
Spirals
Spineless
Rootless in a world that's priceless
Nevertheless
Searching

Afraid without fear
A warrior without a spear
Hear me
See me
Fear me not
But believe me
Whether the weather will or won't change
In a lifetime where love is the strange way
The old ways become pawed ways
And the pay checks come from
Digging coal drilling oil missing daybreak

I say stop the mining
They say mind your own business
No one who only speaks money
Can see that squares are useless
I talk in circles

She cries against my shoulder and I hold her
just as she had held me
She says
It’s too hot
I can feel it
They cannot
Feel

Anything

Harald Gaski and the Language Group

Sánit, govat ja šuoŋat – muhtun jurdagat sápmelaš lohkama, dulkoma ja áddejumi birra

Words, Images and Sounds – Contemplating Sámi Readings, Interpretations and Understanding

We might call this a glossary, for the sake of being understood, but contrary to the glossaries you usually encounter, where the majority (colonial) language determines the definitions and explanations of the concepts in question, we have decided to turn the tables and let Sámi be the defining language, because we are explaining and disseminating knowledge about Sámi art and experiences. What could be more appropriate, then, than to choose the Indigenous language as the foundation for the reference and the source for the experiences described and expressed in art, language and lived life?

The Sámi have three main concepts that describe and explain our existence and continuance on this earth. These are giella, duodji and juoigan, with local linguistic adjustments according to where you are in Sápmi / Saepmie, the Sámi homeland. Giella is language and is the most basic concept, because everything revolves around the way we sense and are able to describe the world in words, visuals and sounds. Sámegiella, saemien – is so much more than just the words and terms that might be categorised in a dictionary. It is the sound and resound of our whole existence on this planet. We don't communicate only through words; we see, hear and sense intuitively; we listen and learn from our co-inhabitants – the animals, birds, fish, the wind, the singing of the rivers and the roaring of the stormy ocean. We are part of the whole – but because of the language we have as humans, we're forced to share the experiences through a vocabulary meant to exceed ethnic and cultural boundaries in an attempt to make the Indigenous voice heard – not as a subaltern one, but as a distinctive one with a clear message to the whole world: listen – like we've always done – and learn.

During the history of assimilation and suppression, our voice was under attack. The oppressive powers wanted to get rid of everything connected with the Sámi: Sámi ways of seeing, ways of being, and ways of doing. But now, things are slowly changing, and a lot of non-Native people are becoming allies, peers and supporters. Now we all seek guidance in traditional Indigenous wisdom, and we turn to our artists because they seem to be the ones expressing this knowledge the most clearly: Guldal, oahpa ja birge (listen, learn and survive).

Duodji provides us with tools, clothing and survival kits, but it simultaneously represents our aesthetics – which is not only limited to what is regarded as beautiful, but to a way of life that praises functionality and accountability as part of aesthetics. It's similar to the Navajo Native American expression 'to walk in beauty' – a way to understand life, to represent basic values of how to 'eallit olmmožin', to be an accountable person, an individual representing a bigger collective, where 'I' extends to 'we' in the local community. In this publication we – Sámi, the Indigenous first person – take control over the definitions. Therefore, art is part of duodji, just as visual representations are part of giella – govvagiella.

Juoigan is the musical way of communicating, from birth to death – and, according to Sámi beliefs, a person does not actually die as long as they are remembered, told about in stories and yoiked. There exists an immediate connection between the one who performs the yoik and the one who is yoiked. The yoik describes the person, the land(scape) or animal through sound and lyrics. The yoiked-one's identity is connected to the yoik, which describes the person and represents a musical portrait of them, which a learned ear will immediately grasp, while for an outsider the yoik may sound strange until the tunes create a room from where to see – wider, deeper and further.

These are a few of the challenges for readers of this book. We want to invite you on a journey, to learn from our perspectives, not to have everything readily explained through 'Western' presumptions and explanations, but based in and on the Indigenous Sámi people's way of life, ways of seeing, understanding and behaving. It all comes together within a realm of kinship among humans and the surrounding environment.

Birget: to manage; have enough food and supplies to be able to live; to master
Dovdat: to feel; to recognise
Dovddiidit: to get to know, acquire knowledge
Giella: language; but also a snare, a trap to catch ptarmigan or hare
Giellat: to put up a snare; but also to trick someone linguistically, disclose inconsistencies in a person's speech or argument
Govva: image; picture; assumption
Gullat: to hear; feel, notice; understand; Gullat geasa nu – belong to someone
Guldalit: to listen to and listen for, using all the senses, not only hearing. Guldalit also means to obey; meaning that the things learnt during the listening process have convinced one to live by this learning
Oahppat: to learn; but also to check the trap or net to see if there's any catch
Oahpahit: to teach
Oaidnit: to see; understand; recognise

Katya García-Antón
To Greet with Respect is to Listen

Ráhkis lohkki, gieries lohkije
Dear Reader,

Indigenous peoples and colonial mind sets have never properly been introduced.[1] Despite the millennium that has ensued since first colonial contact with Sámi people, such an introduction may still take many lifetimes. To greet with respect is to listen. This essay proposes two narratives.[2] The first honours eleven Sámi voices who over different centuries have advocated for Sámi perspectives – listening to and understanding their calls is an essential task for non-Indigenous people who wish to conduct a respectful and informed greeting. In the second narrative, I reflect upon 'The Sámi Pavilion' project as a process for forging sovereignty[3] that sets out some of the parameters needed to make the greeting between Sámi and non-Sámi people a reality today. In these narratives my 'I' is that of a non-Indigenous person mindful of the potholes along the road when building a bi-epistemological position, recognising the limits that this journey will always have when moving towards that space of salutation. The 'we' of my complicity with Sámi perspectives and peoples has been pummelled and tested daily. It has grown (and will continue to grow) through direct action, by deploying with varying success the institutional and individual privileges I have received over time, to confront and unsettle Western colonial structures within which I / we exist in the Fennoscandian region.[4]

The dam is too high
for the hare to jump over,
and if it dared
it would land in the clean and dried death-bed
of a once so powerful river.

Elle-Hánsa / Keviselie / Hans Ragnar Mathisen[5]

1 This point is made by artist Pauliina Feodoroff, in the short film by Egil Pedersen, commissioned in 2021 by the Office for Contemporary Art Norway, as an introduction to 'The Sámi Pavilion'.

2 I am deeply grateful to Prof. Harald Gaski and Prof. Asta Balto for the generous dialogues that took place between us whilst writing this text, and specially for the wise reflections and advice they offered. I am also most thankful for the editorial assistance of my colleague at OCA, Liv Brissach.

3 Sovereignty here is not to be understood in the sense of the nation-state.

4 I am using terms such as 'Western' and 'Indigenous', as ways to show the difference between these two perspectives. It is of course a generalising and reductive approach, since they are both complex and heterogenous categories, with site-specific differences, but useful when talking from a global perspective. This point is eloquently argued in David Garneau, 'What Does or Should "Indigenous Art" Mean?', in *Sovereign Words. Indigenous Art, Curation and Criticism* (Office for Contemporary Art Norway / Valiz Amsterdam), 2018.

5 Published for the first time by KEVISELIE 1981, printed from his handwriting, and with his photos at Øytun Trykk, Alta, 10 December 1981, under the title *JULEVU* (excerpt from pp. 31–32). A revised and shortened version with additional notes was published in *BÁIKI*, Sámi American Journal, ed. Faith Fjeld, in two installments, 2002. This extended poem was written in protest

against the construction across the Luleju River on the Swedish side of Sápmi that resulted in grave ecological damage and land dispossession for the Sámi of that region. Sámi artist Elle Hánsa / Keviselie / Hans Ragnar Mathisen is a central creative figure amongst the Sámi today. For more information on him, see Susanne Haetta, *Mázejoavku. Indigenous Collectivity and Art*, ed. Katya García-Antón (Office for Contemporary Art / DAT), 2020.

6
The notion of Searvelatnja has been pointed out to me by Prof. Balto as a useful term for including the spiritual part of all we know. Created by Sámi scholar Mikkel Nils Sara, in 2003 at Sámi University of Applied Sciences in Guovdageaidnu, in Prof. Balto's words it means 'Traditional learning site where adults, elders, youngsters and children learn and transfer ancestral skills, knowledge, values and the best ways of life for survival in their areas. This intergenerational exchange of teaching/learning combines knowledge, not only from present generations, but from generations who passed, their ancestral skills, assessments, conversations and their mutual connection with the environment. Searvelatnja binds all the Indigenous knowledge together, creates an arena for transferring skills and knowledge between generations and includes both visual and mental and psychological capacities. In Searvelatnja those who have passed away are present. Their voices are carried by the participants and present within those who meet.' Email and telephone exchange with the author, 11 January 2022.

In the last decade since making my home in the north, I have been working on a process of tuning-in to a corpus of defenders who have over centuries stood up against colonial cognitive injustice. Expressed in a variety of interrelated forms that include ancient anti-colonial joiks, animal stories, field recordings, word-weavers, the language of bodily movements, duodji and dáidda, their thoughts compose a Sámi epistemological body that stretches back for centuries. They stand as a family of ofelaččat (pathfinders) each building upon the ancestral knowledge of previous generations in the manner of Searvelatnja[6] to sustain Sámi worldviews. This heritage of collective, hoslitic, Sámi epistemology is to date still insufficiently acknowledged by Western perspectives, and in the first section in this essay I wish to highlight their centrality to worldly being, doing, seeing and thinking today.

The interventions that follow here are mostly in the written form, although they belong to Sámi thinkers who are simultaneously artists, poets, juoigit, duojárat, land guardians, holders of linguistic and spiritual knowledge, amongst other things. They thus think holistically across disciplines, and their reflections enunciate a Sámi world premised upon kinships, dependencies and responsibilities between peoples, lands, waters, fauna, flora, spirits and more-than-human entities. They collapse colonial linear times and conflate biomes and life-forms. The order of the voices that are listed here aims to convey a narrative encompassing the celebration of Sámi land and life, first contact, colonialism, resistance and resurgence.[7] They speak out against the grain of a constructed modernist regime of dualisms (nature-culture, rational-spiritual) and linear time (progress). Living defenders have given permission to share their stories in this text. The stories of defenders who are no longer with us are included here with the wish to respect and honour the gift that their voices represent.

To greet with respect is to listen.
Listen one – the joy of Sápmi, the land is us

Map of Sápmi 1975[8]

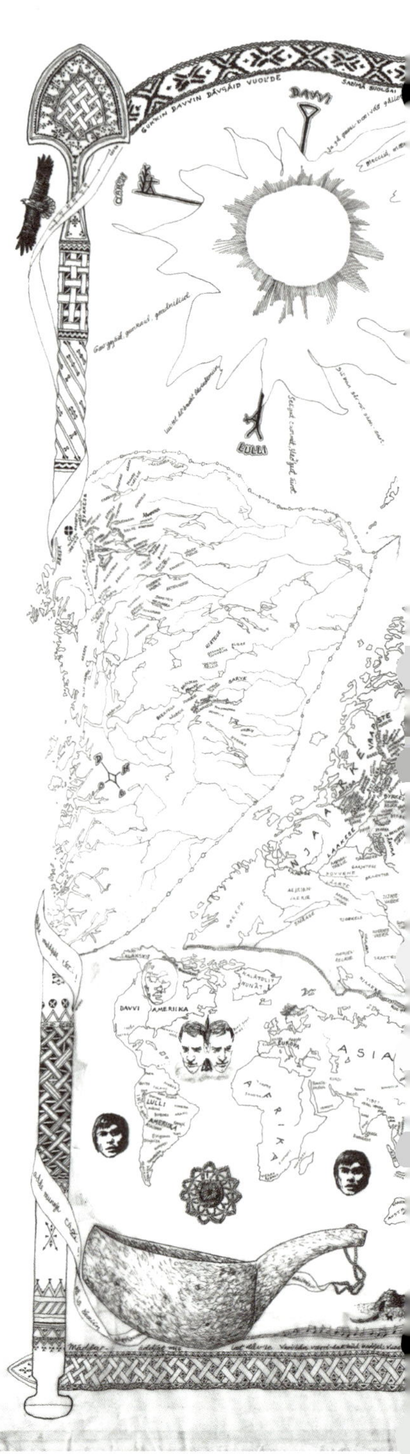

7
For further information on the recent history of resistance in Sápmi, see *Let the River Flow. An Indigenous Uprising and its Legacy in Art, Ecology and Politics*, ed. Katya García-Antón, Prof. Harald Gaski and Prof. Gunvor Guttorm (Office for Contemporary Art Norway / Valiz, Amsterdam), 2020.

8
This map of Sápmi is by artist Elle Hánsa / Keviselie / Hans Ragnar Mathisen, a Sámi Elder participating in 'The Sámi Pavilion' with a series of hand-made Guest Books. Drawn in 1975, the map was made at a time in which Sámi people mobilised with strength, heeding the ČSV call to 'Show your Sámi spirit!', in tandem with the emergence of global Indigenous movements, to claim back the land, life and culture that Nordic and Russian/Soviet colonialism had suppressed for centuries. Keviselie went on to create a vast corpus that re-instated Sámi names into the colonial maps, and that called for a united Indigenous global solidarity. In his work, Sámi languages, cosmologies, spiritualities and stories are reclaimed. These documents of counter-narration also chart the interdependence between language and the land from which it emerges. The kind of erasure Keviselie points to in this work is one of the many colonial damages experienced by Sámi people. Keviselie experienced first-hand, as all Sámi people did, how a Scandinavian nation-state infrastructure (encompassing health, the law, education, economy, religion and culture) intent on assimilation generated high-level ecocide, ethnocide and human dispossession.

Elle-Hánsa / Hans Ragnar Mathisen / Keviselie, *Kart over Sábmi (Kart over Sápmi)*, 1975 © Mathisen, Hans Ragnar/BONO

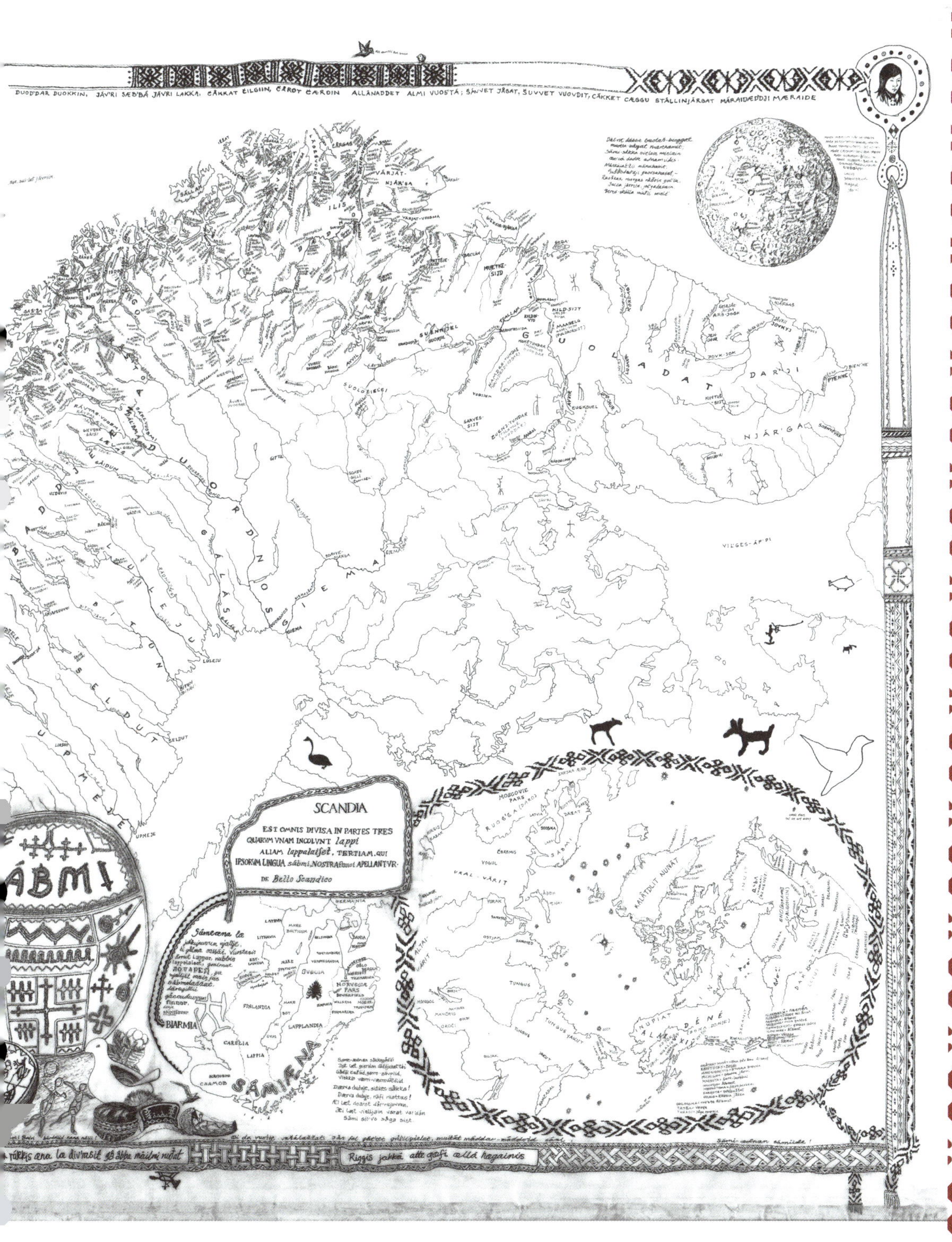

What is more joyous
more healthy and happy
than a boisterous mountain-brook
in the heartland of old SÁPMI[9]
fresh and free
since the first Day of the Earth
sane and sound, yes:
what is more healing to the human soul
when it is overtroubled
coping with suffering and sorrow,
than the cleansing song of a stream?

And when it swells to a mighty river
with shouts of joy and laughter
jumps fearless down the hills
over stones and rocks
spraying the happy herbs on its rim
with a shower of sunblessed dew-drops,
the waterfall invites the strong salmon
to challenge the stream's fall downwards
with a mighty jump upwards,
till it finds rest in a lake
this most sacred spot of calm solitude,
mating ground and cradle for many a creature
playground and home for all the fry,
parents love to see happy children
make the lake their life's delight.
The brook, once so small
now proudly carries its living wealth
to the next lake, then another,
five in all, and between
the mild murmur
and rushing rustle of the river,
a song of love for Creation!

Elle-Hánsa / Keviselie / Hans Ragnar Mathisen[10]

9 Hans Ragnar Mathisen explains in a footnote to this 1981 poem that 'Sápmi is the ancient and correct name of Lappland, in the language of its inhabitants, the Sámi people (plural Sámit). The terms Lapp or Lappland are derogatory and should be replaced by Sámi(t) and Sápmi or Sámieana (Sámiland)'

10 Elle-Hánsa / Keviselie / Hans Ragnar Mathisen, 'Five Friends in Memoriam', published for the first time as 'Julevu' by KEVISELIE, 1981.

11
The old joik lyrics *Suola ja noaidi* were first written down by Jakob Fellmann in Northern Sámi for his *Anteckningar under min vistelse I Lappmarken,* part 2 (Helsinki: Finska litteratursällskapets tryckeri, 1906). They are translated as *The Shaman and the Thief* by Thomas DuBois and included in *From Myths, Tales and Poetry from Four Centuries of Sámi Literature,* ed. Thomas DuBois and Harald Gaski (Kárášjohka: ČálliidLágádus), 2020.

To Greet with Respect is to Listen
Listen Two – Contact

Ane, ane iežat eret
Gos don boađát, dohko manat
Lean, lean mun du badjelii
Manan, manan, válddán, bijan
Suhppen ja deavččastan du eret

Go, go away yourself
Where you come from, there you go
I still have power over you
I go, I go, I take, I place
I'll take and cast you away

Ancient joik text[11]

To Greet with Respect is to Listen
Listen Three – Knowledge from a More-Than-Human world

There are two little birds – cizážat – that the Sámi favour for their singing and the joy they bring: biellocizáš – the bell bird – and rievssatcizáš – willow warbler, who brings summer to Sápmi. There are other birds as well, which are important in different ways, some for their function as messengers and others because they represent a food resource, and still others because they bring beauty in the way they fly, soar and keep an eye on the other inhabitants of the region. Biellocizáš goes by another name as well, giellavealgu – the one who is able to switch between languages. Even in English the bird carries several denominations, the nightingale of the mountainlands, the bluethroat, of course, but also the bell bird because of its singing capabilities.

The Sámi realised early on that biellocizáš is a great imitator, and thus manages to create a lot of confusion in the mating season for the other cizážat. By singing the song of another species, it draws attention from suitors who get confused by finding biellocizáš where they in fact were expecting one of their own kind. In the region of Sápmi where the bird is called giellavealgu, Sámi people obviously found this imitation game amusing, so they saw a trickster in the bird, and named it accordingly, the 'language switcher'. Sámi have always held communication skills in high esteem, so they found inspiration in a bird's song to become multilingual themselves – both in the way

12
A new story written by Prof. Gaski, for this book in 2021.
13
Johan Turi, *An Account of the Sámi, A Translation of Muitalus sámiid birra, as Re-edited by Mikael Svonni with Accompanying Articles*, trans. and ed. Thomas A. DuBois (Kárásjohka: ČálliidLágádus) 2012, p. 132.

they perform juoigan and in their keeping up a two-dimensional conversation with the authorities; trying to snare them with language (giellat) instead of being trapped themselves (gillot) into the majority language – just as giellavealgu has taught the Sámi.

Prof. Harald Gaski[12]

The person who acquires a snake stone will never be defeated in legal matters … When the snakes have their mating or rut season, they throw a white stone about. And the person who goes there in secret to wait for them must grab that stone and run towards the nearest water. And if the person reaches the water before the snake, then that person gets to keep the stone. But if the snake reaches the water first, the situation is dangerous. But the person who has already checked where the nearest water is will make it there first. The snakes are delayed a little while they search for the stone, and in the meantime, the person must run to the water. And the person who has such a stone will be skilled at law for the rest of his life.

Johan Turi[13]

To Greet with Respect is to Listen
Listen Four – Control, How it Happened, and Still Happens

The Land outside the Map

When Ottar the Earl of Håløyg sailed north along the cost of Finnmark to the Kola peninsula in the ninth century, he reported to the King of England that he saw no one other than some Sámi until he rounded the peninsula by the White Sea.

So what happened to this land? How did it disappear? Where did it go?

I live in the land of devils, witches, monsters, they've said, in the land outside the map, in the nothingness, in a history beyond history. The Sámi history made invisible. On the 'real' map the Sámi names are washed out, do not exist. Every mountain, every lake, the remotest places.

Where is my land? Is it a trauma? A dream? A Utopia?

Who are we? Strangers? Foreigners? Guests in our own land? Brainwashed to believe the pseudo stories about ourselves.

A history that the modern Scandinavian states do not want to hear.
No, there were no military forces, no shooting, no killing, they did it in a human way. Their refined cruelty. The assimilation programmes. Loss of language, culture, history, land. The shame brought upon us.

14 Synnøve Persen, *The Land Outside the Map*, 2016. Published in *Art Papers* 40.06 (2016).

Ottar the Earl sails on. The land is explored, the people civilised and tamed to silence. This time they suck the rest of the fjords, the mountains, the fish in the big ocean. All the resources, the natural richness of the Arctic.

She is an extremist. Don't listen to her, we've been supervising her a while. The voice of the poet. The need for a voice.

We've given this people citizenship, equality, welfare, education. What do they want? Back to the Stone Age?

We want stability in the region. Borders. Control. We've saved this uncivilised people from poverty, taught them to read and write our language. The poets should tell stories of beauty, the Northern Lights, the midnight sun.

We have no problems. We've solved them by eating them. We own the land. You're our citizens.

Unsubscribe the map of the colonisers.

Synnøve Persen[14]

To Greet with Respect is to Listen
Listen Five – Colonial Extractivism, the Scourge of Sápmi

No one asked the animals what they thought
when the land was devastated and migration
routes were cut off.

Where trees used to stand, strange alien objects
are now sprouting.
Stiff, hard against the sky.

Close, close together.

Where there used to be a path, now lies an old
disbanded iron road,
rusty against an old migration route.

Where the river ran before, there is only a dry
furrow; one cannot hear its roaring wonder of
a thousand flowing years.

No one asked the river if it hurt when its
arteries were cut, and its circulation long ago
stopped.

The animals are perplexed when the thread of
the migration route turns into a strange, alien
object, stiff, hard against the sky.

Migration routes where they have wandered for
thousands of years, fenced off with barbed wire.

The old heargi cannot understand, standing
there with confusion in his eye watching all the
unfamiliarity that has come his way.

Strange obstacles that hold back what used to
be his annual migration.

15
Britta Marakatt-Labba, 'Et Skôvlat Land' (A Devastated Land), *Nordnorsk magasin* 3 (1981). I am grateful to Sámi artist Susanne Hætta, whose research for her book *Mázejoavku* unearthed this poem; and to my colleague at OCA Liv Brissach, also assistant curator in 'The Sámi Pavilion' project, for its translation. A heargi is a havier (castrated male reindeer) that can be ridden or used for sled pulling.

The old heargi cannot understand, where he used to cool off at the clear spring that runs from the depth of the earth's heart, pulsating through thousands of veins.

Transformed into a dry furrow with stones of a thousand grains of sand.

Grey one early summer day.

Britta Marakatt-Labba[15]

16
I came across this poem in the excellent book by Sámi scholar Vuokko Hirvonen, *Voices from Sápmi. Sámi Women's Path to Authorship* (Guovdageaidnu: DAT) 2008, p. 130. Translated into English by Kaija Anttonen. Originally published: Rauni Magga Lukkari, 'Gå rákkisvuodas juoigasta', *Samefolket* 5 (1967): pp. 99–100.

To Greet with Respect is to Listen
Listen Six – Continuance

They kept yoiking – the ones who knew how to. In love, they yoiked the one they wanted. They knew it was not a sin. Earlier, they had not dared: Læstadius and Tuderus had strictly forbidden chanting. But even a Christian could not help yoiking once he got up on the fells. The fell yoiked, and the lake and the creek, the wind howled its troubles and it was impossible to live the way Tuderus and Læstadius had told them. Humbly, he first yoiked the wind, then the fell, and, feeling sad, thought about the powerful clergymen and their lack of judgment. How could they know what it meant to live on the tundra and chant the same yoik as the wind? How could they have known what it meant to live on the river? But he, he knew how to yoik, and had to yoik. And as if to prove his thoughts he said to his son: 'Go ahead and yoik! When you're in love and you yoik a friend, it's the same as when they sing their hymns. Yoik, my son, and remember your friends!' The son yoiked.

Rauni Magga Lukkari[16]

17 Áillohaš / Nils-Aslak Valkeapää, sonic excerpt from *Goase dušše (Loddesinfoniija/The Bird Symphony)*, (Guovdageaidnu: DAT),1994.

To Greet with Respect is to Listen
Listen Seven – Life, an Art to Live

Áillohaš, excerpts from *Goase dušše* (*Loddesinfoniija/ The Bird Symphony*), DAT, 1994.

Áillohaš / Nils-Aslak Valkeapää[17]

18
This poem 'Dij åhpadijda muv tjállet' (You Taught Me to Write) is by the Lule Sámi actress Harriet Nordlund. It first appeared in the anthology *Vårt liv. Samiska dikter* (Our Lives: Sámi Poems, 1991). I came across it in the excellent book by Sámi scholar Vuokko Hirvonen, *Voices from Sápmi. Sámi Women's Path to Authorship* (Guovdageaidnu: DAT, 2008), p. 124.

To Greet with Respect is to Listen
Listen Eight – Trickstering Oppression into Survivance

You taught me to write
Thank you!
Now I will write about everything
we had to go through
I will write exactly what you did
How you scorned and laughed at us
How you tortured us with your laws
and with what you thought was good
The only useful thing you taught us
was how to write
Thank you!
And even if the sentences
are in a strange language,
for we never learned to write our own,
your failings will appear
And I will forget nothing
not even because of your recent benevolence
It is good that you taught me to write
Thank you!
I will write for all the young people
who are the way I once was
And they will feel proud
of their real selves
Never again will they be
ashamed of their slanting eyes
or colourful shoe bands
You who taught me how to write
Thank you!
A new era has begun and nothing can hold us back
We demand a life on our own terms
and a life for our children
We have kept silent too long
we have trusted you too long
But now our patience is exhausted and we say
Thank you!

Harriet Nordlund[18]

19 First published in Anna-Stina Svakko, *Virvelvind*, (Jokkmokk: Sámi Girjjit, 1991). I came across this poem in Hirvonen, *Voices from Sápmi*, pp. 169–70.

To Greet with Respect is to Listen
Listen Nine – the Futurity of Ancestral Knowledge

The goat willow
must part with its bark.

The alder
with its roots.

The moon is full,
a powerful force.
Nature gives
what we need.

Skins billow
in the clear water
of the creek.

For generations
our days
have become filled with
the rank smell
of skins.

I continue,
pass tendon thread
Through needle
and finish sewing.

The coffee pouch
in my father's backpack…

The handbag hanging
from my mother's shoulder…

The trousers around
a friend's legs…

An inheritance…
in a pair of hands.

Anna-Stina Svakko[19]

20
Niillas Holmberg, 'Indigenous Manifesto', in his *The Way Back* (London: Francis Boutle Publishers, 2016).

To Greet with Respect is to Listen
Listen Ten – a New Generation Resurges, the Water is Us

What can I say
to you who tend gardens
making a flowerbed of my mouth
ready for the big sleep

what on earth

you poor children
so used to noise
you get nervy
at the sound of quiet breathing

stop throwing stones into water
don't bury me
I might have not blinked all day
but I'm not ready to be buried

stop throwing stones
for the water is me
when there is stillness I will show you
the flowers you have planted

Niillas Holmberg [20]

Ofelaččat, The 'Indigenous Paradigm' and 'The Sámi Pavilion'

Ofelaččat

A Northern Sámi word meaning pathfinder. Sámi pathfinders pave the way and innovate, to sustain Sámi ways of being, doing, seeing and thinking in the world today, that have been and are being eroded, devalued, suppressed, erased by past and current colonial systems.

'Indigenous Paradigm'

A concept proposed by Sámi Prof. Rauna Kuokkanen, the 'Indigenous Paradigm' is, in her words:

> 'a way of both decolonizing Indigenous minds by "re-centering" Indigenous values and cultural practices and placing Indigenous peoples and their issues into dominant, mainstream discourses which until now have relegated Indigenous peoples to marginal positions … the main objectives of such a paradigm include the criticism of Western dualistic metaphysics and Eurocentrism, as well as the return to the Indigenous peoples' holistic philosophies.'[21]

'The Sámi Pavilion' comes late in the day. The Nordic Pavilion was inaugurated in 1962; it took 60 years for Sámi artists to be honoured in this way. Nevertheless, the project is a historic step born from a broad and long-lasting movement led by the Sámi, with support along the way from non-Sámi partners, to deconstruct the damage of colonialism on the Sámi people. For the Sámi, as for the Indigenous world, there can be no postcolonial; the historic practices of exploitation and dispossession of Sámi lands and peoples remain standing, albeit in different forms from in the past. Colonialism endures, absorbed

21 Prof. Rauna Kuokkanen, 'Toward an "Indigenous Paradigm" from a Sámi Perspective', *The Canadian Journal of Native Studies* 20.2 (2000): pp. 411–36. Prof. Kuokkanen highlights the need to treat this concept with some caution, since it is not a term directly derived from Indigenous modes of thinking, but rather a constructed linguistic spaceholder for decolonising actions.

22 See Susanne Hætta, *Mázejoavku. Indigenous Collectivity and Art*, edited by Katya García-Antón (OCA / DAT, 2020) and Katya García-Antón, Harald Gaski and Gunvor Guttorm (eds.), *Let the River Flow. An Indigenous Uprising and its Legacy in Art, Ecology and Politics* (OCA / Valiz, 2020) for further context.

internally in Sámi society, imposed externally. It continues to devalue Sámi perspectives and push them towards the edge of extinction.[22] 'The Sámi Pavilion' is therefore part of the Sámi people's struggles for self-determination and the decolonisation process that works to empower it. It regards Indigenous presence as uncontainable in its powerful reverberations, ingenuity and playfulness, as well as challenges the Western art field's role in defining and promoting colonial perspectives, in colonising Indigenous bodies, minds and spirits. Its conception is part of Sámi advocacy for the right to maintain and develop Sámi cultural practices and for the restitution of spiritual and intellectual material culture, and it resonates within the world-wide calls for reparation and rematriation today. It is part of a broader movement politically and artistically towards Indigenous self-determination and the Indigenisation of the arts and polis globally that incites co-existence and does not privilege one worldview at the expense of another.

However, to present 'The Sámi Pavilion' in the pavilions section of the Venice Biennial brings its own challenges. Outstanding among them is the nation-state premise of the Giardini. The grandmother of all biennials, the Venice Biennale models the Giardini upon the very World Fairs that exhibited and transacted Indigenous bodies, lands, technology and resources to strengthen the nation state model. Pavilions come with the trappings of national flags and the names of nation-states emblazoned in elegant bronze letters on their exteriors as ineludible brandings. Over the years, artists from all walks of life have presented projects in the Biennale and the Giardini section that are critical of Western modernity's supremacist impulses and projects that have claimed their own home-grown modernity. The Biennale has been enriched by a critique that reflects international ethical, aesthetic and socio-political shifts, and that is increasingly arguing in favour of a multiplicity of worlds and perspectives. And yet, walking up the central avenue of the Giardini, crowned by a trinity of empires of old (Great Britain, Germany and France), still makes one's hairs stand up on end. The Nordic Pavilion is positioned on this avenue, facing the Russian Pavilion, next door to the Danish Pavilion (also a former coloniser of Sápmi).

Nation-states aside, the Venice Biennial has expanded its Eurocentric perspectives over the years towards a progressively broader global arts showcase. However, the lenses of the Western mind-set remain distinctly present. Within the Western canon (and here I recognise the canon's gradual bid for inclusion and expansion, problematic in its own way), artists coming to the Biennial have presented over the years powerful projects that claim land, call for political justice, narrate discrimination and exploitation, and demand reparation. But what happens when the proposition is that art is life is land?[23] When artists are life are land? When the three are one, indivisible? When cultural resurgence is tantamount to land resurgence? The philosophical meta-categories of Sámi word-views have for centuries been marginalised into ethnographic quaintness; what happens when they are the very reference points for the artists presenting in Venice? How do holistic Indigenous epistemologies and Western dualistic epistemologies greet each other within the framework and restrictions of a distinctly Western space? How is the notion of the Indigenous Paradigm activated and safeguarded from becoming yet another appropriated resource within this context?

> The way we experience life in and of itself is art: clothing, colours, the way to dress, and even the way to sit, squat and walk: how the campfire is – to keep it tidy around the camp – to work graciously. Life – an art to live. To live without leaving traces behind.[24]

23 Land in this case is used to stand for all of the natural environment.

24 Nils-Aslak Valkeapää, 'Keviselie', in *Hans Ragnar Mathisen / Elle Hánsa / Keviselie* (Guovdageaidnu: DAT, 1998), p. 154.

25
Aileen Moreton-Robinson, *Sovereign Subjects: Indigenous Sovereignty Matters* (London: Routledge), 2007.

Within the matrix of these challenges and opportunities 'The Sámi Pavilion' proposes a project that sets out first and foremost to serve as a space of sovereignty for the artists. The term is not to be misunderstood within the optics of the nation-state. Those of us, Sámi and non-Sámi, working on 'The Sámi Pavilion' as a project of Sámi sovereignty have contributed our respective knowledges (bringing together Sámi scholarship, Sámi politics and activism, land guardianship, duodji, and understanding of the Biennale mechanics and Western history of art and its display) in order to structure the project from the perspective of reconnection to Sámi concepts, values and knowledge systems, as well as to rethink a curatorial experience specific to the project. Feminist scholar, Aileen Moreton-Robinson, an Aboriginal woman of the Goenpul tribe, part of the Quandamooka nation explains Indigenous sovereignty clearly:

> Our sovereignty is embodied, it is ontological (our being) and epistemological (our way of knowing), and it is grounded within complex relations derived from the inter-substantiation of ancestral beings, humans and land. In this sense, our sovereignty is carried by the body and differs from Western constructions of sovereignty, which are predicated on the social contract model, the idea of a universal supreme authority, territorial integrity and individual rights.[25]

The objective is that this understanding of sovereignty in 'The Sámi Pavilion' will contribute to decolonisation processes in Sámi, Finnish and Scandianvian societies; that it will empower the intellectual imagination and practicality of self-governance and self-definition. 'The Sámi Pavilion' is not a categorical project; others have existed in Sápmi, in the Giardini and in the central exhibition of the Biennial, and others will follow in different shapes and forms. Neither has everything that was discussed in this project amongst the artists, elders, curatorial group, extended programme collaborators and team members worked, and nor was this expected from the outset. However, much has been learnt along the way; what has proved generative will endure and enable others to build further.

'The Sámi Pavilion' project revolves around three key elements: trans-generational relations, holistic Sámi epistemology and Sámi spiritual perspectives. Colonialism results in a severing of bonds between generations. The project has thus sought to create a space of relations that fosters transmission and continuity of knowledges across generations. The residential schools of the past prevented Sámi children from learning their language, cultural and land-based practices; the children were instead indoctrinated with Western values. Today, there are no residential schools, but it is still challenging for Sámi children to be taught their language, history and worldviews in school, as is preparing them to deal with the pressures of a dominant consumer society, land encroachment and extractivism. Amongst many examples to be cited is the experience of youth seeking to make their livelihood in reindeer herding or fishing. They are challenged by Finnish and Scandinavian laws that either ban them outright or push them to bankruptcy, thus eliminating the most fragile, yet most important links in the continuity of these knowledges and practices. They also face the consequences of the long term christianisation politics that still stigmatise Sámi spirituality and prevent it from thriving in public.

With this backdrop in mind 'The Sámi Pavilion' sets out to strengthen the links between artists, elders and youths. In tandem with the dialogues between artists and the curatorial group, the artists have been enriched by individual conversations with community Elders of their choice. Artist Pauliina Feodoroff has connected with Sámi spiritual holder, educator and Professor Emerita Asta M. Balto; Máret Ánne Sara with reindeer herder and Sámi knowledge bearer Káren E. M. Utsi; and Anders Sunna with Ánde Somby, Sámi Professor of law, noaidi and juoigi (practioner of juoigan/joik the Sámi musical practice). The elders have shared spiritual, legal, reindeer herding and other knowledges with the artists, and been close dialogue partners every step of the way. As eloquently explained by Prof. Balto's notes in this book: 'As a teacher of Sami and Indigenous knowledge I know that teaching is more than sharing information. Learning happens when your teaching is rooted in love, speaking from your soul to other souls. It is sacred.'

In addition, Sámi Pathfinders from across Sápmi have prepared (through workshops and dialogues with the curatorial group, the elders and the artists) to mediate 'The Sámi Pavilion' and offer visitors a point of view of Sámi youth today. The youths are part of a programme run by Sámi allaskuvla (Sámi University of Applied Sciences), Guovdageaidnu, with The Sámi Parliament in Norway, that brings Sámi perspectives to schools. Their objective in 'The Sámi Pavilion' is not only to transmit knowledges collectively forged, tested and adapted over time that help bring context and understanding of the artists' works, but also to encourage bonds of meaningful connectivity with audiences.

'The Sámi Pavilion' advocates for understanding and generating knowledge from a Sámi perspective. Ancestral Sámi knowledges have been central to the work of the artists, and the dialogues with Elders, youths and the curatorial group. Their premise is powerfully outlined in Prof. Gaski's essay in this book, 'Sánit, govat ja šuoŋat – muhtun jurdagat sápmelaš lohkama, dulkoma ja áddejumi birra (Words, Images and Sounds – Contemplating Sámi

26 Aslak Holmberg, 'Conserving Sámiland'. trans. Tommi Kakko, in *Rehearsing Hospitalities. Hospitalities of Security, Safety and Care,* ed. Yvonne Billimore and Jussi Koitela (Berlin: Archive Books / Frame Contemporary Art), 2021, p. 136.

Readings, Interpretations and Understanding)', from which I quote the following introductory reflection: 'The Sámi have three main concepts that describe and explain our existence and continuance on this earth. These are giella, duodji, and juoigan, with local linguistic adjustments according to where you are in Sápmi/ Saepmie, the Sámi homeland.'

In Prof. Gaski's notes, giella refers to Sámi languages and juoigan to a form of musical communication. Duodji is the philosophy from which Sámi material culture and creative practices emerge; it is key to 'The Sámi Pavilion' project and informs all of the artists' work. Often mistranslated as 'craft' by the Western arts field, duodji encompasses a specifically Sámi and complex worldview, combining spiritual, material and environmental knowledge, concepts of aesthetics and beauty, but also utility and manual work, that converge in the processes of making objects, the behaviour they elicit and in the objects themselves. Knowledge holders and practitioners of duodji are called duojárat, a title that is never self-proclaimed but collectively awarded. Giella-juoigan-duodji is a Sámi conceptual triumvirate that is inextricably connected to land. This indivisibility is clearly explained by Sámi nature guardian, fisherman, and vice-president of the Sámi Council Aslak Holmberg:

> The Sámi lands are not wilderness. There is no word for 'wilderness' in the Sámi languages. A wilderness is uninhabited, deserted, wild. What we do have is 'meahcci': territories without permanent habitation that are used for various purposes. There is 'muorrameahcci' (tree-felling area), 'luomemeahcci' (cloudberry-picking area), a meahcci for reindeer herding, fishing, picking other kinds of berries and foraging. Our so-called wildernesses are in fairly intensive use. Our natural landscape is our cultural landscape.[26]

Centring these knowledges is a crucial element of 'The Sámi Pavilion' concept. Indigenous knowledge is often described as 'traditional' knowledge and this can lead to misunderstandings, since the term 'traditional' is after all a Western invention of the nineteenth century deeply imbricated in the trappings of modernity and Empire. As a result of this, traditional knowledge can be thought to imply something stuck in the past or whose purity cannot be altered, excluding the fact that all knowledge is fine-tuned as it is lived to avoid becoming obsolete. In this regard, the term 'ancestral knowledges' may be more appropriate because it relates to knowledge inherited over time rather than bound by the frame of a tradition. The last decades of Indigenous scholarship and creativity have contributed to clarifying for the Western field that their knowledges – grounded in a life informed by ancestral ways of being, doing, seeing and thinking – are the time-tested bedrock of Indigenous existence, a point that 'The Sámi Pavilion' strongly upholds.

It is also important to note that Sámi epistemology has a holistic approach, constituted collectively and actively, the way in which this underpins the work of the artists in 'The Sámi Pavilion' stands in a parallel and distinctive contrast to Western artistic practices of ecological art and relational aesthetics. In addition to which the Sámi artists also forge their work through other forms of received knowledge from spiritual sources and narratives, as Prof. Kuokkanen has explained:

> There are other forms of receiving knowledge, which could also be termed as intuitive or shamanic knowledge. These forms of knowledge, which are received through altered stages of mind such as shamanic trances or sudden glimpses of 'seeing', are largely dismissed by Western epistemologies. Sámi knowledge,

27 Kuokkanen, 'Towards an "Indigenous Paradigm"', p. 419.

> like any Indigenous knowledge, is reflected in language and disseminated through storytelling and ongoing dialogue.[27]

The transmission, constitution and activation of these spiritual and cosmological knowledges within the conception, production and presentation of the artists' works in 'The Sámi Pavilion' is significant but is something that mostly, and necessarily, remains in the private realm. However, this publication and the project's overall graphic proposal give a public face to them. Many of the contributions in this book – poems, plays, stories, reflections and essays – emerge from Sámi spiritual and cosmological knowledges, amongst them the powerful narrations by fellow curators Beaska Niillas and Liisa-Rávná Finbog, the excerpt from Máret Ánne Sara's novel, the poems by Pauliina Feodoroff and Anders Sunna, as well as the reflections of Prof. Balto, Prof. Somby and Prof. Gaski. Sámi artists and duojárat Fredrik Prost and Inga-Wiktoria Påve contributed their deep knowledge of Sámi spiritual practices and cosmologies to the design of this book and communication material for the project, structured along three elements that tell a story about Sámi ways of perceiving the world.

The first is a symbol representing beaivváš, the sun, derived from old Sámi weaving patterns. The sun is a central force across the diversity of Sámi communities and thus brings unifying power. The second is the concept of parallel worlds. Represented through the mirrored letters in the design of the logo of 'The Sámi Pavilion', it pays homage to the inhabitants of sáivu, the inverted world, who walk with the soles of their feet against those of Sámi people and thus constitutes a mirror image of our world. The third element relates to the most important star constellation in Sámi cosmology, the pole star boahjenásti, which given the high latitude in which Sápmi is situated, always shines at the centre of the

28
Ibid., p. 416.

night-sky. In addition, the Sámi creation story speaks of the hunting of the wild reindeer stag sarvvis, which after an arduous chase is tied to the pole star. The third narrative also illustrates the Sámi cosmological way of describing the world through the reindeer: the fur is the forest and everything that grows within it; the veins and the blood constitute the rivers and lakes, the pole star is the entrance to the upper world and the Sámi noaidit (spiritual leaders) climb the antlers of the reindeer to reach it. The three worlds exist in tandem, and in so doing bind the past, present and future into a circular relationship.

As Prof. Kuokkanen states, incorporating these knowledges forms a notable critique of Western dichotomical thinking: 'taking the Sámi cosmology as a basis of Sámi criticism allows us to be aware of the trappings of Western rationality and positivism which since the Enlightenment have separated the spiritual aspects of life from the material world and denied the existence of other realms that our visible daily reality that can be placed under "scientific scrutiny".' [28] It is also an essential practice in asserting Sámi epistemologies in the world today. Indeed, it is one that is shared across the Indigenous global artistic world, uniting both in a thorough questioning of colonial assumed notions of aesthetics, civility and religious hegemony. The moment of a spiritual reflection is central in global society and the arts, and it emerges from a history in which colonial religions were forced upon Indigenous people in the name of their self-appointed 'civilising' mission. Their impact installed dichotomical and patriarchal perspectives, as well as those of sexual binarism, the latter deeply affecting the fluid and complex gender politics of Indigenous societies. Anishinaabe (Ojibway) artist and curator Raven Davis speaks of art as a tool of healing and communicating a different sort of civility. Indigenous spirituality within the arts is, in his words:

> … one that is not confined in space to a house

29
Max Haiven, 'Beyond the Violence of Colonial Civility. Examining the Art of Raven Davis', in *The Art of Civil Action. Political Space and Cultural Dissent*, ed. Philipp Dietachmair & Pascal Gielen (Amsterdam: Valiz, 2017), p. 128

> of worship or in time to one day a week. Informed by discussions with Indigenous elders [one can] … understand spirituality as a practice that can happen in any place, located in the body, and that is a force of transformation. This means that political art can also be forms of prayer: 'Every protest is a prayer, every fight is a prayer, in a prayer', they informed me. Prayers don't necessarily mean being in a church … Activist art is also a tool of healing and protest, and can also include prayer.[29]

In this sense, 'The Sámi Pavilion' is an ofelaš (pathfinding) project reflecting upon a working process and generating artistic projects that centre healing, repairing and re-remembering Sámi ways of being, thinking and doing in the world. It creates a space that seeks to give primary importance to the pursuit and activation of Sámi sovereignty. Fundamental to that endeavour is an understanding that Sámi people and land are one, indivisible, that what happens to land happens to people; that what happens in 'The Sámi Pavilion' is interlinked to what is happening in Sápmi / Saepmie today, and that all are encompassed and defined by a Sámi spiritual worldview that is eloquently celebrated with these words by the Sámi artist and wordweaver Synnøve Persen.

30 Synnøve Persen, *poems poemas* (Karasjok: ČálliidLágádus), 2016. English translation by Pekka Sammallahti.

To Greet with Respect is to Listen.
Listen Eleven – to the Core, Spiritual Matriarchisation

The Four Dream Sisters

the four dream sisters
keep the corners of the world with their silky fringes
pound the shaman's drum
outline the souls' journey back home

the dream sisters catch me
when I fall
stretch out their arms
hum consolations
put their arms around my aching shoulders
weave a web of golden hair
for shelter

their soft singing
creeps into my body's cells
flies my soul off to the sunny peak
kindles my boldness

the dream sisters save my life
with their lively songs
their cheerful humming
itching pleasures urge up my back
to the neck and little brain
wake up my nerves

Synnøve Persen[30]

Biographies

Brook Garru Andrew's matrilineal kinship is from the kalar midday (land of the three rivers) of Wiradjuri, and Ngunnawal on his mother's father's line, both Aboriginal nations of Australia, and paternally Celtic. He is an artist and scholar who is driven by the collisions of intertwined narratives, often emerging from the mess of the 'Colonial Hole'. In 2020, he was artistic director of 'NIRIN', the 22nd Biennale of Sydney. As well as an artist, Andrew has, amongst others, been co-curator of *We Are Not All Just Human After All: Care, Repair, Healing,* scheduled to open in September 2022 at the Gropius Bau, Berlin; Associate Researcher, Pitt Rivers Museum, Oxford, UK; participant in the ARC Special Research Initiative for Australian Society, History and Culture Grant with Dr Brian Martin: 'More than a guulany (tree): Aboriginal knowledge systems'. Together with Wanda Nanibush he is International Indigenous Advisor to 'The Sámi Pavilion' at Biennale Arte 2022.

Katya García-Antón is director/chief curator of the Office for Contemporary Art Norway. She graduated as a biologist, and transitioned into the arts with a master's degree in nineteenth- and twentieth-century art from The Courtauld Institute of Art, London. She has worked at The Courtauld Institute of Art, Museo Nacional Reina Sofía Madrid, ICA London, IKON Birmingham, and the Centre d'Art Contemporain Genève. She curated the Nordic Pavilion, Venice Biennial in 2015 and the Spanish Pavilion in the Venice Biennial 2011. In OCA, García-Antón has generated significant Indigenising practices and programmes. In August 2022 she becomes director of the Northern Norway Art Museum (NNKM).

Harald Gaski from Deatnu on the Norwegian side of Sápmi is Professor of Sámi Culture and Literature at Sámi allaskuvla / Sámi University of Applied Sciences and at UiT The Arctic University of Norway. He is the author and editor of several books on Sámi literature and culture and has also translated Sámi literature and the poetry of legendary Sámi artist Nils Aslak Valkeapää into Norwegian and English. Gaski's research focuses on Indigenous methodologies and Sámi oral and written culture. He has been instrumental in establishing Sámi literature as an academic field and has been awarded for his research and writing. Gaski will serve as Mentor in TBA–21 Academy's Ocean Fellowship 2022, a programme organised in collaboration with OCA, aabaakwad and Artis that gathers participants to consider our kinship and duties of care toward the Ocean and its relations in multi-species communities and with diverse lifeforms.

Timimie Gassko Märak is a poet, feminist and Sámi queer activist based in Stockholm. Märak puts just as much in between the lines they write as in the words they choose to share. Like them, their poetry is a combination of deep roots and connections, read at a big-city pace. They are the Word Weaver, also known as a Poet in Residence at 'The Sámi Pavilion' at Biennale Arte 2022, in a role that emphasises orality.

Northern Sky above Venice

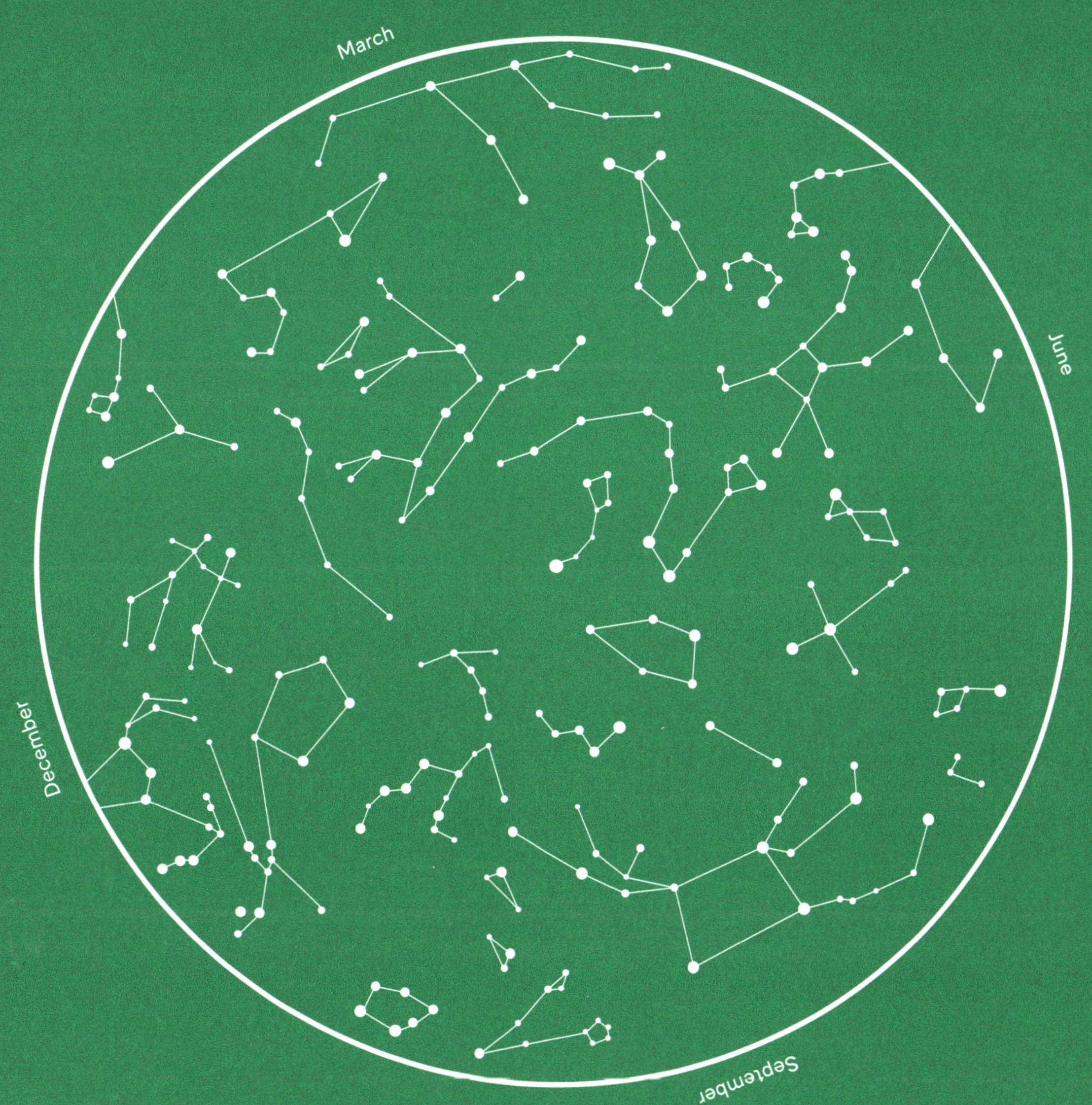

Čatnosat. The Sámi Pavilion, Indigenous Art, Knowledge and Sovereignty takes as its starting point a ground-breaking moment in the history of the Biennale Arte in Venice: the Indigenisation of the Nordic Pavilion in 2022, by 'The Sámi Pavilion' project. Featuring the creative practices and worldviews of Sámi artists and land guardians Pauliina Feodoroff, Máret Ánne Sara and Anders Sunna, the project represented a sovereign call for Sápmi (the Sámi homeland spanning Norway, Sweden, Finland and the Kola Peninsula) and revolved around three elements: transgenerational relations, holistic Sámi knowledge and learning, and Sámi spiritual perspectives.

Čatnosat, whilst inspired by 'The Sámi Pavilion', stands on its own feet to reflect on Indigenous sovereignty within the interconnected spaces of land, art and knowledge and to consider the centrality of story-telling, sound and the spoken word in Sámi perspectives. The book is conceived in three sections, neither beginnings nor ends, highlighting the importance of non-linear time in Sámi life. One section is dedicated to the artists' work and writings; a second section presents an experimental short play, poems, as well as stories interlinking Sámi spiritual, political and philosophical perspectives. A third section reflects upon Indigenous and Western concepts of land, the long history of Sámi epistemology, the relationship between Sámi land, people and language and the curatorial practices in 'The Sámi Pavilion' that seek to empower the above mentioned notions. An exercise in Sámification, *Čatnosat* advocates for the importance today of Indigenous holistic perspectives, and Sámi Indigenous wisdom in all fields of art and living.

The Sámi Pavilion

Editors:

Liisa-Rávná Finbog
Katya García-Antón
Beaska Niillas

Assistant editor:
Liv Brissach

Contributors:

Brook Garru Andrew
Asta Mitkijá Balto
Liv Brissach
Pauliina Feodoroff
Liisa-Rávná Finbog
Katya García-Antón
Harald Gaski
Timimie Gassko Märak
Beaska Niillas
Máret Ánne Sara
Sigbjørn Skåden
Ánde Somby
Anders Sunna

Valiz, Amsterdam
www.valiz.nl

OCA
Office for Contemporary Art
Norway / www.oca.no

ISBN 978-94-93246-12-6

‘To all those who came before us,
and to those who will come after us’

‘Pukid si′jjid, kook jie′lle mij ooudpeä′lnn,
da si′jjid, kook puä′tte mij mââipeä′lnn’

‘Buohkaide guđet min ovdal bohte,
ja buohkaide guđet min maŋŋel bohtet’

‘Gaajhkesidie gïeh mijjen åvtelen böötin,
jïh gaajhkesidie gïeh mijjen mænngan båetieh’

Čatnosat (Northern Sámi) means connections, attachments or bonds. The dedication on this page is in the following languages: Skolt Sámi, Northern Sámi and Southern Sámi.

Sigbjørn Skåden
Guške for Lunch

THEIR LIEGE Ah, here comes the bird!

THEIR GOOD MAN As ordered, my liege.

TL I can hardly wait to sink my teeth into that plump leg. Open the lid, my good man, open it!

TGM Yes, my liege.

TL What is this?

TGM They said guške, my liege.

TL What?

TGM Guške.

TL What's a guške?

TGM The bird, my liege.

TL This one?

TGM Yes.

TL Who said that?

TGM The people who brought it.

TL It's a guške?

TGM Yes.

TL What's a guške, then?

TGM I don't know.

TL What do you mean?

TGM They only said guške.

TL Go and ask them then, my good man!

TGM They left, my liege.

TL So we don't know what this is?

TGM No, my liege.

TL I requested a great auk.

TGM Yes, my liege.

TL Is this a great auk?

TGM I couldn't say. They only said guške.

TL And we don't know what guške is.

TGM No, my liege.

TL It doesn't look all that much like a great auk.

TGM It doesn't.

TL It's too small, for starters.

TGM Yes, my liege.

TL Is it a little auk?

TGM It might be.
TL The shape seems a bit off.
TGM Yes, my liege.
TL Why doesn't it have any legs, first of all?
TGM I clipped them before I prepared it.
TL Yes, yes, but you know what I mean. Why doesn't it have any plumpy meaty leg parts? Look at this, there's nothing. Where are the plumpy meaty leg parts?
TGM I don't know.
TL I don't think this is an auk at all.
TGM You might be right.
TL So why wasn't I brought a great auk as requested?
TGM I heard someone say great auks have run out.
TL Run out?
TGM There aren't any left.
TL What do you mean, aren't any left?
TGM They can't be found.
TL Sounds like a load of horsewallop. There've always been plenty of great auks to go around.
TGM The good news is that there are scores of little auks still. Someone said, so this I know for a fact. Funnily actually, the same person said that when Linnaeus was going to make a species name for the little auk he made a name that derived from the South Sámi name for the bird. So he thought. But then it later turned out he'd mistaken the little auk for the long-tailed duck, so the species name for the little auk, which is *Alle alle*, has in fact no connection to the little auk at all; it's the South Sámi name for the long-tailed duck. Confusing, but also amusing.
TL Linnaeus, that old tosspot. Where is he nowadays anyway?
TGM I don't know, my liege.
TL And what's the purpose of this shower of words you just gave me?

TGM Just an anecdote. I thought you might find it humorous.

TL I don't.

TGM Sorry, my liege.

TL So back to this bird at hand, then.

TGM Yes.

TL What did you call it?

TGM Guške, my liege.

TL Right, guške. And what language is this?

TGM I don't know.

TL Of course you don't. I'm sorry to ask, but what *do* you know?

TGM I know how I prepared it.

TL Let's hear then.

TGM So, I wrapped it in a seal skin, heaped stones over it and left it in the heap for some months.

TL Wait, you've had this for some months?

TGM Yes, my liege.

TL Under a pile of stones?

TGM Yes, or a heap.

TL A heap, yes. Well that explains the long wait. So, you've fermented it?

TGM Yes.

TL Why?

TGM That's what I was told to do.

TL By those who brought the bird?

TGM Yes.

TL Whom we can't identify, and neither what they brought?

TGM No.

TL How did you come up with the skin?

TGM It came with the bird.

TL Did the seal also come with the bird? Maybe I could eat some of that instead.

TGM No, just the skin and the fat for the fermentation.

TL Too bad. Well, what then? After some months you heaped the bird out, and now we're here?

TGM Well, first I plucked it and chopped its head off.

TL So, you got it whole?

TGM Yes.

TL Well, then you've seen what it looks like in real life.

TGM Yes, but I'm not so good with birds.

TL *Quelle surprise*. Let's see the head, then. Maybe we can identify it somehow.

TGM I gave it away.

TL You gave the head away?

TGM Yes.

TL To whom?

TGM A person asked to have it.

TL What person asks to have a fermented bird's head?

TGM I didn't know them, my liege.

TL And now they're gone.

TGM Yes, my liege.

TL Of course. So, all we have is this … what did you call it?

TGM They did, my liege.

TL Yes, what did *they* call it?

TGM Guške, my liege.

TL Guške, right. And we have no idea what guške is.

TGM Still not, my liege.

TL Nor the slightest clue what language or cultural circle we're dealing with.

TGM No, my liege.

TL Is it somehow connected to what you told me before about Linnaeus and … what was it? South Sámi something?

TGM I don't know.

TL Why did you tell it then?

TGM It was just a humorous anecdote about Linnaeus.

TL Right, old Linnaeus. He could've helped us.

TGM Presumably not, since he can't tell a little auk from a long-tailed duck.

TL Valid point.

TGM Also, he might very well be dead.
TL Has something happened?
TGM No, but you know. He lived way back when.
TL When when?
TGM When there still were great auks.
TL And now there are not?
TGM Right.
TL When is it now, then?
TGM Later. Much, much later.
TL And now all we have is this guške.
TGM Yes.
TL And we don't know what it is.
TGM No.
TL And I'm supposed to eat it.
TGM Right.
TL Is there a North Sámi, since there's evidently a South one?
TGM That would be logical. But let's not get into cardinal directions again. It's a blind alley.
TL Right. Maybe I'll just try some? Get it over with?
TGM You're welcome, my liege.
TL This is an exceptionally acquired taste.
TGM It *is* fermented.
TL Have you ever had anything fermented?
TGM No, my liege.
TL Neither have I.
TGM Right.
TL So, we don't know what fermented tastes like.
TGM I suppose not.
TL I'm thinking that whatever this guške bird naturally tastes like, the fermentation process probably has a say in the matter.
TGM They say fermentation is a practical way for hunters to prepare food. That way they already have a stack of food waiting for them when they return next hunting season.

TL Which is fermented a full year?

TGM Indeed.

TL Who says this?

TGM The ones who brought the guške.

TL But we're not hunters, are we?

TGM We're not, my liege.

TL So, for us, in principle, fermentation is neither necessary nor practical.

TGM I only followed instructions.

TL Want a bite?

TGM Thanks, I've just eaten.

TL You could've at least gotten some little auks, instead of this dreadful guške.

TGM I lied.

TL You lied what?

TGM Little auks have run out too.

TL Who told you that? Wait, never mind: the ones who brought the guške.

TGM Yes, my liege.

TL That's a disappointment. But some luck for Linnaeus at least.

TGM At least that, my liege.

TL Well, my good man. What can one say? How did we end up here, eh?

TGM There was a drought.

TL I was trying to be colloquial. Don't you think I know there was a drought?

TGM I thought maybe you'd forgotten.

TL I had not.

TGM Neither have I.

[So how *did* they end up here? Who knows, really, how anyone ends up anywhere? It felt practical. Or necessary. First came rainstorms that wiped the land clear. Then the long drought. It's been foretold since long before Ketil Ketilsson on 3 June 1844

accidentally stepped on the last egg of the great auk: at one point there will no longer be a better place to migrate to. There's a saying in Sámi that time doesn't pass, it comes. It's a mode of existence that cultivates prophecies. Some will be pleasant, some will be grim. Common to all of them is that they aren't about the future; they're about our time. Foretold to help us steer our lives now so that our descendants will have the future that belongs to them. The grimmest prophecy of all, great or small, is that one day there will be only one prophecy.
So, we return to our two characters, wherever and whenever they might be, to give them one last line.]

TL & TGB both When I woke up this morning I'd never foresee that this was our ultimate quay.
Cuuuur-cur-cur-leeeeeee-leeeeee-leeeee-leeee-leee.

Beaska Niillas

Mirkkospeajal

Ođđa áiggi stáluid fámostallama njálgga doarggástusaid návddašeapmi.

Sii bukte govaid alddiiseaset

Ja mii, geahččaimet daidda dassážii go speadjalin navddiimet

Mas iežamet oaidnit

Behtolaš mirkkospeajal

De bassalehppet oappát ja vielljat čalmmiideattet

Vaikko čiežain čáziin

Vaikko čuđiin

Vai mierká loktana

Vai speajal cuovkana

Go áicát

Go gávnnadit

Go čoahkkanit

De lea bálggesčuovga

De lea doaivva

Oaidnetmeahttun oktavuođat

In han ealášii jus ehpet livčče

dii

geat lehpet

ja leamašan

Ieža eai ba dieđe ge

Dat geaidda dorvvastan

Oaidnemeahttun jávohis doarjja
Dárbbaslaš jávohis oktavuohta
Ráhkisvuođa báttit
Ruvdejuvvon
Bárgiduvvon
Čanastuvvon

Veahkkin savdnjilehppet čáhppes idjabalvvaid
čuovganeapmin

Loktebet, bassabet ja girddititehppet

Giitosat

Áicat

Dovdat

Muitit giitit

Giitit muitit – muitit giitit

Ráhkásat

Moarsit

Eamidat

Oappát

Vielljat

Fuolkkit

Máttut

Eadnanvuložat

Háldit

Vuoiŋŋat

ja
Ipmilat

Giitu áhčči

Giitu eadni

Giitu

Giitu

Fámuideattet juogadeamis ja várjaleami gokčasiin

Giitu

Giitu

Ráhkisvuođa skeaŋkkain ja buot dan buorrevuođas

Giitu

Go mii ain leat

Poisonous Mirrors

The stállus in this new time enjoy the sweet shaking of power.
They brought pictures of themselves

And we stared at the pictures, until they turned into mirrors

And we saw ourselves

A betraying, poisonous mirror

Sisters and brothers – wash your eyes
With seven waters
Even a hundred

So the mist might clear

So the mirror will shatter

When we see

When we join

When we gather

Then there is light

Then there is hope

Invisible Bonds

I would not be alive without you

you

who are

and have been

They don't even know it

The ones I hold on to

Invisible silent support
Necessary silent connection
Braided ropes of love – link us

You help me clear the dark night clouds for light
You uplift, wash and make me fly

Gratitude

To notice

To feel

To remember to thank

The

Loved ones

Girlfriends

Wives

Sisters

Brothers

Kin

Ancestors

The ones we don't see

The Spirits

and
The Gods

Thank you Father
Thank you Mother

Thank you

Thank you

For sharing your powers and for the carpet of protection

Thank you

Cause we are still here

Timimie Gassko Märak

To Remember

I want you to remember
it was never about blood.

I want you to remember that it was never
about blood.
The conversations always include blood due
to colonialism and racial biology.

I want you to remember
Spirituality.

I want you to remember
that in the same way that music or smells or
pictures can take you back to memories
of the past or dreams about the future,
drums, rituals and seances can work
as an extension when reaching out for
connection.
But no drum, chant or seance will act as a
tool for someone not knowing what they
are doing or why.
Because as with a knife when crafting or
words in a conversation, we risk hurting
ourselves and others if we are unwilling to
learn from others and our mistakes.

I want you to remember
Connection.

I want you to remember
We will make mistakes and that pride when closely connected to shame rather than community will try to stop us from asking for help.

So I want you to remember
It is about love. All forms of love.

We learn from each other and spirituality is the connection you get when love goes deep enough for you to care for your surroundings and all things and people in it.

I want you to remember
To care.
Spirituality is the love you feel when connection goes deep enough for you to care for your surroundings and all things and people in it.
That is when you grow, that is where you find reflection and love.
And in a place with rules and laws set to divide us, we must break them
without breaking ourselves.

That means you mustn't rush.
Keep going, let it take time, resting doesn't mean stopping.
You already have so much to be proud of so just
drop the shame.
Let it give space to instead
learn the names of the places and people and needs who made you

and speak them.
They will not know you are calling them
if you do not know their names.

Break the colonial tongue and illusion of
power.

Spirituality is connection
Is care
Is community.

I want you to remember
It was never about blood.

For Us

What we want

To be acknowledged as a people treated as an
equal

What they do

They cut our hair and our forests
They say they are doing it for us
Always ignoring the chorus crying out facts
and feelings

Let's face it we are dealing with the rootless

Labour camps on our homelands

The old ways become paved ways
Love is seen as the strange way still treated
as an illness

Let's face it we are dealing with the ruthless

They want to breed us to be kneeling feeding
greed leading everyone to thinking
healing is hiding behind face masks and
productivity

Let's face it we are dealing with a useless
system. It is working for them
but because of us.

Digging coal drilling oil missing daybreak
Blood money paycheck

They will never walk in our shoes
Because let's face it we are dealing with the
soulless

Labour camps on our homelands
They don't care about the borders
They are killing us killing our reindeer.
They are killing us killing our languages
They are killing us making wind millions

Labour camps on our homelands
The irony that nothing will grow and the
only thing they know to fear is to be
fruitless
Only the ones without future can afford to be
truthless

Calling it law and order
Fascism knows no borders
Labour camps on our homelands
They say they are doing it for us

For Us, by Timimie Gassko Märak was previously published by the Goethe-Institut in relation to the project *The Right to be Cold: Climate justice for the Arctic* (July 2021).

Liisa-Rávná Finbog
Seeing the Unseen

Once, while walking in solitude by the eternal waters, the creator, Jubmel, found the peace disturbed by shrieks of hatred, and evil chants invaded the calm of the eternal void. Disturbed, Jubmel decided to create a new world, a universe so peaceful and harmonious that love and compassion would reign and the evil spirits would flee.

He wanted the beautiful body of his favourite creature, a gentle reindeer doe, to be the matter from which the new world would be shaped, and he wanted her loving heart to inform the new creation. So he called the lovely Vaja, the reindeer doe, from Passevaari, the holy mountain upon which she grazed. As the radiant reindeer came running, her golden hooves sparkled like shafts of sunlight, delighting the creator's heart.

Turning to the gentle Vaja, and looking into her tender eyes, Jubmel said: 'You my little Vaja, have infinite sadness in your eyes: and from your body I will shape the world to set my Savio-aimo (the home of holiness) apart from the nether regions.'

So the creator took a tiny bone from the body of the reindeer doe and built a bridge that spanned the abyss between the light world and the nether regions.

The innermost structure of the new earth was fashioned from Vaja's bones and became the rocks and boulders and the peaks and mountain ridges.

Her flesh became the fertile soil, and her blood and veins the flowing rivers. From her hair the

mysterious forests were created. Her skull became the sky, which shields the earth from the blazing brightness of the holy heavens.
The reindeer's deep, sad eyes became the morning and evening stars to guide the songmakers, the dreamers and the parted lovers and to give them hope.
Finally, Jubmel hid Vaja's still-beating heart in the centremost depths of the earth to remind the lost wanderer, the lonely mountaineer, and all those in sorrow, that help would always be there.
Vaja's heart would be the heartbeat of the earth, so that when peace and love reigned, the reindeer doe's heart would beat with joy. But if hatred and greed disrupted the earth's harmony, her heart would convulse in pain, and tremors would shake the earth from top to bottom.
The beauty of the new earth was abundant.[1]

At the Árran – Convening the Collective

Our ability to listen to or for 'messages from Nature, from our fellow creatures, animals, birds, winds, sky, and the Earth', to Eana (Earth), goes back to this muitalus, the story of the splendorous Vaja, whose gift created the foundation of our world(s).[2] 'Muitalus', the Sámi word for story, shares its root with the verb 'muitit', meaning to remember.[3] When stories are told, the muitaleaddji, the storyteller, thus shares the memory of and with the searvevuohta, the collective.

To gather at the fireplace,

sharing and coming together. We tend to ourselves – our knowledges and spiritual needs –

in the same way that we tend to the fire.

1 Excerpt from Linda Schierse Leonard, *Creations Heartbeat: Following the Reindeer Spirit* (Bantham: Bantham, 1996).

2 Harald Gaski, 'Indigenous Elders' Perspective and Position (Nordic Colonialisms and Scandinavian Studies) (Viewpoint essay)', in *Scandinavian Studies* 91, 1-2 (2019): p. 262

3 Coppélie Cocq, *Revoicing Sámi Narratives: North Sámi Storytelling at the Turn of the 20th Century* (Umeå: Institutionen för språkstudier, 2008), p. 41.

Stories, then, make up our archives and libraries, as the place we keep our knowledge. As a society, we all own these stories, yet they belong to no one. When the stories are shared, the muitaleaddji opens space for the listener to learn and understand the world(s) we live in and the realities they spawn.[4] Yet, the muitaleaddji never shares stories in a set form. Rather, the stories are told all at once, growing into one another, manifesting as a circular weave that may touch upon multiple aspects, but that always relate to the central point.[5] In our story, and the many stories that will follow, we embrace the role of the muitaleaddji in all its complexity, inviting you to gather at the árran, the fireplace, where Sáráhkká, she who is the mother of inspired creation, lives, to open a space in which we convene our pasts, futures and presents. Entering the nexus, what we call the 'Native slipstream', we thus travel the lands, the waters and the skies, to manoeuvre across, throughout and within the pluralities of time, connected by Vaja's heartbeat, giving you a glimpse of the beauty of this 'new' world, which is abundant.[6]

4
Julie Cruikshank, *The Social Life of Stories: Narrative and Knowledge in the Yukon Territory* (Lincoln University of Nebraska Press, 1998), p. 2; Margaret Kovach, *Indigenous Methodologies: Characteristics, Conversations and Contexts* (Toronto: University of Toronto Press, 2009), p. 94.

5
Harald Gaski, *Sami Culture in a New Era: The Norwegian Sami Experience* (Karasjok: Davvi girji, 1997), p. 199.

6
Grace L. Dillon, 'Imagining Indigenous Futurisms', in *Walking the Clouds: An Anthology of Indigenous Science Fiction*, edited by G. L. Dillon (Tucson: The University of Arizona Press, 2012), p. 3.

Jearrat Biekkas

The story of Vaja is not simply one of creation, however. It is also a story of how we in Sápmi, the homeland of the Sámi, value the capacity to listen: to hear what is being truly said.

We listen,
we hear so as to know what is being said.
This is good practice.

Learning to listen to the land, to the heartbeat of Vaja, takes great commitment. Not in so far as you must become a conduit, with dedicated ceremonies, rituals and specific acts to help you reach such a state. There is no need to dress it up, because all it takes is the simple act of opening mind and heart – be humble, be still and listen. The commitment we speak of is spiritual. And yet it is simple, demanding only that you allow yourself to breathe, to stand in place, and to listen.

Here is the sound of the crows
– they speak of their travels to distant shores, far away,
but they nest in our home, close to the heart.

Can you hear the heartbeat? Does it resonate joyfully, or does it tremble in convulsions?

The elders often say,
go out into the woods, all you need you will find there.
Yes, this is where we listen to Vaja.
This is where the sound of her heartbeat is loud.

If we listen to the whispers of the wind, they speak, sharing both stories and feelings across and throughout borders of time and space. Whether we hear those stories and connect with those feelings, however, depends on our ability to take a breath – inhale, exhale – be still and listen.

There is sound all around us.
It's easy to dismiss these sounds, to think that they do not matter.
But consider this:
the build up of a storm at sea, the calm after the storm,
– we all know this sound –
and when we hear it, we also know what's coming.

This is a gift.

The Gift

In his now canonical book on the gift, the French sociologist Marcel Mauss writes that the gift is little more than 'a polite fiction', and that the present that seems to be so

'generously given is [...] a social deceit [as] there is obligation and economic self interest'.[7] The idea that because I have gifted to you, so too must you gift unto me, is a perversion.[8] It is born from the thought that Indigenous communities are 'societies of a backward or archaic type', which compels the gift 'that has been received to be obligatorily reciprocated'.[9] This is an understanding born in a colonial world, which is a strange world, where capitalistic and opportunistic ideals are at the centre.
Nevertheless, the gift is not an archaic practice. It is not the remnant of life-before and a society that we (who are Indigenous) have never (seemingly at least) managed to evolve beyond.[10]

> There is a horn of wood unearthed from its place in the ground, a šiella that for generations has been hidden in the Earth as a symbol of the alliance we who live here have had with the world below.[11]

A gift once given is always a reminder.

It is the heartbeat of our world(s), of Vaja's gift to us, and an acknowledgement of the part we all play to generate the 'specific ways of knowing, relating to, and being in the world', that make kin.[12]

'Making kin is to make people into familiars in order to relate.'[13] This is a truth for many Indigenous philosophies. In a Sámi context, the worlds we live in and besides (or below and on top) are created through an intricate web of connections, extending from the complex relations between and to people, land, skies, spiritual entities and other beings as well as objects and things.[14]

> De oainam go ovtta vuogje boatta oudald
> – bajas jotta, viđain hergin, ovdemuš vel læ
> ruoša-jievja. Go boares Gersela ragjai goastai,

7 Marcel Mauss, *The Gift: the Form and Reason for Exchange in Archaic Societies, Essai sur le don* (London: Routledge, [1925] 2002), p. 4.

8 Rauna Kuokkanen, *Reshaping the University: Responsibility, indigenous Epistemes, and the Logic of the gift* (Vancouver: UBC Press, 2007), p. 66.

9 Mauss, *The Gift*, p. 4.

10 Rauna Kuokkanen, 'Láhi and Attáldat: The Philosophy of the Gift and Sami Education', in *The Australian Journal of Indigenous Education* 34 (2005): p. 266, also see Jelena Porsanger, 'The Problematisation of the Dichotomy of Modernity and Tradition in Indigenous and Sami Contexts', in *Working with Traditional Knowledge: Communities, Institutions, Information Systems, Law and Ethics* edited by Jelena Porsanger and Gunvor Guttorm, (Guovdageaidnu: Sámi allaskuvla/ Sámi University of Applied Sciences, 2011), pp. 225-252.

11 Beret (anonymous by choice) Northern Sámi area. Oral communication, 17 April 2017.

12 Kuokkanen, 'Láhi and Attáldat', p. 265.

13 Kim Tallbear, 'The US-Dakota War and Failed Settler Kinship', in *Anthropology News* 57 (9), *sfaa.net*, 2016.

14 Jelena Porsanger, 'Indigenous Sámi Religion: General Considerations about Relationship', in *The Diversity of Sacred Lands in Europe: Proceedings of the Third Workshop of the Delos Initiative – Inari/ Aanaar 2010* (Gland, Switzerland: IUCN and Vantaa, Finland: Natural Heritage Services, 2012), p. 38.

de dam garvveli mædda ja de javkai jokka rogge sisa. Varas vacca vel læi. Mon vurdden ja vurdden atte dola itta dam roggest bajas, muotto i dat itta, goassege.[15]

These relations are what makes up the social structure of the world. They are what defines the place of individual and of community, and they are always manifested through the practice of gift giving. The gift, however, may take many shapes; it can be a physical object, but it can also be a song, a dream or a whisper on the wind.[16]

They showed me how to make a drum. They came many nights, giving me knowledge until they told me that I was ready to make one.[17]

But no matter the form, the intent behind a gift is always to make the receiver aware that they are part of a world-of-relations, and that they are responsible for maintaining these relations in a good way. In turn, this presumes the responsibility of the recipient to act accordingly by respecting those relations and honouring them.[18] This is a relational accountability, and it is the backbone in a system of kinship.[19]

This system of kinship – the act of making your relations kin – is not singular to a Sámi context and indeed, it is a basic principle in many Indigenous philosophies. In the Lakota and Dakota philosophy of Turtle Island for instance, we find the 'Mitakuye Oyasin' meaning, 'all my kin' or 'we are all related'.[20] In the Wiradjuri philosophy of (what is now known as) Australia, there is the 'yindyamarra', a way of life where everything is respected.[21] In (Southern Sámi) Sápmi, we find a similar expression of such kinship in the concept of *guelmiedahke*.

15 Ondre Jakvitsch, quoted in Isak Saba, *Čállosat: Isak Saba álbmotmuitočoakkáldat*, edited by Line Esborg (Oslo: Spartacus Forlag/Scandinavian Academic Press, 2019), p. 187.

16 E.g. Marlene Brant Castellano, 'Updating Aboriginal Traditions of Knowledge', in *Indigenous Knowledges in Global Contexts: Multiple Readings of Our World*, edited by George J. Sefa Dei, Budd L. Hall and Dorothy Goldin Rosenberg (Toronto: Toronto Universty Press, 2000), pp. 23-4.

17 Násti (anonymous by choice), quoted in Liisa-Rávná Finbog, *It Speaks to you – Making Kin of People, Duodji and Stories in Sámi Museums* (PhD. Department of Culture Studies and Oriental Languages, University of Oslo, 2020), p. 202.

18 Rauna Kuokkanen, *Reshaping the University: Responsibility, Indigenous Epistemes, and the Logic of the Gift* (Vancouver: UBC Press, 2007), p. 65; e.g., O. P. Pettersson, Louise Bäckman and Rolf Kjellström, *Kristoffer Sjulssons minnen: om Vapstenlapparna i början af 1800-talet / upptecknade af O. P. Pettersson*, edited by Louise Bäckman and Rolf Kjellström, Vol. 20, *Acta Lapponica* (Stockholm, 1979), p. 134.

19 Shawn Wilson, 'What Is an Indigenous Research Methodology?' *Canadian Journal of Native Education* 25 (2001): p. 177.

20 Nick Estes, *Our History is the Future: Standing Rock Versus the Dakota Access Pipeline, and the Long Tradition of Indigenous Resistance* (London: Verso Books, 2019), p. 12.

21
Bernard Sullivan, *Yindyamarra Yambuwan: Respecting Everything.* (Bathurst: Charles Sturt University, 2016).

22
Maja Dunfjeld Aagård, 'Symbolinnhold i Sørsamisk ornamentikk', Hovedfag i duodji/ Master in Duodji (Oslo: Statens Lærerhøgskole i forming, 1989), p. 90; Jorunn Jernsletten, *Bissie dajve: relasjoner mellom folk og landskap i Voengel-Njaarke sïjte* (Universitetet i Tromsø, Fakultet for humaniora, samfunnsvitenskap og lærerutdanning, Institutt for historie og religionsvitenskap, 2009), p. 168.

23
Inga Olsdatter quoted in Saba, *Čállosat*, p. 128.

24
Maria Puig de la Bellacasa, *Matters of Care: Speculative Ethics in More Than Human Worlds* (Minneapolis: University of Minnesota Press, 2017), p. 1.

Guelmiedahke – The Mirror Of The World

Today, the direct translation of the word is 'mirror' or something that reflects. Nevertheless, of old, *guelmiehdahke* has the specific meaning of 'reciprocity in all our relations'.[22] Even though there are borders of space (and perhaps even time) that divide the Mitakuye Oyasin, the yindyamarra and the guelmiedahke, the philosophies that they represent are similar in that they encourage a 'duty of care', calling upon our responsibilities as human beings, living on Eana (Earth), to honour and acknowledge all our relations.

But do not confuse the idea of care with one of Western make.

In the Oxford dictionary, care is defined as 'the provision of what is necessary for the health, welfare, maintenance, and protection of someone or something'. Though this seems to be an understanding that is benign, the fact of the matter is that it embeds itself in asymmetrical power relations. Framed by a Western understanding of the word, care is thus given because someone or something is unable to care for themselves, or they lack the necessary means to do so. But there is a sense of ambiguity in caring for someone or something. On the one hand, you may provide care because you have the means to do so, but on the other hand, you may also provide care because you believe that your care is superior to the care others may provide. A slippery slope then, care.

> Muttu go son lei gullam ette maŋŋases i galga gæčastet, de son eitu i gæčastam maŋŋases.[23]

Care 'can be identified, researched, and understood concretely and empirically, [and] remains ambivalent in significance and ontology'.[24] The ways in which care is understood, may as such mean vastly different things. When we speak of care in the context of a Sámi duty of care, what we are speaking of is an Indigenous ethics that teaches us that we are already involved in and together with land and waters, with the sky and the horizon, with other humans and spiritual entities, with other animals and living organisms, and with objects and things.[25] Our worlds, which are of relations, are made up of relationships to and between all of these.[26] The way to a good life, whether socially, economically, spiritually and in respect to health – what we call *birgejupmi* – is to care equally for all of these relations, which in turn transforms you into an *eallit olmmožin*, an accountable person.[27]

Indigenous knowledge systems (our epistemologies) and concepts (our methodologies) materialise from this system of kin, forged by a duty of care, as ways of being, knowing and doing. It is this system of kin, constituting the various relationships that make up the many worlds of existence, but always embedded in the land, that create the foundation for Indigenous realities and perspectives.[28]

This is a 'grounded normativity', or 'the modalities of Indigenous land-connected practices and longstanding experiential knowledge that inform and structure our ethical engagements with the world and our relationships with human and nonhuman others over time' and it materialises as a 'system of reciprocal relations and obligations', or as a duty of care.[29]

Nonetheless, with the onset of colonialism, these relations and the system of kinship that they create has been made invisible, or at best marginalised. This is a strategic erasure of Indigenous ways of being, knowing and doing, our ontologies, epistemologies and axiologies. 'One might call colonization a way of war', and the war waged on Indigenous peoples has many prolific (some more than others) strategies of erasure.[30]

> I know we must speak of colonialism, but there is great sorrow in doing so because it means that we did not make our world better for those to come.[31]

25 Ibid.

26 Kuokkanen, *Reshaping the University*, p. 65.

27 Porsanger, 'Indigenous Sámi Religion', p. 39.

28 Aileen Moreton-Robinson, *Sovereign Subjects: Indigenous Sovereignty Matters, Cultural Studies* (Crows Nest, N.S.W: Allen & Unwin, 2007), p. 2.

29 Glen Sean Coulthard, *Red Skin White Masks: Rejecting the Colonial Politics of Recognition* (Minneapolis: University of Minnesota Press, 2014), p. 13.

30 Jernsletten, Kristin, *The Hidden Children of Eve: Sámi Poetics: Guovtti ilmmi gaskkas*. PhD. (University of Tromsø, 2011), p. 45.

31 Ande (anonymous by choice) Northern Sámi area. Oral communication, 15 February 2015.

'We have never been conquered in war and we have never signed agreements with any state', but still the land has been divided, borders delineated in colonial treaties that we were never party to, enforced onto the land on which we live.[32] The colonial legal geographies implicated in this process – what we might term an epistemic injustice – have a vital part to play as a very specific strategy of erasure; manifesting as the alienation of the body from land.[33]

'For a long time, we have been alienated from the organism to which we belong – the Earth. So much so that we began to think of Earth and humanity as two separate entities'.[34] This binary created the 'Lapps' of what has always been the Sámi. Of the land itself, this alienation made Sápmi part and parcel of Norway, Sweden, Finland, and Russia.

> We never stopped being Sámi, and our land is always Sápmi. But those that wished for our destruction did not honour our terms and instead created their own.[35]

Never mind that 'the politics and struggles of Indigenous peoples are partially oriented by the need to convey their existence as polities in the context of settler-states assertion of jurisdiction over them and their lands'.[36] We continue to articulate practices of living in sovereignty that challenge said assertion.[37] Care, as we understand the term, is a vital part of that because care is a doing, it is a chosen perspective, a much loved value, that shapes and forms how we move in the world, but also with it.

> We care for our relations because they care for us.
> We live together, and that means that we all have a balance.
> That we all live in the understanding of the good life, of birgejupmi.

32 Ole Henrik Magga, 'Sami Past and Present and the Sami Picture of the World', In *Awakened Voice: The Return of Sami Knowledge*, edited by Elina Helander (Guovdageaidnu: Nordic Sami Institute, 1996), p. 76.

33 Jernsletten, *The Hidden Children of Eve*, p. 4.

34 Ailton Krenak, *Ideas to Postpone the End of the World* (Toronto: House of Anansi Press, 2020), p. 22.

35 Suvi, (anonymous by choice) Northern Sámi area. Oral communication, 9 June 2019.

36 Mark Rifkin, *Beyond Settler Time: Temporal Sovereignty and Indigenous Self-Determination* (Durham: Duke University Press, 2017), p. 39.

37 Elizabeth Carlson-Manathara and Gladys Rowe, *Living in Indigenous Sovereignty* (Halifax: Fernwood Publishing, 2021).

Our care, that which we know as the guelmiehdahke, initiates the understanding 'that humans are not the only ones caring for the Earth and its beings', the dominant crusaders subjugating a wild, yet passive entity.[38] It destroys the cartesian 'idea of the earth as humanity's backyard', which 'we cling so stubbornly to', impressing the truth: that we are but one small part of a much larger system.[39] In this system, the duty of care grows from the certain knowledge that 'we are [already] in relations of mutual care'.[40]
So while colonialism attempted to alienate us from the land, our bodies remain 'landed', rooted in, formed of and by the land and our presence in it for generations.[41] And so, the 'Indigenous experience is spatial, connected to places, to Earth, to the ground on what seems an almost personal level'.[42]

> Njavddamest bajas, Suoma rajast, læ jokka, mai láddek goččuk dal Bakanan-joki (Bákken-jokka). Mutto i dat namma vuolge bákken -anest. Dat boatta dast atte dolen Nuorttalažak čuppe bákkanis dam joga lakkasin [...] Dast læ bákkan-jokka ožžum namas, go dolen læ bakkanid čuoppam dam joga aldde.[43]

38
de la Bellacasa, *Matters of Care*, p. 161.

39
Krenak, *Ideas to Postpone the End of the World*, p. 60; Joe Kincheloe, 'Critical Ontology and Indigenous Ways of Being', in *Key Works in Critical Pedagogy: Bold Visions in Educational Research*, edited by Hayes K., Steinberg S.R., Tobin K., Vol 32 (Sense-Publishers, 2011): https://doi.org/10.1007/978-94-6091-397-6_25 accessed 13 January 2022.

40
de la Bellacasa, *Matters of Care*, p. 161.

41
Pirjo Kristiina Virtanen and Irja Seurujärvi-Kari, 'Introduction: Theorizing Indigenous Knowledge(s)', *Dutkansearvvi dieđalaš áigečála* 3, 2 (2019): pp. 1-19.

42
Jernsletten, *The Hidden Children of Eve*, p. 43.

43
Jak Ondrei, quoted in Saba, *Čállosat*, p. 186.

Aagård-Dunfjeld, Maja. 'Ornamentikk of dafliglivets gjøremål.' In *Far etter fedrane. Årbok for Vefsn, Grane og Hattfjelldal*, pp. 42–53. Vaapste: Vefsn Museums, 1991.

Aagård-Dunfjeld, Maja. 'Symbolinnhold i Sørsamisk ornamentikk'. Hovedfag i duodji/ Master in Duodji. Statens Lærerhøgskole i forming, 1989.

Carlson-Manathara, Elizabeth and Gladys Rowe. *Living in Indigenous Sovereignty*. Halifax: Fernwood Publishing, 2021.

Castellano, Marlene Brant. 'Updating Aboriginal Traditions of Knowledge.' In *Indigenous Knowledges in Global Contexts: Multiple Readings of Our World*. Edited by George J. Sefa Dei, Budd L. Hall and Dorothy Goldin Rosenberg, pp. 1–36. Toronto: Toronto Universty Press, 2000.

Cocq, Coppélie. *Revoicing Sámi Narratives: North Sámi Storytelling at the Turn of the 20th Century*. Umeå: Institutionen för språkstudier, 2008.

Coulthard, Glen Sean. *Red Skin White Masks: Rejecting the Colonial Politics of Recognition*. Minneapolis: University of Minnesota Press, 2014.

Cruikshank, Julie. *The Social Life of Stories: Narrative and Knowledge in the Yukon Territory*. Lincoln: University of Nebraska Press, 1998.

de la Bellacasa, Maria Puig. *Matters of Care: Speculative Ethics in More Than Human Worlds*. Minneapolis: University of Minnesota Press, 2017.

Dillon, Grace L. 'Imagining Indigenous Futurisms'. In *Walking the Clouds: An Anthology of Indigenous Science Fiction*. Edited by G. L. Dillon, pp. 1–62. Tucson: The University of Arizona Press, 2012.

Estes, Nick. *Our History is the Future. Standing Rock Versus the Dakota Access Pipeline, and the Long Tradition of Indigenous Resistance,* p. 24. London: Verso Books, 2019.

Finbog, Liisa-Rávná. *It Speaks to you – Making Kin of People, Duodji and Stories in Sámi Museums*. PhD. Department of Culture Studies and Oriental Languages, University of Oslo, 2020.

Gaski, Harald. *Sami Culture in a New Era: The Norwegian Sami experience*. Karasjok: Davvi girji, 1997.

Gaski, Harald. 'Indigenous Elders' Perspective and Position (Nordic Colonialisms and Scandinavian Studies) (Viewpoint essay)'. *Scandinavian Studies* 91, 1–2 (2019): p. 259.

Jernsletten, Jorunn. *Bissie dajve: relasjoner mellom folk og landskap i Voengel-Njaarke sïjte*. Universitetet i Tromsø, Fakultet for humaniora, samfunnsvitenskap og lærerutdanning, Institutt for historie og religionsvitenskap, 2009.

Jernsletten, Kristin. *The Hidden Children of Eve: Sámi poetics: guovtti ilmmi gaskkas*. PhD. University of Tromsø, 2011.

Kincheloe, Joe. 'Critical Ontology and Indigenous Ways of Being'. In *Key Works in Critical Pedagogy: Bold Visions in Educational Research*. Edited by K. Hayes, S. R. Steinberg, K. Tobin, Vol 32. Sense Publishers, 2011: https://doi.org/10.1007/978-94-6091-397-6_25 accessed 13 January 2022.

Kovach, Margaret. *Indigenous Methodologies: Characteristics, Conversations and Contexts*. Toronto: University of Toronto Press, 2009.

Krenak, Ailton. *Ideas to Postpone the End of the World*. Toronto: House of Anansi Press, 2020.

Kuokkanen, Rauna. 'Láhi and Attáldat: The Philosophy of the Gift and Sami Education'. *The Australian Journal of Indigenous Education* 34 (2005): pp. 20–32.

Kuokkanen, Rauna. *Reshaping the University: Responsibility, Indigenous Epistemes, and the Logic of the Gift*. Vancouver: UBC Press, 2007.

Leonard, Linda Schierse. *Creation's Heartbeat: Following the Reindeer Spirit*. New York: Bantam, 1996.

Magga, Ole Henrik. 'Sami Past and Present and the Sami Picture of the World'. In *Awakened Voice: The Return of Sami Knowledge*. Edited by Elina Helander. Guovdageaidnu: Nordic Sami Institute, 1996.

Mauss, Marcel. *The Gift: The Form and Reason for Exchange in Archaic Societies, Essai sur le don*. London: Routledge, [1925] 2002.

Moreton-Robinson, Aileen. *Sovereign Subjects: Indigenous Sovereignty Matters, Cultural Studies*. Crows Nest, N.S.W: Allen & Unwin, 2007.

Pettersson, O. P., Louise Bäckman, and Rolf Kjellström. *Kristoffer Sjulssons minnen : om Vapstenlapparna i början af 1800-talet / upptecknade af O. P. Pettersson ; red. av Louise Bäckman och Rolf Kjellström*. Vol. 20, *Acta Lapponica*. Stockholm: 1979.

Porsanger, Jelena. 'The Problematisation of the Dichotomy of Modernity and Tradition in Indigenous and Sami Contexts'. In *Working with Traditional Knowledge: Communities, Institutions, Information Systems, Law and Ethics*. Edited by Jelena Porsanger and Gunvor Guttorm, pp. 225–252. Guovdageaidnu: Sámi allaskuvla/ Sámi University of Applied Sciences, 2011.

Porsanger, Jelena. 'Indigenous Sámi Religion: General Considerations about Relationship'. In *The Diversity of Sacred Lands in Europe: Proceedings of the Third Workshop of the Delos Initiative – Inari/Aanaar 2010*, pp. 37–45. Gland, Switzerland: IUCN and Vantaa, Finland: Natural Heritage Services, 2012.

Rifkin, Mark. *Beyond Settler Time: Temporal Sovereignty and Indigenous Self-Determination*. Durham: Duke University Press, 2017.

Saba, Isak. *Čállosat. Isak Saba álbmotmuitočoakkáldat*. Edited by Line Esborg. Oslo: Spartacus Forlag/Scandinavian Academic Press, 2019.

Sullivan, Bernard. *Yindyamarra Yambuwan: Respecting Everything*. Bathurst: Charles Sturt University, 2016.

Tallbear, Kim. 'The US-Dakota War and Failed Settler Kinship'. *Anthropology News* 57 (9)*, sfaa.net,* 2016.

Virtanen, Pirjo Kristiina, and Irja Seurujärvi-Kari. 'Introduction: Theorizing Indigenous Knowledge(s)'. *Dutkansearvvi dieđalaš áigečála* 3, 2 (2019): pp. 1–19

Wilson, Shawn. 'What is an Indigenous Research Methodology?'. *Canadian Journal of Native Education* 25 (2001): pp. 175–9.

Beaska Niillas
Stállu ođđa máilmmis

Dolin ledje stálut ja stállu lei dakkár guhte válddii maid ieš dáhtui. Stállu lei gal vašánis sivdnádus mii gottii ja givssidii. Muhto dat stálut eai lean menddo jierbmát ja daiguin gal sápmelaš dávjá birgii. Jus mat stállu lei fitnen gitta de sápmelažžii lei juonain ja gávvilvuođain vejolaš beassat. Dolin dáiddii lean álkit, dalle go stállu bođii okto. Vaikko vel lei stuoris, gievra ja issoras. Lihkus ii lean nu menddo jierbmái, de mii basttiimet fillet. Muhto stálu ii galgan iežas niibbiin čugget, go dalle gal eallái ja šattai vel gievrrat.

Duháhiid jagiid leat mii sápmelaččat eallán ja birgen Sámis. Oktii áiggis leat máttut ge leamaš joavdan amas duovdagiidda, ja sii šadde oahpahallat ja gulahallat. Go dál manná meahccái, ja go duolmmada eatnama ja go gállá jogaid, de diehtit ahte dáid eatnamiid ja dáid jogaid leat sii duolbman ja gállán, sii guhte vázze min ovdal.

De mii leat doložis otnážii huksen čiekŋalis gulahallama ja oktavuođa iežamet máilmmiin. Mii leat huksen vieruid, árvvuid ja máhtu mii birgehii ja ain birgeha min dáin iežamet eatnamiin. Ja iešguđet gulahallamiid ja gielaid bokte lea vejolaš áddet máilmmi obbalaččat. Go ádde máilmmi mas vánddarda ja dainna máhttá gulahallat de lea vejolaš birget vaikko mainna ja vaikko geainna. Mii leat ođđa máilmmiid uvssaid rahpan ja ođđa áiggiid ieža huksen.

Rievddalmas máilbmi ja rievddalmas
čuolmmat leat gal ovdal ge gáibidan
sámiin heivehandáiddu ja sápmelaš
leamaš beaktil ja vitmat, go vel stáluiguin
birgii.
Muhtumat jáhkket ahte stálut eai šat gávdno.
Muhto dat ii leat duohta. Áiggit rivdet ja
Stállu maid, ja ii boađe gal šat okto. Dat
bohtet máŋggat ja mojinjálmmiid, vai eat
ballá. Dat leat juonalaččat maid šaddan,
iige daid leat álo nu álki dovdat šat. Sis
leat máŋggalágan hámi, go stálut máhttet
háma lonuhit.
Ja go bohtet, de leat sis máŋggalágan
vearjju, koanstta ja reaiddu maid geavahit.
Sii leat oahppan čállit, nu olu ahte masá
heavvanat daidda báhpáriidda. Lea nu
maid ahte stállu ii dárbbaš ba ieš ge
boahtit, go fillejit min bargat sin ovddas.
Stálut gal ain geahččalit njielastit sámiid ja
dáin stáluin lea sakka vearrát birget.
Muhtomin mii šaddat fuomáškeahttá
bártái, go navdit iežamet oadjebassan min
ruovttuguovlluin ja eatnamiin.
Muhtumin mii eat áicca áiggil ja
fuomáškeahttá mii sáhttit gielastuvvot
stálu sátnesuohpanii. Lea dat gal buorre
lihkus muhtumin nu ahte fuomáša
sátnesuohpana ovdal giella čavgá. Ja dalle
bastá vel dávjá dan garvit.
Mii leat dađistaga oahppagoahtán dovdat
sin vugiid ja mo sii jurddašit ja mii leat
fuobmágoahtán goas ja mo galgat duostut.
Mii leat geavahišgoahtán iežamet reaidduid
ja vearjjuid, maid mii dađistaga leat
iežamet oktasaš bargguid bokte lokten

čuovgga ovdii, ja daid mii gal dárbbašat
ge, juohke beaivvi.
Mii eat leat nu galle olbmo, muhto jáhkán
stálut navdet min čuđiid duháhiid mielde,
go jo eai bastte.
Mii leat ain dás

Scan the code to hear this story read by the author

Ánde Somby
When a Predator Culture Meets a Prey Culture

I'm going to present a metaphor that will help to explain the complex ways in which colonist societies oppress Indigenous cultures such as the Sámi. We'll be looking at a story where a predator culture meets a prey culture.

One of the oldest fables in Western civilisation is Aesop's tale of 'The Wolf and the Lamb'. The Wolf comes to the Lamb on the bank of a woodland stream and says, 'Last year, you grossly insulted me.' The Lamb says, 'But I wasn't born then.' 'You feed on my pasture', the Wolf continues, to which the Lamb replies: 'I haven't yet tasted grass.' Then the Wolf comes up with a third and final argument: 'You drink from my well', and the Lamb says: 'I never yet tasted water, since my mother's milk is both food and drink to me.' The Wolf then attacks and eats the Lamb.

There is an interesting question here: why does the Wolf bother to try to establish that the Lamb has violated its interests? This is a question that the Italian novelist and philosopher Umberto Eco discusses in one of the essays in *Turning Back the Clock* (2007), a book on political rhetoric. According to Eco, when a bigger and stronger entity wants to claim a smaller, weaker entity, it will attempt to use rational arguments to justify its intentions. This could be considered one of the demarcations between humanity and the animal kingdom. In the animal kingdom, the bigger fish eats the smaller fish without concern. Among people, morality will sometimes prevent the 'Wolf' from attacking the 'Lamb'. Or, occasionally, the rule of law might encourage the stronger one to look to his humanity in order to ensure that he is making reasonable and rational decisions.

It's interesting that one of the oldest texts in Western civilisation is the story of a dictator. How should we read such narratives about cultures consuming other cultures? There are several different ways to look at a text and the many different dimensions, layers of meaning that it contains, such as post-text, meta-text, inter-text and subtext. To be able to read a text, we need to do a certain amount of work to acquire the skill of literacy. But what about cases where what we are supposed to read is not on the surface of the text, but is hidden in its structure and processes? Perhaps we can approach these in a similar way. We would then have to ask, when reading Aesop's fable, what kind of rationality is at play?

As a lawyer, I'm familiar with normative rationality, which presents the rules under which one is allowed to operate. One has to remain within the norms, not outside them. Normative rationality, for example, prohibits torture. Then, we have teleological rationality. In contrast to normative rationality, teleological rationality is based on focusing on the goal with no ethical concerns. Let's say the goal is to get information from a person. When considering the best ways to get information, we have options such as 1) asking him; 2) torturing him; and 3) giving him drugs that will make him talk. According to teleological rationality, there are just two parameters involved: will it work and how expensive will it be? In other words: efficiency and cost are the only concerns.

So what might the goals be when a predator culture meets a prey culture? When looking at it in the framework of teleological rationality, the goal is clearly for the predator culture to get access to the gold – the natural resources. There are several ways for the Wolf to try to get the gold.

Convincing

The Wolf can try to make convincing arguments to claim that the Lamb is in the way and should move. This can be done by using the family metaphor. A national state, for instance, could say to an Indigenous nation that they are all one big happy family. Naturally, all members of the family have to contribute to its well-being. So, since the Lamb happens to be standing on the gold, could it please move a little for the benefit of everyone?

In Norway, the king essentially confiscated Finnmark in this way, and welcomed everyone to the party of the natural resources in the North. Now, a very complex process of handing back Finnmark to the Sámi people is ongoing. Here, the family argument comes in again, with the claim that privatising the commons isn't nice.

Another example of the family argument used against the coastal Sámi population is to think cost-efficiently. Since Røkke and other Norwegian trawler companies are much more effective at fishing than the Sámi with their small boats, why not hand the right to fish to them? According to the Wolf, that would be good for the well-being of the whole family.

Switching the Language

The Wolf might also try to use another language – 'Legalese' – to argue that the nomadic Indigenous people, who were traditionally constantly on the move, lack the concept of ownership. This idea that the Indigenous territory is no-man's land legitimises the confiscation of land, dignified under the legal-sounding doctrine of 'Terra Nullius'.

Propagandising

If the smooth talk and all the reasonable, rational and legal arguments don't work, the Wolf needs another strategy. Propaganda has proved to be a useful tool in the appropriation of land. The Wolf can romanticise the mining industry, promoting it as the new technology, while reindeer herding is decadent, dirty and belongs to the past.

The Wolf can also argue that the Sámi are claiming special rights to these lands based on ethnicity. In this way, he can exploit all the negative connotations attached to nationalism, and even racism, to milk some propagandist juice from the cow.

The prey culture can also be made invisible using propagandist methods. The Wolf can move the prey culture into the margins so that it doesn't appear in the main text. It might exist between the lines, words or letters, where no one sees it. In his book *How Propaganda Works* (2015), Jason Stanley describes a situation that is very familiar to the Sámi and is one of our biggest obstacles: 'A school that produces partially informed citizens who believe they are fully informed is a vehicle of propaganda, even if it never produces any actual propagandistic claims.' In his doctoral thesis in 2006, Hadi Lile executed empirical research proving that Norwegian children are very poorly informed on the policy of Norwegianisation of the Sámi.

Sometimes I face this problem when litigating a Sámi case. Often, the judge doesn't know anything about the Sámi because the Sámi have been hidden somewhere between the lines. One can understand that a nation doesn't want to see its ugly parts reflected in the mirror. This, unfortunately, leads the judge to be ignorant about Sámi history – the history of confiscation, boarding schools and other painful phenomena. This then forces me into a situation in which I find it necessary to explain the most basic things about the Sámi. I point out to the judge that the Sámi are a people who inhabit four countries, not all of whom live by reindeer herding, and that there are urban Sámi living in cities etc. While explaining this, the time allocated for me to discuss the matter at hand runs out. I'm given a task that should have been executed by the school system, but because of the propaganda of silence, is a burden that is left to me.

This is an issue that a lot of Sámi people face daily in different situations. Teaching the non-Sámi about the Sámi culture and political situation becomes their burden. And when communicating with non-Sámi, every Sámi, regardless of their field, seems to be expected to answer questions about all aspects of Sámi culture, politics and rights.

Force

Finally, if propaganda doesn't work, the Wolf can use force – just as Aesop's Wolf attacked the Lamb. The case of the hydroelectric power plant in the Alta river, for which the Sámi were moved away by force, is a classic example. It has repeated itself many times in other contexts.

So, getting the resources is the main goal of the Wolf. In order to get the resources, it needs to have a sub-goal. That is, territorial control. Territorial control can be achieved by military means or semi-military means. However, getting territorial control is one thing, but getting control over the people calls for internal control. Without internal control, the people might become rebellious and sabotage the territorial control and even change the minds of the predator culture. To secure the stability of control, internal control is crucial. To do that, the Wolf needs to kick the prey culture out of its own world, to alienate it from its own background. Religion has served as a powerful tool in that respect. The Wolf also wants to get control over the knowledge of the prey culture. This phenomenon has manifested itself in the boarding-school system into which our children were captured.

When the Wolf has achieved both external and internal control, what more is needed? Surely, at the moment of opposition, it's important for the Wolf to show who is in charge. But the Wolf also needs to be able to live with itself. He has to be able to look into the mirror, so he needs a blameless self-image. To maintain a blameless self-image while maintaining control over the prey culture through the methods described above, one way is to exist in denial. That calls for hiding the ugly facts of history.

In 2006–07 there was a big debate in Norway about whether Norwegian children should be taught the Sámi language in school. It was a huge debate, for it was widely considered a violation of pure Norwegian children. When defending itself from criticism of violating Sámi children, the Wolf can turn to new rhetoric and admit that the prey culture has been wronged in this way and that way, but was it all for the bad? Yes, you lost your language, but this is a very trivial problem. Is it really worth whining about?

Now the Wolf has achieved the appropriation of natural resources, the external and internal control, as well as an acceptable self-image. But how to achieve an acceptable external image, which is also very important in maintaining control?

When a culture has been colonised, it faces problems that need solving. The Wolf then needs to colonise the problems too. This manifests itself in the predator culture showing a willingness to have the situation surrounding the prey culture analysed, to Wolf-support and promote projects in the prey culture that appear nice but at the same time represent no danger or threat to the predator culture. The Sámi people and Sámi culture have been the subjects of uncountable research throughout the decades, but very often it has been useless and even harmful for the Sámi themselves, since they themselves are not the presenters of the story, but those who are represented.

And what could be cleverer than establishing a democratically elected representative body that doesn't have any decisive power, such as the Sámi Parliament, in its beautiful buildings? The Wolf has also promoted its external image in Sápmi by establishing the Court of Inner Finnmark, which appears to be a Sámi court, but in reality is a regular Norwegian court. What about establishing a body whose stated aim is to reverse the land confiscation, but in reality continues the practice of confiscation? This is how Finnmárkkuopmodat (FeFo, the owning and managing body for the land areas in the Finnmark County) works.

Now that the Wolf has the natural resources, internal and external control, an acceptable self and external image, what more is needed? Can it exploit and make use of the remains of the prey culture? Cultural appropriation, such as manufacturing cheap copies of the prey's cultural riches and selling this corrupt picture, is an effective way to squeeze the last drops out of what is left of the beauty of the prey.

So there we have it. This is what happens when a predator culture meets a prey culture.

Asta M. Balto
My Traditional Teachings

Testimony – On 'Gal Dat Oahppá Go Stuorrola' Philosophy

My lessons are based on the guiding principles of 'Gal dat oahppá go stuorrola' philosophy. This traditional saying, which translates loosely as 'I'm sure they will learn when they are older' celebrates the capacity to learn, upholding that every individual can learn anything, and that this depends only on the opportunities and adjustments offered. I am so happy to be part of this ancestral heritage and I like to think that I carry this wisdom as an educator and transfer it to others. As a teacher of Sámi and Indigenous knowledge, I know that teaching is more than sharing information. Learning happens when your teaching is rooted in love, speaking from your soul to other souls. It is sacred.

Testimony – On Language

Sámi language, my mother tongue, is a communicating and connecting phenomenon. It connects me with my ancestors. Part of their ways of knowing, ways of being and ways of living is in me. I can strengthen the ties or weaken them because language is a living process. It moves with me and impacts on my relationships with those who have left, with those who are here, and with those who are coming. My language shapes, upholds and changes my own ways of being, of living and knowing the world. This precious heritage can speak without words, be silent and still connected to all I see and all I do not see, to the land, to living beings, to myself and to outer space. My language is a living sound in my body, floating warmly with my blood and heating the emotions that dwell in me. I live my language until I die, devoted to the hope that it will flourish.

Testimony – The Land, The Earth is Healing
I am continuously in 'gal dat oahppá' is learning mode. I listen to my friend, an elder Sámi woman, Sárgon Sara, who shares her connection to Mother Earth. She says that she can feel how her feet are in an intimate connection with the land on which she steps. 'This closeness is healing me, giving me strength and making me feel well. It is like a remedy, therefore I am always longing to be outdoors in Nature [meahccái]', says Sara, as do I.

Asta Mitkijá Balto is a Sámi Professor Emerita and freelancer, awarded an Honorary Doctorate by WINU (the International Indigenous University in 2018) for her lifelong work for Sámi and Indigenous education. She is Pauliina Feodoroff's chosen Elder for 'The Sámi Pavilion' project. Committed to combining academic knowledge with knowledge rooted in traditional Sámi society, her books, articles and countless lectures she provides in Sámi content, perspectives and decolonizing perspectives to teacher training, schools, kindergartens, administrations, amongst other institutions. The general lack of Sámi knowledge has also led her into counselling in health, administrative, court, art, political, and church sectors, assisting them to build Sámi perspectives into their activities.

Balto was a rector, vice rector, lecturer and professor within a period of 20 years at The Sámi University of Applied Sciences and was also director of the Sámi Education Council under the Ministry of Education, researcher at the Nordic Sámi Institute and lecturer at Finnmark University College. Currently she chairs the board of the Sámi Cultural and Language Centre in Kárášjohka and serves on the boards of various cultural and educational institutions, while also working on her books and articles.

Liisa-Rávná Finbog is a Sámi archeologist and museologist from Oslo/Vaapste/Skánit on the Norwegian side of the Sápmi. She is currently a Post-Doctoral Researcher at Tampere University, Finland. She completed a PhD in museology at the University of Oslo in 2021. In her doctoral project, she looked at the relation between Sámi identity and duodji within a museological framework. She is also an accomplished practitioner of duodji and teaches both courses and workshops in traditional Sámi arts. She has recently contributed to the collective work Research Journeys In/To Multiple Ways of Knowing (2019).

Timimie Gassko Märak is a poet, feminist and Sámi queer activist based in Stockholm. Märak puts just as much in between the lines they write as in the words they choose to share. Like them, their poetry is a combination of deep roots and connections, read at a big-city pace. They are the Word Weaver, also known as a Poet in Residence at 'The Sámi Pavilion' at Biennale Arte 2022, in a role that emphasises orality.

Beaska Niillas from Deatnu in the Norwegian part of Sápmi, is among other things a father of two, Sámi duojár, hunter, gatherer, nature guardian and politician. Nature has been at the centre of his life since childhood. When growing up, the land was his playing field and his friend. He has done a lot of different things in his life, but the only formal education he has is a certificate of apprenticeship in duodji. For some time, he also worked as an actor in both Beaivváš Sámi National Theatre and Giron Sámi Theatre. After that he was a teacher and then went on to work as a fisherman. For the last ten years he has been active in Sámi politics and also defended Indigenous land and waters in Sápmi and beyond.

Sigbjørn Skåden is a Sámi author from Skånland based in Tromsø. He authors books in Sámi and Norwegian and published his debut epic, *Skuovvadeddjiid gonagas* (The King of the Cobblers) in 2004, for which he was nominated for the Nordic Council's Literature Award 2007. Since his debut he has published a poetry collection, a children's book and two novels. In addition, Skåden has authored texts for various interdisciplinary artistic projects. He was young artist of the year at the Indigenous festival Riddu Riđđu, prologue author for the Arctic Arts Festival, and among the chosen authors at the European poetry platform Versopolis. He was awarded the Havmannprisen in 2014 and nominated for the P2 listeners' novel of the year prize for the novel *Våke over dem som sover* (Wake Over Those Who Sleep)

Ánde Somby is a Sámi juoigi, noaidi and Associate Professor of the Faculty of Law at the Arctic University of Norway. He is artist Anders Sunna's chosen Elder for 'The Sámi Pavilion' project. Somby has been an active joiker since 1974. In 1985 he produced the LP record and MC cassette *Ean Máššan* with his father Aslak Somby (1913–2008) and mother Karen Kristine Porsanger Somby (1920–2017). In 1991 he produced the record *Ravddas Ravdii* with Inga Juuso. In 2000 he produced the record *Deh* and in 2003 *Deh* with his uncle Ivvár Niillas. Somby is one of very few Sámi with a Ph.D. in law (dr. juris). Somby's Ph.D. thesis is titled *Juss som retorikk* and his project 'Is the Legal Medium the Legal Message?' (2009) attempted to apply Marshall McLuhan's mantra of the medium being the message to jurisprudence. Somby is also one of the cofounders of the Sámi publishing house and record label *Dat* (www.dat.net). Together with the band Boknakaran from Tromsø and the acapella group Rosynka from Petrozavodsk in Russia, Somby participated in the project 'moya på Tvoja' (1998–2002). From 2003 to 2007, Somby was a member of the group Vajas (Echo) and was the vocalist and joiker for the band. The polyphonic sound project *Yoiking with the Winged Ones,* initiated by Somby, was recorded and produced by Chris Watson and was released by *Ash International* as a vinyl record in January 2016. 'Yoiking with the Winged Ones' has also been presented as an art installation at Tromsø Kunstforening in 2016 and Sámi Dáiddaguovddáš / Sámi Center for Contemporary Art in 2019.